I0104613

FIND YOURSELF
-OR-
THE KEY TO CHANGE YOUR FATE

BY ALEXANDER PINT

Translated by Emin Kuliev, MD

www.pint.ru

https://caterpillartobuterfly.wordpress.com

skyrocket press

ISBN: 978-1-944722-07-4

Visit www.SkyrocketPress.com

Cover art by Freydoon Rassouli

TABLE OF CONTENTS

CHAPTER 1
WHAT DO YOU WANT TO UNDERSTAND, AND WHO IS GOING TO UNDERSTAND THAT?

●◄●•►●◄●•►●◄●•►●◄●•►●◄●•►●◄●•►●◄●•►●◄●•►●◄●•►●◄●•►●◄●•►●◄●

A human being is a radio

— Let's start with those of you who have come to the seminar for the first time. What brought you here?

— *My name is Inness. I am from Kazan. Recently, I was at a seminar where the instructor criticized and chastised Elena Rerix and Leo Tolstoy. I was shocked. I thought he was crazy. On my way home, I developed an excruciating headache. I decided not to attend his seminars anymore. A few months later, I discovered your book* Caterpillar to Butterfly. *It shocked me. I recalled the seminar I attended and what I felt afterwards. I realized that the moderator tried to shake us up, like a dentist tries to shake a diseased tooth from side to side to pull it out. He was not able to pull me out. I will have to do it on my own. After reading your book, I ran to his seminar again. I've been attending his seminars for the last six months. I am not sure why.*

— What are you receiving there?

— *I don't know. He doesn't tell us anything. We just sit there crying and discussing our problems. One of my many problems is my husband. He drinks. How can I stop fighting this situation? How can I accept it? How can I live with it?*

— *My name is Nataly. I found your books two years ago. Someone presented me with a copy of* We Are One. *I've read all your books. Your last book,* Who Are You? *really shocked me. It made me come here. What*

1

you write about the regeneration of DNA excites me. I am also very interested in self-observation. I am learning how to use it in stressful situations. I am trying to understand myself better.

— Great. What do you mean when you say you want to understand yourself better, and who do you think you are?

— *We experience multiple thoughts, feelings, and sensations. We react to them differently in different situations.*

— When you turn on a radio, you hear splashes of electromagnetic waves, which the radio transforms into sounds and voices. When you turn the tuning knob, these voices and sounds change.

— *Yes, that is the function of the radio.*

— Are not you the same thing? You have just defined yourself as a radio.

— *Okay. Whatever is inside me will manifest itself one way or another.*

— A radio can also say that every wave it catches will be transmitted into one sound or another. A radio is a reproducer. It can be tuned in to accept one station or another. If these radio stations were to stop transmitting their signals, the radio would be silent.

— *So? There are many things in me.*

— What's in you?

— *My current life experience, as well as the experience of my many past lives, are in me, and they manifest themselves.*

— What kind of experience is it, and how does it manifest itself?

— *I am not sure how to describe it. My life experience manifests itself somehow. It contains certain thoughts, feelings, sensations…*

— It is similar to a glass of water. If you drop it, it breaks, and water gets spilled.

— *The result is a puddle of water with pieces of glass.*

— You insist your body is filled with experience. What if your body were to die? What would happen? Where are you?

You have said you wanted to understand yourself. I am a self-investigator, and I want to figure out *what* exactly you are. What are you going to understand, and who is going to understand it?

— *The one who will see it … that's who will understand …*

— Who is it?

— *Someone who will see my feelings and name them. Someone who will see my thoughts and name them.*

— Who is this someone? Is it you? Who is it? Who can observe? Is it you?

— *Yes, it's me.*

— Is the one your observer observes also you?

— *The observer observes a part of me.*

— Let me get this straight. One part of you observes another part of you. And who are you in this picture?

— *I am the one who wants to observe.*

— Are you the one who wants to observe or the one who observes?

— *I observe.*

— And what does your observer observe?

— *My observer observes my interest in the game. It observes the sensations of pleasure and fear.*

— Okay, and how does one human being differ from another?

— *By his experience.*

— What kind of experience? We have our own games, interests, and fears. But how do we differ from one another?

— *We differ in our relationship to all of this.*

— And who creates these relationships?

— *I have lived a substantial portion of my life without observing myself. I am learning to observe myself and what happens around me. I am learning not to identify with my roles and states.*

— Great. Let's work with what you just said. You have said you learned to observe. I suppose you observe, and as a fellow

3

self-investigator I ask you a specific question: "Who is it that observes, and what does this observer of yours observe?"

— *I am observing myself—a woman who reacts emotionally to certain events.*

— Are you a woman?

— *Yes! Who do you think I am?*

— I don't have anything against it.

— *She reacts according to ...*

— According to her feminine nature.

— *She reacts according to her life experience, upbringing, and the education she received. She has certain habitual reactions. She also experiences another, non-emotional state, a state where there is no separation between a man and a woman. This is a quiet, balanced state, out of which she can see what is going on here.*

— Okay. If your observer can see all of this, what does it see now?

— *It sees me getting drawn into a negative emotion. It sees me getting angry...*

— How does it see it?

— *It sees it calmly. It says, "Are you getting crazy again?"*

— Does it talk?

— *Sometimes it does.*

— What does it say?

Husband is a mirror of irritation

— *There are certain habitual reactions to events. There is a habit to get upset and to hold a grudge. There is a division inside. There is a voice that says, "Overcome the state of sulking, the state of not understanding and fear of making someone upset. You are afraid of making someone upset again. You feel guilty again." That's what this voice says. For example, when my husband comes home, I get irritated. As soon as he comes—it is irrelevant what he says and does—every word he says make me angry. I understand that my state is caused by his "falling into guilt". When he feels guilty, my system starts to swing. I want to kick him. I want to scream at him.*

4

— Do you want to blame him for something?

— *I want to confirm his guilt.*

— You want to blame him, so he would feel guilty. A man feels guilty when he is blamed for something or accused of something.

— *Blamed? Accused?*

— You just told us that you want to scream at him and kick him.

— *I want to tell him, "Here you go. You've left your shirt and socks on the floor again. You've made a mess again."*

— Is not this an accusation?

— *Yes, it is.*

— Pay attention to this. This is very important. Unless you clearly see the working mechanism of what you observe, you will not be able to describe it well.

— *I would not say that this is an accusation. This is agression or unmotivated anger.*

— Okay. What is aggression?

— *Irritation. Anger.*

— Okay. Something irritates you. What does it mean? It means something does not satisfy you. Am I correct?

— *Yes. It does not fit my notions. I must find a reason for this to happen. A man comes home. He is calm, and he is in a good mood. He does everything the way he usually does, but this irritation is already in me. I observe and I see it. I just have to switch myself out of this state. I have to say to myself, "What are you getting angry about? What is wrong with you?" I understand that this happens because he got into a state of guilt for one of his own reasons.*

— And why are you there? Are you there for a reason or not?

— I just happened to be there.

— He is in a state of guilt, and you just happened to be there for no reason. And for some reason you get more and more irritated with him.

5

— I may ask him to stop blaming himself. There is no reason for that. He should not blame himself for whatever happened at work.

— Why are you irritated by him being in a state of guilt? Let him experience it. Why do you care?

— *Until I see it, it does not depend on me.*

— If it does not depend on you, why does it irritate you? You react to him this way, and it appears to me that it must have something to do with you. Why do you say that it does not concern you?

— He is the closest human being I have.

— So, he shows you something that is in you.

— *Obviously.*

— You cannot separate from him because he shows you something that is in you.

Love—dependency

— *I came to this seminar to untie my familial dependencies.*

— We are dealing with many dependencies here. It is easier to see dependencies that arise within families. They are more pronounced.

— *I would like to start with my inner circle. You write in your books that we have an opportunity to live in a state of love with people who are close to us, in a state where love doesn't limit us but makes us stronger. I want to experience this feeling. I want to support a man who is next to me irrespective of what he does. It is far from what I currently experience in my life. I keep seeing how this so-called love makes us more and more dependent. We constantly owe something to each other. I am on my third marriage, and I have a child from each one of my husbands. I am afraid to destroy what I have now.*

— Is every subsequent marriage of yours the same as the prior one?

— *No. They are all different.*

— What's the difference between them? How do they differ in terms of your relationships with your husbands? Did your first and second husband experience the feeling of guilt?

— *No, it's not about that. Everything has changed.*

— What has changed?

— *Should I talk about my husbands?*

— Have any of them satisfied you? Have you experienced the state you have read about with any of them?

— *No. I have not.*

— It looks like something dissatisfied you in all three relationships. Otherwise, why get a divorce? What exactly didn't satisfy you? I am interested in the reason behind your dissatisfaction with your husbands. That's what you need to see.

— *I can tell you that. It appears I form a dependency on a human being right away. It was very important for me to feel needed in every one of these marriages. It is important for me to be the one for my man. I would reinforce this dependency, reinforcing his notion that it is me who he needs. I am good at making a man feel that I can do something that no other woman can. I can make a man's life very comfortable.*

— "You will not make it without me".

— *Yes. Soon, a man I am with cannot live without me. He comes to understand how much better off he is with me.*

— He is not just better off with you, he would not be able to live without you now. How do you do that? How do you create such a relationship?

— *I learn to understand him very well, and I make sure he feels it.*

— What does it mean, "I understand him very well?"

— *It means, I clearly see his weak spots.*

— And you play on these weak spots. "I give you something you don't have. I am the only one who can give it to you. I will keep a close eye on you and make sure no other woman gives you that, because if another woman were to show up and to give him more than I am giving him, she would take my spot." This is not love, this is dependency.

7

— *Dependency?*

— Yes. You call it love, but this is a dependency. When you come to City Hall, you don't say, "We have decided to get married to reinforce our dependencies. People call their relationship love, but they get into dependency.

— *This dependency starts to irritate me pretty fast.*

— You think this is his dependency, but this is your dependency too. Both of you get stuck in this dependency.

— *The desire to be needed.*

— Yes. It seems to you that you satisfy his dependency, but in reality, he satisfies your dependency too.

— *I agree.*

— Why don't you satisfy each other's dependences? Your back and his fingernails are itching. Why don't you scratch each other? What's the problem?

— *Are you asking me about my last marriage or about the prior two?*

— You have been divorced twice, and as I understand it, presently you are not happy either. Looks like something was not working in your prior marriages and something is not working in your current one.

— *We are trying to make it work.*

— Try, by all means try. Why did you come to the seminar?

— *I need your help.*

— We have just determined that what you call love is a mutual dependency. What are you fighting for in this so-called loving relationship?

— *I am not fighting for anything anymore.*

— You are lying. You have started your conversation with, "My husband is in a state of guilt. That irritates me. I am irritated by him not doing things right and not saying the right things." Is not this a fight?

— *Yes, you are right. He came home yesterday, and he got on the couch right away. He spent the entire evening there watching TV. That irritated the hell out me. I kept asking him what's wrong with him.*

— Is not that a fight?

— *Yes. That is a fight. I can see that now.*

— Wait a minute. Let me correct you. You don't see that, you do that. When you see something, you can explain why it happens. That's what the word "see" means in my terminology. If I do something and say that I see what I do, I call it seeing. **What I call Awareness or Clear Seeing is clear and precise seeing of the mechanisms that create a conflict.** You cannot describe these mechanisms yet.

— *I can do it sometimes.*

— I have not seen you describe one mechanism yet. If you can do that, tell us about one of your mechanisms. It's very important to understand that "I am the way I am now. I don't understand anything yet." This is the first step with which the process of self-investigation starts. When you make this step, you start seeing the mechanisms of your inner conflicts. If you don't make this step, you remain in the sleep of consciousness.

To understand yourself, you need a new language.

— *Let me share a common scenario with you. It's Sunday. My husband lazily walks around the house from one TV to another. I am angry, and I tell him, "When will you finally do what you really want to do?!"*

— That's exactly what he does. He does what he wants to do, but he doesn't know who he really is. **He is not aware of the fact that he is living in the dual reality in which every desire has an anti-desire. We live in a paradoxical reality.** This is the main idea that I transmit to you. You have just manifested the state of a "sleeping" human being who has an impulse to wake up. How does it look from the outside?

— *It looks like an attempt to use a well-known terminology to describe something that is not totally clear yet.*

— What well-known terminology are you talking about? You are using street language, and you don't even understand the meaning of the words you are using.

— *When she hears a familiar word, she fits it into the system of notions that is familiar to her.*

— I want you to notice that the system of notions that she has cannot be used to describe her problems. When I asked her what love was, she couldn't answer my question. She would not be able to answer my question related to the other words she uses either.

— *Are you saying I cannot explain the meaning of the words I use?*

— We are not in court. We are reviewing what we have now. As you can see, the situation we are in is not very pleasant. At the present time, you do not understand what you think, feel, or do. This is a shock to you, but you must pass through this shock if you want to start the process of self-investigation. Everyone who walks in here receives such a shock. Afterwards, you either submerge deeper into the sleep you are in or start to move toward self-awareness. The process of self-investigation is long and cumbersome. You will have to move step by step here. I show you the direction of your movement toward yourself, but you will have to move on your own here. Don't wait for me to come up with Truth that would instantly change you. This is not going to happen. No Truth can be expressed in this dual reality with the language that was created by the dual mind. You will perceive everything I say as a shock. What I say to you doesn't improve your understanding of yourself. On the contrary, it destroys the notions of understanding you currently have. That's how it is going to be, but it will create an opportunity for you to truly understand yourself.

— *So, your every phrase is going to destroy something, eh? Go ahead, destroy.*

— What is your emotional reaction to my words?

— *I am irritated.*

10

— What irritates you?

— *I am irritated by your statement that I couldn't explain a single word I said. I doubt that's true.*

— Which word can you explain?

— *I can explain what love is.*

— Okay. If you know that, explain it to us.

— *The meaning of which word that I used do you want me to explain?*

— I'll ask you to explain any word related to your main problem. I am not asking you to explain to us what a table or a chair means.

— *Dependency.*

— What is dependency?

— *Mutual obligations, fears.*

— What is fear?

— *Fear is an emotional state. When I am afraid, my physical body gets constricted. I expect something bad, something that I don't want to happen will happen.*

— So, something happens in a way you don't want to happen. Give us an example.

— *I don't like family conflicts.*

— What is a conflict?

— *Mutual accusation.*

— How do mutual accusations arise? What's a conflict, in general?

— *It's a collision of notions of two human beings about how something should happen.*

— Collision of which notions? I steer you toward the essence of our conversation. Currently, you are talking quite superficially.

— *Those are my notions.*

Conflict is a disharmony of the opposites

— Why does conflict appear?

— *It appears because our notions are harsh. I have my notions and he has his notions. Our notions are different.*

11

— They are opposite. Your husband lies down. You tell him, "Don't lie down!" He starts to read his paper. You tell him, "Don't read the newspaper!" You tell him something opposite to what he, as it appears to him, wants. **A conflict is an interaction of opposites.** This is extremely important for us to understand. Otherwise, we will never be able to figure out and understand why things that happen in our life happen. Why do we suffer? Why do we experience fear? Those are the basic questions. We have come to the point in our Process when we should start to understand these questions.

So, a conflict is an interaction of opposites.

— *Some harsh, opposite tendencies don't allow us to compromise. We can't come to a mutual understanding.*

— He wants to go south, but you tell him he needs to go north. If he goes north, he would do the opposite of what he wants to do. Conflict appears when two opposite interests collide, and it may arise in relationship to anything in the life of human beings. You don't have to chastise him for lying on a couch; you can, for example, join him.

— *No, I can't. I can't lay on the couch for a whole day.*

— I just show you how a conflict may appear and how you can resolve it. If he reads something, you can sit next to him and read something. Later, you can discuss what you have read. It's our unacceptance of the opposites that creates basic problems in life. It's opposites that bring people together. If we didn't have the opposite understanding of what we need to do, feel, and think, we would not have conflicts.

— *Yes. You say people are attracted by opposites. It follows then that when we decide to unite, we pretend we don't have these opposites.*

— What does it mean to unite?

— *It means to live together as a family and to have children. We assume that we are going to live together for many years.*

— What we assume and what happens in reality are two totally different things. Your problems confirm that and cause

12

you to suffer. I am helping you to sort out how your life problems appear. That's why people come to the seminar.

— *Suffering is an exaggeration. There is a certain discomfort …*

— What do you mean by an exaggeration?

— *Suffering is something global for me.*

— Is it a state when you commit hara-kiri?

— *It's when you hit your head against the wall.*

— There are different degrees of expressing suffering: one man cries quietly, another one cries loudly. Those are different manifestations of suffering.

— *For me, suffering is something very strong.*

— Okay. Are you suffering now?

— *I am not suffering right now.*

— Then why are you here, at the seminar?

— *Why should I suffer? I didn't come here to suffer.*

— You don't think you came here to suffer? Can you do anything else?

— *I can enjoy life. I can find pleasure in life.*

— Aha, and what does pleasure lead to?

— *It leads to the absence of pleasure.*

— Is not the absence of pleasure suffering? Did you notice that sooner or later something you like transforms into something that you don't like?

— *If there is too much of it, I get bored with it.*

— Too much or too little, but in the beginning you liked him.

— *I did. He was caring and attentive.*

— Later on, his care and attention started to irritate you. This is the suffering every human being will experience. First, people like something greatly. Then they get irritated and outraged by the thing they liked. Finally, they get angry with it. It is the presence of duality that leads to conflict. We love people for the same qualities that we later come to hate. We should thoroughly feel the situations that give birth to our conflicts and to become

13

aware of the lawful nature of their appearance. A life that a human being spends asleep is not perceived by him holistically. It seems to him that he experiences pleasure and displeasure. He doesn't see that pleasure and displeasure are two sides of one coin.

— *It follows then that the best way to build a family is to build it with someone who you don't care for, someone who will not cause you to experience any emotions.*

— Everything you interact with causes you to experience emotions. Even the absence of emotion is an emotion. Boredom is an emotion. Depression and indifference are emotions. Indifference is the absence of discernment.

— *Indifference. I don't care.*

— When you don't care, you don't discern what everything you deal with is made of.

— *Or I don't want to discern and understand.*

— The sleeping man doesn't understand what he does, how he does it, or why he does it. He forgot who he really is. I am trying to bring clarity into that, and this is very difficult work. Right now, you are raving.

— *I do what I can.*

— I understand. This is neither an insult nor a condemnation. It's a fact. You rave the way any sleeping human being would rave.

— *What is raving? People usually rave when they have high fever. They speak in incomplete and unrelated sentences.*

— Yes, you come up with unrelated sentences. You talk and you don't understand what you say. You don't see the connection between the things you say. You don't see the mechanism of your suffering.

— *I come up with associations that are connected to what you say.*

— When a radio is switched from one radio station to another, it does the same thing. We hear news. Then, we hear music, followed by distant, unrecognizable voices. What is the interconnection between all of this? Can you see the interconnection between all these fragments you come up with?

— *Some channels transmit advertisements.*

— This is another fragment. How does it connect with the previous ones?

— *You are providing the advertisement theme. You are flipping the channels.*

— Yes, I am. I am turning the knob of the radio, and you describe what you receive. You receive fragments of totally unrelated parts, transmitted by different radio stations. That's what you do now. That's what every sleeping man does. Do you intend to sort this situation out? Are you capable of seeing yourself as a radio that flips from one channel to another, constantly producing fragments of sounds without any understanding of what it produces?

— *As I have said already, I verbalize my thoughts in trying to answer your questions. This is a direct reaction to your message. You throw something at me. My thought comes back as a reaction to your words.*

— That's why I compare you to a radio receiver, and myself to someone who flips through the channels of that receiver.

— *How can we lead a different dialogue if you are asking the questions?*

— You cannot lead a different dialogue when you are in a sleeping state. The "sleeper" raves about his reactions on different channels. If you continue to identify with the "sleeper", you will take everything I say as an insult.

— *I don't take it as an insult. You tell me I am raving. I doubt that, but you know what you are talking about. I trust you.*

— Okay. Can anyone explain why I call what she says raving?

— *You call it raving, because her thoughts jump from one place to another. She starts talking about one thing and she immediately jumps to the next. She doesn't notice these jumps. A woman starts talking about her husband, "My husband is sitting in the kitchen. He is watching TV. News are being broadcasted. We have a 32-inch Sony."*

15

— "My kettle is boiling over. I forgot to buy eggs. I got to work late yesterday. Peter upset me last night. He said I was stupid. My shoes are red. Oh, no, they are burgundy in color."

— *When a human being talks this way, he doesn't see his association chain.*

— Exactly. I call it raving, because there is no interconnection there. There is no logic there. I am not talking about the logic of sleeping people. I am talking about the logic of the awakened one, which a sleeping man cannot grasp. A sleeping man raves in the stream of unconnected associations. He doesn't see the interconnectedness of the events that happen to him. A thought pops in—it is a phenomenon that happened to him. Another thought appears—it is a phenomenon that happened to him. An action or bodily sensation is a manifestation of something that happens to him. What is the pattern of their appearances?

— *Thoughts, feelings, sensations, and actions are usually interconnected.*

What is the difference between an awaken man and a sleeping man?

— Thoughts, feelings, and actions are connected to the experiences you receive. What kind of experiences are they? The sleeping man cannot answer this question. He can only regurgitate portions of the experiences recorded in him. A voice recorder records everything it can catch and then regurgitates it, but a voice recorder doesn't understand what comes out of it.

— *So, if we were to take a thought, connect it with a corresponding feeling and action …*

— We would get a sleeping man. This is an apparatus that has its own, associatively connected thoughts, feelings, and actions. Every human being contains certain fixed associations. A sleeping man is a recording device that has a peculiar way of recording what is happening around him. If we were to take three or four such devices and record one situation, each one of them will record and reproduce this situation differently. Every one of these recording devices has a different attunement for recording and reproduction, but each one of them just records what is happening around him, not understanding how he does it. To record what's going on and to understand it are two totally different things. The sleeping man records things. Then, he expresses them according to his associations. We cannot demand a recording device to explain what it records and how it records it. It can only reproduce what has been recorded on it every time you turn it on. If you were to ask it, "What exactly are you bringing up?" it will not be able to say anything. It will continue to bring up what was recorded on it. I pose the most difficult question for a sleeping man to answer. I push him to see the experience he creates and records instead of simply reproducing it. The ability to see the experience which was created, experienced, and recorded by you is a peculiar feature of an awakened human being. A sleeping man cannot understand what he records. He can only bring up and regurgitate what was recorded in his structure. This is the difference between an awakened man and a sleeping man.

— *I got it. I still don't understand what it means to accept.*

— You regurgitate your experience to me. I invite you to become aware of it.

— *That's the reason I came here.*

— Correct. But you don't understand what we are discussing now. You talk without any understanding of what you transmit. You can start to discern between what a sleeping man says and what a self-investigator, who works with his experience, says. Can you make this discernment?

— *I need a specific situation.*

— Okay. Let's say your husband is slouching on the sofa. Is your reaction to this situation always the same?

— *No. When he spends too much time on it, I become aggressive.*

— Is that when your irritation appears?

17

— I get nervous. Is he getting sick? Did something happen? Is he depressed? I want to shake him up.

— Why don't you let him lay there as long as he wants?

— Because I can't do it myself.

— You are not aware of this situation. You just react. When he spends more time on this couch than you consider to be normal, you experience irritation. In reality, you are irritated with yourself.

— Yes.

— This is how you react to what happens around you. You don't understand why you get irritated when he spends more time on the couch than you think he should. You don't understand that. Do you?

— I have an image of a man in my head in whom I am interested. He is very active and energetic.

— Okay. Why did you find a couch potato who would cause you to experience irritation?

— He didn't do it before. He used to be very active.

— Why did you find a man who turned into a couch potato?

— Did I make a couch potato out of him?

Explanations of the mind can diminish the severity of a
conflict for a while, but they will not

Resolve it

— And what did he make out of you? He irritates you when he is lying on the couch. Neither one of you understands what is going on; you just react. If I were to push you hard, you would explain why you react the way you react. If I don't push you, you will simply react. When I ask you a question, your mind comes up with an explanation as to why you do what you do. But your mind's explanations do not explain why you react the way you react.

— My mind tries to explain why it reacts the way it reacts.

18

— The mind searches for the answer, and it will find it. The mind can explain everything, but it's explanations do not explain the mechanism of what is really happening between the two of you. You can have hundreds of different explanations, but the situation doesn't change.

— *You are right; it doesn't change.*

— It doesn't change, and it will not change. So, what do your explanations mean? Do they offer you an opportunity to resolve this conflict or to just reinforce it?

— *These explanations allow me to lower the voltage of the conflict for a brief period of time.*

— Yes, but your fear doesn't disappear, and it is fear that creates your reactions— irritation, anger, and aggression. Not seeing the real reason behind your irritation leads to the reinforcement of this state. By bringing up certain explanations for the conflicts that happen around you, the mind just lowers the level of emotional manifestation of fear; it doesn't remove it. It cannot remove it. You need to better define the reasons behind the conflict you experience. Only then will you be able to resolve it. Can you see that your explanations do not solve the problem?

— *I was able to resolve this conflict before. How did I do that? I did that by doing what I wanted to do. I didn't drag him anywhere or push him into doing anything. I would get on a bike and go to the beach.*

— That was a temporary solution—you just unplugged from him for a short time. You can't do that all the time.

— *I cannot.*

— Therefore, this is not a solution to the problem. You can spend two weeks on the beach, but then you will come home and find him on the couch. You will be even more irritated this time.

— *He unplugs from you on the couch. You unplug from him on the beach.*

— You can divorce him, but this will not solve the situation either. You will find a carbon copy of him. Why do you find and

19

marry men who irritate you? You find them yourself. Each one of you finds what he needs.

— *Looks like we have a lot of anger inside us, and this anger is searching for an exit. My husband simply offers me an opportunity to let this anger out.*

— It follows that we do not unite for love. We unite to let our anger out.

— *Not only anger. We unite to allow every emotion that appears in us to get out.*

— Which emotions? You are hallucinating again. You need a garbage can to dump your aggression. That's what you need a husband and kids for.

— *I definitely don't get married for that reason.*

— No? Then why did you get married?

— *I married to be happy.*

— You deliver kids to be happy. Then, you dump your aggression on them.

— *I never said that I dump my aggression onto my kids. You said it.*

— Everything I say is based on what you say. If you get married for happiness and give birth for happiness, you should be happy. Why did you come to the seminar? Did you come happy, or did you bring us your problems?

— *I have both. I cannot say I only came with a problem.*

— Okay. Do you want me to help you sort out your happiness?

— *I came with problems.*

— So, you do have problems. And that is what I am trying to sort out now—your problems. You don't understand what I mean when I talk about a problem. **A problem is an interaction that occurs between two opposite sides of a duality.** Your entire life points to the presence of opposites. They cause you to experience conflict, fight, aggression, and pain. I invite you to "take the bull by the horns", but you keep insisting that the bull only has one horn. You talk about unhappiness, but when I

20

invite you to sort out the reasons behind this unhappiness, you say everything is great with you.

— *I am not saying that everything is great, but there are other things aside from anger and hatred. You exaggerate the situation when you say that I got married in order to dump the hatred I have onto my husband.*

— Yes. That's precisely what you've said. I just repeated it.

— *I am saying there is more to my marriage than anger and hatred.*

— What else is there?

— *I am telling you: boredom, impatience.*

— Can you use one word to describe boredom and impatience?

— *No.*

— Both are negative emotions that you don't want to experience. You call them problems. You want to have positive emotions all the time, but you are not successful at that. Am I right or not? One can find positive and negative sides in everything around here.

— *Of course, I want to experience positive emotions.*

Every "sleeper" wants to have a positive experience but
winds up having a negative one

— Of course. Every sleeping man wants to have a positive experience but winds up having a negative one. So, what do we do with all this negative experience? You want to acquire positive experiences. As a result, you acquire negative experiences.

— *Should we yearn for negative experience then?*

— I am not here to tell you what you should yearn for. I am here to sort out everything you bring and to discuss it with you. I want you to see every positive and every negative experience you have acquired throughout your life and to understand how they are interconnected. Unless you understand that, you will not be able to change anything in your life; you will continue to act the way the rest of the sleeping population acts, i.e. to accept and insist on having only a positive side. People like different things, but they only like positive things. At the same time, they are

21

submerged in negative experiences. They keep asking how to get out of it. This is the craziness of a sleeping man, who thinks it is possible to get rid of the negative states by reinforcing the positive states. Everyone tries to do that. People try to do that in their families, the corporations they work for, government structures, etc. They want to have positive experiences, but wind up getting negative experiences.

— *Yes. I have a notion of how my husband should behave. When he behaves according to this notion, I accept him. When he doesn't, I don't accept him.*

— When he behaves the way you want him to behave, he is positive for you. When he doesn't behave the way you want him to behave, he is negative for you. You have both the positive and the negative in you. I assert that you want to experience both of these states: positive and negative. Therefore, when your husband spends the entire day laying on the couch, he fulfills your desire. You don't think that's the case yet. You equally need both love and hatred. How do our opposite sides interact? How do our positive and negative sides interact? How do good and bad interact? How do love and hate interact? Are these sides interconnected?

— *They transfer from one side to another.*

— Exactly. They transfer from one side to another. Can you get rid of something without losing its opposite side?

— *Is our task not to enter the extreme points of duality?*

— What is the "the extreme point" of duality? The sleeping man is looking for a "golden middle", but in reality, he is afraid of exacerbating his inner conflicts. One man cries a little bit and laughs a little bit, another cries inconsolably and laughs without restraint. Their extremes are different, but the interaction between the negative and the positive sides in everyone is the same.

— *In that case, let's not call something positive and something negative.*

22

— We can't do that. We have to use things that have been named and exist as a result. We need to sort this out. What dissatisfies you exactly?

— *I am dissatisfied by the irritated state I am in.*

— As you have just said, positive states and negative states flow one into another. What is opposite to the state of irritation?

— *It is the state of pleasure.*

— So, if you want to experience pleasure, you should also experience irritation. This is what flowing from one state into another is all about. If you don't understand how opposite states interact, you will not be able to do anything about these states. If you understand that, you should start seeing what is happening to you, according to this new understanding. You have just said that positive and negative states flow one into another, but do you investigate your problems based on this understanding? I don't think you do.

— *In connection to the situation I experience at home, I thought it would make sense to feel my irritation as hard as I can and then move to another state. But to do that, I need to see these states.*

— Do you accept your irritation?

— *I don't like myself when I am in the state of irritation.*

— Okay. You don't like yourself in the state of irritation. It means you do not accept this side of yourself. Who experiences irritation?

— *Irritation is being experienced by an older woman. She is always irritated.*

— Who is this older woman?

— *Well, it's me.*

— So, it's you. You experience irritation, not someone else.

— *Yes. It is me. It is this older woman in me who grocery shops and runs around the house cleaning up after kids. This older woman experiences irritation.*

— And who experiences pleasure?

— *It's another lady. She is calm.*

— What lady are you talking about? You spoke about the old woman. Where did the lady come from? The older woman who does grocery shopping and cleans up after kids experiences the negative state. A well-dressed high society lady experiences pleasure.

— *She is not neceserely a high sociey lady. She is just calm and relaxed.*

— Who are you talking about? Are both of these characters—an older woman and a lady—in you?

— *Yes, I have both of them in me.*

— Okay. So, who are you?

— *I am the one who sees both the irritated older woman and the calm lady.*

— Okay. You are the one who sees yourself as both. Can you relate to what this older woman sees and what the lady sees?

— *Yes, I can.*

— So, you are the irritated older woman and the calm lady. You are also the one who sees both of them.

— *I am totally mixed up now.*

— Are these three characters in you?

— *Yes. These are my parts.*

— So, all these parts are you?

— *These are my parts. These are parts of my ego.*

— These are your parts. The older woman who experiences the negative states and the lady who experiences the positive states are your parts. Is that the case?

— *There are many other parts in me.*

— Okay. Let's sort out these three parts for now, because everything else is as dual as this. It looks like these parts of yours are opposite to each other. Am I right?

— *The older woman is constantly irritated, stressed, and tired. She forgets to buy things she needs to buy at the store. Her kids are hungry. They are screaming. She is late with dinner.*

— This older woman experiences the negative state. How about the other one, the high society lady?

— *The lady is calm, "It's Okay. I'll buy it later. The kids will be okay."*

— It looks like one of them experiences positive states and the other experiences negative states.

— *I feel more comfortable in a state of calmness and pleasure.*

— Which "i" are you talking about? There are three of you here.

— *There are many more of me here.*

— Let's sort out this trio for now. You say you feel better when you are calm. Who is saying that?

— *The one who is observing those other two parts of me is saying that. The calm lady doesn't cause the observer to be irritated. I want to pat the calm lady on her back and to tell the irritated old woman to comb her hair.*

— It looks to me like this third part of you condemns your irritated old woman.

— *Yes. The third part condemns the older woman and approves of the calm lady.*

— If the third part condemns one part and aproves of the other part, it is not the Observer. The Observer doesn't condemn anyone. Let's sort these two parts out. One of them, the calm lady, likes tranquility. How about the second one, the irritated older woman—what does she like?

— *She likes tranquilty too. She yearns for it.*

— Does the irritated older lady want tranquility?

— *Of course, she does. She wants to bring everything to order.*

— What does this irritated older woman create?

— *She is trying to clean up the house.*

— What kind of a state is she in while she is doing that? What does she create around her? What kind of a state does the irritated older woman create in this house of yours?

— *She creates chaos and condemnation.*

— Irritation. She creates irritation. She is an irritated older woman.

— *Yes, she is.*

25

— Then this is the state that satisfies her. If she creates irritation, it means irritation satisfies her.

— *But it appears to her that she wants to get rid of this state of irritation.*

— What does she create? What satisfies this irritated older woman?

— *She creates and she is satisfied by the state of irritation.*

— Yes. She creates the state of irritation. She is irritation. You say she wants to transform irritation into tranquility. No, she doesn't want to do that. Why didn't she do it yet?

— *Because in order to transform her state into a state of calmness, she needs to...*

— She needs to be irritated. She needs to experience the state of irritation.

— *She needs to do a lot. She needs to change the world around her according to her notions of how it should look.*

— Will calm and tranquility only arrive when it's done? You will never bring the world to correspond your notions. Therefore, you will always remain in the state of irritation. Therefore, you need irritation.

What about your calm lady? Why is she calm?

— *She is calm because she doesn't need to change the world. She is not trying to adjust it to her notions.*

— That's why she is calm. Those are two totally different approaches and they create two totally different states. The irritated older woman needs irritation. The calm society lady needs calmness. Each one of them creates exactly what they need. You are both the irritated older woman and the calm lady. Do you understand that?

— *Yes. Moreover, I see myself in both roles.*

— Yes, you need to experience both irritation and calmness. How will you find what calmness is if you don't know what irritation is? Calmness is absence of irritation. How will you find what irritation is? Irritation is absence of calmness. You have two

26

sides to compare. You will not be able to feel irritation or calmness if either one of these sides is absent. You are both of these states, but presently you create these states mechanically: you don't understand how you create them.

— *Yes. I cannot control these states.*

— How can you control something that you don't even see?

— *No, I see it. I don't like myself when I am in the state of irritation. I see myself starting to get irritated and I say to myself, "You are going crazy again."*

— When you condemn yourself in such a way, you cause the state of irritation to appear. That's what we are discussing now. Your irritated older woman needs irritation. That's your method of bringing up this emotional state. To have irritation, you have to be dissatisfied with something. This older woman finds something she is not satisfied with, and as a result, she gets irritated.

— *Yes, there are many things she is not satisfied with.*

— And that is what she needs. That's exactly what she needs.

— *What does she need it for?*

— Are you asking me? This is happening to you.

— *I am asking myself. Let me take a break and think about it for a while.*

— Okay. Does anyone want to share his perception of our conversation? What did you see?

— *I saw that I am never in a part that creates calmness. The only way for me to create calmness is to run away from irritation. That's what I see now.*

A man who is asleep cannot see himself from the outside

— I will ask you to pay attention here. What is basic here? **The personality or the ego structure of a human being is built dually. It consists of two opposite sides, which fight each other. One side of a duality condemns the other,**

27

which feels guilty. Then, the second side condemns the first, and the first side feels guilty. That continues eternally. This is the only thing that happens in the old matrix of divided perception. Nothing else can happen here. This is not easy to grasp. I keep talking about this all the time, but our conversation occurs at the level of superficial explanations. We cannot get to the essence of the question. Why is it so difficult for us to see the essence of things that happen to and around us?

— *It is difficult for me to grasp it because it deals with me and only with me. It deals with my basic perception of myself.*

— In order to see the the essence of things, you have to change your perception of yourself. You cannot do that if you are asleep. A man who is asleep cannot see himself. That's exactly what our long conversation shows.

— *I would like to discuss a similar case. I don't know whether I have experienced a right thing or not.*

— What does it mean: "a right thing or not"?

— *I don't know whether I was I able to get out of it or not.*

— You haven't gotten out of anything yet. You keep asking me, "Did I get out or not? Did I exit or not?" You cannot exit out of anything until you start to see the mechanism of your sleep, i.e. to see what exactly you are trying to exit. I keep talking about this mechanism. Who can describe the mechanism of a sleep he is currently in? What you spend hours describing in minute details can be described in a short, concise form. But it can only be done when you understand the essence of the events that happen to you. Who can do that?

— *The mechanism of sleep consists of our identification with one side of a duality and our insistence on fighting its opposite side. Let me share what happened to me today. I knew I had to come to this seminar, but I didn't have the money to pay for it. Trying to find the necessary sum, I started to manipulate my husband. I observed this inner conflict. I asked myself, "What are you afraid of? Why are you so fearful?" It turned out I was afraid to transfer from the decent part to the indecent part. These two parts were fighting inside me. There is more to it. I couldn't discern between what my feelings were saying and what my mind was saying. My feelings were resisting: "Don't do to others what you don't want them to do to you." My insistence to come to the seminar brought me here anyway. I went to it purposefully. I was riding a bus when I saw this conflict. My heart was constricted. I was suffocating. I was afraid to transfer to this indecent part. I got stuck in the decent part, and I didn't want to yield to the indecent part.*

— No personage wants to awaken from sleep. Everyone here experiences the thoughts you have experienced and acts the way you acted. Some of you don't talk about it, and the appearance is created that they are fine. But if they were to talk about it, they would find themselves in the same shoes.

— *Olga talks about this mechanism, but she only talks about her inability to see her feelings clearly. She doesn't say that being in the decent part, she is afraid to move into the indecent part.*

— *That's exactly what I have said.*

— *Yes, you have vocalized it. You spoke a lot about feelings and the mind. You felt constriction, and you saw what you needed to do. But you did something else. One part says one thing now, while another side manifests the same thing in relation to the opposite part. That's what's happening here. That's what I see here. I felt resonance with Natasha when she spoke about her relationship with her husband. You, as I can see, are identified with a certain activity, and as a result, your husband manifests passivity. Naturally, being in the active part, you feel irritated by your passive part. Not accepting it in yourself, you project it onto your husband. That's why you are constantly irritated. You keep asking him to be active all the time: "Be like me!" He, on the other hand, expresses your opposite, passive part. You represent two opposite parts. That's why you irritate each other. Your husband is your second part.*

— *I understand that. My son doesn't cause me to experience this irritation.*

— We got stuck in the dream. I invite you to sort out what's going on here.

— We are playing the game of awareness. Without awareness, we will never understand what's going on. We condemn our resistance, but without resistance, we will never understand what resistance is. The meaning of life is in its meaninglessness. Life is paradox and movement. Behind everything is fear. Fear comes from the mind's inability to trust. It overshadows the opposite side—trust. Oh! I am shaking!

— Take a look everyone. Total chaos.

— It seems to me, we simply describe something. We don't keep ourselves accountable for what we create. We don't see it.

— We are seeing the release of associations recorded in the recording device of your body-mind. This seminar is not the first seminar for many of you. We have only two new students, but we start everything as if anew. Do you see how difficult and painful this work is? This is neither an insult nor a condemnation. This is a fact. I am describing my own state now, and I am describing it from my current position. We have gathered here to see something new. And I need to see it too. This is not a process of education. This is a process of investigation.

— Can one always express what one becomes aware of in words?

— The difficulty of this reality is in its paradoxical, dual nature. Different worlds were constructed as complicated structures that mirror each other. This reality is made dually— two mirrors are looking at each other. To see yourself as a whole, you need a third mirror, which will reflect what is being reflected in two parallel mirrors. That's the paradox of this reality. You never see the whole thing. You only see half here. That's where all our problems stem from. What is a conflict? We have already discussed that. **A conflict is an interaction of two opposite parts of a duality. You cannot see both of your opposite parts simultaneously without using the third mirror that reflects two opposite mirrors. Getting on the side of one part, you fight the other part of a certain duality, and vice versa.**

The language that we use in this reality is also dual. It is impossible to describe anything holistically using a dual language. It was created to be used in the world of illusions, and it is impossible to describe anything real by using illusion. One can only create a certain system of pointers here. That's what I do. Using this dual, illusory language, I create a system of pointers for you, which you can use by moving on the road to yourself.

— *Our ancestors spoke about themselves using a plural word: we. They didn't divide themselves.*

— Yes, but we have since been divided. **While in the consciousness of duality, you cannot understand yourself holistically. I invite you to join me on the road to wholeness by seeing every duality and the dual nature of this reality all the time. You can only exit duality when you clearly see and can concisely describe its mechanism.**

Sufferings of a consumer of kaif* love

— *I will talk about two sides of a duality that brought me here. I am involved with two groups. Yours is one of them. About a year ago, I joined another group. From the standpoint of duality, it makes sense. When I am there, I don't have to be a personage. I don't have to think about who I am. I don't have to think about who is sitting in front of me, and what they mirror in me. I don't have to think about whether I say a right thing or not. You don't have to walk on your tippy toes all the time there. I feel kaif there. While there, I am not concerned whether it's a man or a woman who is sitting next to me, or whether they are close to me or not. All the masks are off. One just sits there and experiences kaif of a high level of vibrations. Recently, I clearly saw that our school conducts logical work, the work of the mind. We are constantly dealing with our negative sides. We express everything bad and negative we have that we don't want to acknowledge and accept. While in the other group, I don't have to do that. One can simply receive the kaif of Unconditional Love there, i.e. the state of bliss where you have everything. Suddenly, a thought came to me. Here, in this group, my action is to observe what is happening to me and around me, while in the*

31

other group, I don't have to do anything. Everything is there already. However, something is missing. There is no action there. I came to the conclusion that in Pint's group the work of the mind is being conducted and negative states are being released, while in the other group, I get into a state that is outside the mind. I get into the heart there. This is what I sense. I took this physical sensation for the state of love. I am not sure how to express it. While being there, I thought that perhaps that was the state of separation. I am dealing with the mind here and with the heart over there. How can I connect these two states? Where did I get this sensation that I am only in my mind here and in another state over there? Action is necessary here, and no action is required of me over there. Another thought flashed through my mind: "Perhaps we don't have enough people here. Perhaps that's why the channel is so unsteady." The love I receive there, I do not receive here. Love just flows there without me doing anything. Everyone there knows what the source of love is. Everyone knows it doesn't belong to him but just passes through him. I know that as soon as I say that it is mine, it would stop.

— We are working simultaneously with three centers: mental, emotional, and physical. The fact that you don't understand that tells us that you are not whole. Why don't you describe the leader of that group to us?

— *He is hard to describe. There is nothing special about him. He uses very simple words. This is not important either. I experience kaif there.*

— In that case, why are you here? You have already found your love.

— *I saw dependency behind it. I am getting attached to this positive state. I don't need anything else. I can just sit there for hours. I don't even need to listen to what he says. People in Osho's group experienced a similar dependency. They were just sitting around him in a state of bliss. I saw this and thought, "Wow. It's great I have learned something from Pint. I will be able to sort things out here. It's great that I learned about all these parts of mine." For some reason, it was important for me to connect all of this. I chose to come here today. I can discuss anything I want there too. I spoke about what I felt with him, and he was happy for me. After my conversation with him, I developed a strong desire to come here and to figure out what it was. But this is another dependency. I see that, but I cannot decide on my own—whether to stay there or to run here. I swing between one side and another. After I said everything to him, I experienced a state of tranquility. Perhaps I can connect and combine these things. I experience a state in which I can act, but I also experience a negative state. I am in my mind a lot. I also saw quite clearly that while here, I accept everything. I accept everything from the group and from you. After talking to some of the students, I feel guilty. Later, I understood that after I have a deep conversation with someone, I exhaust something inside myself, and I move forward. The result there is the same. While over there, I also feel love coming from someone, and I feel like I don't give anything in return. While here, I feel that I use these conversations with people while I am totally closed myself. I am a machine that sucks everything in as a consumer. When I realized this, I ran here.*

— I feel the same. I come here. I consume and consume, but whatever I consume disappears. That's how I feel. You have helped me to see my intellectual center. There is no feeling there. It is huge. It is interesting, but it is dry. Something is missing there. Love. That's what is missing. While Natasha was speaking, I understood that I see things only through my mental center. My emotional center is closed.

— For me, love represents positive emotions: the states of calmness, tranquility, and relaxation.

— For me, on the other hand, love is action.

— What is love? I want you to pay attention to the way your mind, which always needs two opposite halves, works. You need someone who will irritate you the same way you need someone to love. These people create two opposite sides, which are necessary for you. You cannot have one without the other here. That's what you spoke of. This is your perception of what is happening here, but you also need the opposite. From my standpoint, while over there, you are just a stupid "saint". You are sitting there loving and loving. Then what? You are sitting there loving everything: one day, two days, three days … What's next? As you rightfully said, "Something is coming through him, but he himself doesn't know what it is."

— There is no attachment to the roles of a "man" and a "woman" there.

— Nevertheless, some kind of an attachment is present there, right? You have mentioned there is love there. A certain emotional state is there. What do I do *here?* I irritate you all the time, pushing you to see what's going on within you. He, on the other hand, sits there—all goodness, doing something totally opposite to what I do.

— Something very unusual happened yesterday. I was able to have a conversation with him that was very similar to the conversations I have with you. The main difference is that you immediately trample and destroy our illusions, while over there something is being shown and done to me and I start to experience kaif. I don't even have to listen to what is being said there. Not even perceiving information on the intellectual level, I experience a certain physical kaif there. Something is off there. I don't like it.

— Why do you say that something is off there? This is what duality is all about. The way you define what happens here forces you to search for the opposite side, and you will find it. You are a system of two mirrors. You need both sides. That's the only way for you to discern between them.

— It's great over there, but I have to run here to sort it out.

— You just went bananas from being high. Your mind is thinking, "What's next?" This interest can be satisfied here, but you also need to experience the emotional state you experience in that other group.

— It's funny. While in that state, I don't have any objections to anyone or anything. There are no stupid attachments there.

— Are you saying you are not attached to anything or anyone? You have spent some time there. Don't you feel condemnation there? Don't you feel guilty there?

— I do. I do. But it is not manifested so strongly anymore. When I observe what is going on in my life from this kaif side, I can see the whole game and I realize how tired I am of this show. I am bored with it. I am not interested in it anymore. I feel apathy.

34

— You experience kaif and love there. Perhaps that's what you need?

— *I am afraid of this state; one doesn't need anything while in this state; everything is there already from the get go.*

— It appears to me, you have found what you need.

— *This state doesn't lead to any action. That worries me.*

— Why not organize a commune and have fun?

— *This state is great in terms of physical sensations, but I want to experience some action. I want to have results. This is a result of me not giving anything back. I just sit and receive there. I want to give something back.*

— You say something comes through him. You receive this something, and all of you are happy.

— *This is bullshit.*

— Why?

— *If we were to combine this state with the ability to give, we would be able to move mountains. I want to look at people without judgment and be able to give them something at the same time. I am unable to give people anything there. I only consume there.*

— He is giving you everything. You take everything from him. Everyone is happy. But why is he giving you this something that you call love? Why is he supporting your consumer attitude?

— *As I have said already, I am a consumer here too. I am using everything and everyone here. People discuss their personal stories, but I am stuck in my inner world. I cannot express myself at all.*

— So, go ahead. Express something.

Search for negative experiences and you will find yourself having a positive experience

— *What can I express? I can't give anything. I understood something yesterday. I don't need money. I don't need material things. But I can't give anything to other people.*

— What does he give you there? What do you accept from him?

35

— *He provides us with an unexplainable physical sensation.*

— Okay. He provides you with an unexplained physical sensation. Why don't you give it to us? What kind of a sensation is it? Did you receive it? If you have really received it, you should be able to transmit it to us.

— *A few days ago, I asked him, "Why do I experience this sensation only when I am around you? As soon as I am out of here, it disappears." He answered, "You should not wait for this state to come. It may not come for many years. It can only arrive spontaneously." The way I understood him—everything happens coincidentally, and no one knows how.*

— This is a game. If you like this game, continue to play it.

— *They say it is a state of emptiness. They say it doesn't belong to them.*

— Okay. And what do I do?

— *You return me to myself. You say that I am the reason for everything.*

— Perhaps you don't need to be here. Perhaps these mental reviews with which we occupy ourselves here just hurt you. You have a guru there who gives you love. You feel kaif there. Perhaps you need to be there, not here. We are not calm here, and we will never be calm here.

— *A thought has entered my head that this is a similar dependency. Here, I get dependent on constant excitation from the inner digging.*

— Is there a difference between what I do and what he does?

— *There is a big difference between what you do and what he does. Nothing is being done there. I just sit there. I am a consumer there. No one hurts anyone there. This is the most important thing that he stresses—we should not hurt each other. No one cries there; tears are not acceptable. Here, on the other hand, we bring up and discuss everything we want. We can discuss our negative experiences.*

— Why do I accentuate your attention on the negative instead of positive experiences? I could have easily done just that: "Look how great you are. Let's look at your beautiful essences." We can hug, kiss, and compliment each other. I, on the other hand, always direct your attention toward seeing the negative experience. I keep reminding you that positive experiences and negative experiences are two sides of one coin, but I primarily work with your negative experiences. Why?

— *Negative states submerge into sub-consciousness and start to create from there.*

— *I understand that you speak out of love. You show us our illusions and you destroy them. I think, "Why don't I experience this physical kaif being here? I know you do it out of love too."*

— Perhaps I don't do it out of love. Perhaps I am a false teacher. Perhaps I do everything out of hate. You think you don't have hate in you, but I say you do. You are full of it. So, why do I accentuate your attention on hate, on the negative experience?

— *You do that because we don't want to see this negative experience in ourselves.*

— Yes. You don't want to see it in yourself. You don't want to see your negative side. That prolongates your separation. You are convinced you are positive, and positive only. As a result, you cannot understand why you experience all these problems in your life. Why are you irritated by certain things? Why are you dissatisfied with certain things? You cannot understand it. You consider yourself to be good, and you only want to have positive experiences. "Why do I feel irritated when my husband spends the entire Sunday on a couch?" "Why does my boss scream at me? Why does it irritate me?" "I will spend some time with the love guru and experience kaif there. But as soon as I leave him, I start to experience irritation again. I come to Pint, but he talks about the negative stuff I carry inside me. I don't think I have that negative shit in me. I go to my guru, and he says I don't have any of it. Why?" I tell you, "Go to your guru and remain in the positive state with him if you can."

— *We are flipping from one state to another.*

— *There were moments when I was crucified between love and hate, but presently, these two states have collided in me head to head.*

37

— This is your inner separation.

— *Collision is also a separation.*

— You accept only positive states, and you fight the negative states. That's how you maintain your inner separation. You come out of the presupposition that you can be on the positive side and smell the roses all the time. That's what all sleeping men think. They constantly seek pleasure, happiness, love, cosmic vibrations, and gurus who would appear out of nowhere and enlighten them. At the same time, they are submerged in the negative states.

— *That's what I experience now—only the negative states.*

— Okay. Are you satisfied by this situation?

— *No.*

— What do you want? Do you want to experience positive states?

— *Yes, I do.*

— Here you go. Everyone here wants to experience only the positive states. "I am surrounded by shit, but I want to smell the roses." Everyone is looking for recommendations on how to reinforce his positive states. You are constantly searching for positive states, while you happen to be in the negative states.

— *We do.*

— I constantly push you into the negative experience. If you start to search for the negative states, you will experience positive states. That's the way duality works. You don't understand it yet, but for some reason you come here. Why do you come here? Why don't you go to the gurus that carry goodness? Why don't you go to the psychotherapists who talk about and promise positive states? Why don't you spend your day repeating positive affirmations? Why don't you do that?

— *I have spent months doing that.*

— However, your state has not changed. Moreover, you experience even more negative states now. The more positive your talk is and the more positive your actions are, the more negative states you see and experience. Why is that?

It's simple. A human being contains two sides: positive and negative. But for some reason, he accepts his positive side and fights his negative side. Thus, he is always unhappy. This is a concise description of the life of a sleeping human being.

— *It sounds simple, but personality cannot see that. So, this is not so simple. Moreover, this is impossible.*

— This is so simple that the mind cannot grasp it. Unless you accept your negative side, you will not be able to manage the duality "positive—negative". When you face a serious problem, you start to rave, insisting only on one explanation of what is happening to you. Why does a man rave? He raves because he only accepts one half of himself. He doesn't accept his second half. He raves because he doesn't know himself holistically. As a result, a man cannot navigate through the circumstances of his life. This is it. As soon as you grasp that, our work here will be done. You will become instantly enlightened.

— *The fight between two opposite sides of personality starts as soon as I enter a personage. As long as I look from above, everything is clear, but as soon as I enter the personage, I am torn apart.*

— So, why do conflicts appear in personality? They appear because the positive side doesn't accept the negative side, while the negative side doesn't accept the positive side. That's it. You cannot understand yourself unless you accept this basic tenet— you have both sides in you. In that case, the investigation of your dual personality turns into an investigation of its positive and negative sides. But you don't want to investigate the negative side. Am I right? Why do I constantly talk about the negative side? Why do so many people have the impression that I belittle and insult them? It happens because they don't want to accept their negative parts. These parts are in you, but you don't want to accept them.

— What if I were to see, to accept, and to allow myself to manifest my negative side? If I were to do that, I would appear to be bad, as from the positive side's point of view, the behavior of the negative side is unacceptable here. Condemnation would immediately follow.

— Are you implying that you don't manifest your negative states?

— Yes, I do.

— Then why are you afraid to start seeing what you do? What did you just say? "If I were to accept it, I would allow myself to manifest it." As if you don't manifest it already.

— Beeing in my good, positive side, I don't see myself manifesting it. I don't see it. My positive side doesn't see it.

— Exactly. "I pretend it doesn't exist." When I am told, "Start to see it," the positive side screams, "Horror! Horror! I am about to start to manifest the negative side. This is unacceptable!" But you are already doing it. People around you are screaming because they experience it. That's what each one of you is doing already. You need to see how simple this mechanism is and how difficult it is to become aware of it.

— Can you be a bit more specific? What exactly did I do? Who did I inflict pain upon?

— We cannot grasp it because our personality is dual.

Loyalty is a sprout of betrayal

— Yes. We return to the dual makeup of the personality. Unless we understand this dual mechanism, we will not be able to go further. While trying to figure it out, we will experience resistance, which reflects what we happen to be in. As we are one, I do not separate myself from you and you from me; I bring this situation to our attention. What are we going to do with it?

— I am afraid to accept the part of me that I call a traitor. Something prevents me from accepting it. I simply reject the thought that I can be a traitor.

40

— "I don't consider myself to be a traitor. I constantly betray people, but I don't see it. When I commit an act of betrayal, I look for a scapegoat and for an explanation as to why I was betrayed. I don't even accept the thought that it was I who betrayed." What does it mean to see my negative side? In this case, what prevents you from seeing this side's one-sided conviction, "I am not a traitor." But you do carry the opposite side of this duality in you. It is in your sub-consciousness, and it is called a betrayer or a traitor. You have both sides. How do you betray? You betray the same way you manifest loyalty. The root of these two words—betrayal and loyalty—is the same in Russian language. Can your mind comprehend that?

— *I have a question. We have discussed that creation in this reality occurs through a thought, the verbalization of it, and a resulting action. In that case, how does our subconscious side create if there are no thoughts, verbalization, or actions there? Is this another paradox?*

— *A horrible fight occurs there. One side of a duality always acts as a betrayer in respect to the other side.*

— They betray each other every minute. Right now, not talking about your betrayer side, you betray yourself. I want you to pay attention to this. This is a paradox. This dual reality is paradoxical. You are as truthful as you are a liar. You are as loving as you are full of hate. But such a perception of yourself contradicts the matrix of one-sided perception. When you start to see yourself holistically, you start to break your habitual matrix of one-sided perception, i.e. of the sleep of consciousness. When you start to see yourself holistically, you cannot play the game of "sleep" anymore. Actually, you can still play it, but you start to see it as a game you create. In not seeing it, you play it without accepting the responsibility for your own actions, and suffer as a result.

How Pint manages to balance on the razor edge of sleep and wakefulness

— I don't know how to make you see that. Perhaps you can help me. I am going to ask for your help. Can anyone of you see how to do this work differently, not the way I invite you to do it? Can we do this work any other way? I cannot get you out of sleep. I accept my weakness. I have done this work for a long time, but I have not moved anywhere. I want you to know that. I am not condemning you or try to make you feel guilty. I see this as a very difficult period of our Process. I am asking you to mirror me.

— *Perhaps this has to do with the format of the seminar itself? We come to the seminar as if it was a week-long vocation. Seminars are not integrated into our life. While we are here, we understand and become aware of many things, but as soon as we are back home and enter the real life, we immediately identify with one of our sides, the side we are in habitually.*

— Okay. But I am also submerged in a state of sleep. My personage is also asleep, the same way each one of you is asleep.

— *Every personage is deeply submerged into a state of sleep. For some reason, we have lost the connection with our Supreme Aspects.*

— Okay. Have I lost this connection? I invite you to see me as a part of you. That may help you to figure out something. You are saying that when you leave the seminar, you fall asleep again. I am also a human being, and I also happen to be in the reality of sleep and illusions. Do I lose the connection? I invite you to investigate this situation in relationship to me, so you can understand something about yourself.

— *Let me disccuss my understanding of how it happens in your case. I think you can regulate the degree of your de-identification. By entering a certain experience, you can regulate the degree of your de-identification and make decisions that depend on your intention to identify with something or not.*

42

— When I enter a situation with which I am not familiar, I submerge into sleep, the same way you do.

— *Do I understand you correctly? You cannot regulate the de-identification process?*

— Yes. That's what I said. When I submerge into a state of sleep, I identify with it.

— *Wait a minute. I thought you do everything in a state of awarenes. I thought you observe the state of sleep and people who are asleep. I thought that was the meaning of your life.*

— How can I do that? How can I, while submerged into a state of sleep, fail to submerge in it completely? I have to submerge into sleep to sort certain things out. Once I figure out what I intend to figure out, I come to the surface and share the results of my investigation with you.

— *Are you connected to whatever is outside the sleep when you are asleep?*

— *I think you are experimenting with sleep. You investigate something, and as a result, knowing that you are an investigator, you cannot fall asleep.*

— Okay. And what about you?

— *For you, this is the object of investigation. You are de-identified from it.*

— *As a personage submerges into a sleep, he starts to search for the positive states. An investigator dives into a sleep for a different reason. He does it to become aware of something, to become whole. A personage always wants to receive something "good". The aim of a self-investigator is different. The aim of a self-investigator is awareness.*

— Great.

— *That's why an investigator is happy to encounter any situation, even though his personage may see and experience the situation as horrible.*

— As you know, I have experienced and continue to experience multiple negative states.

— *That's what you need. You can only see something through the negative states. The heavier the experience you enter, the more valuable is the gift of awareness you receive at the door.*

43

— Okay. So how can I, while submerged in a negative state, exit out of it?

— *You operate based on the intention to see your personage as a personage.*

— **Yes, this is the basic idea I live for here.**

— *The most important thing for you is to become aware of who you are, and you are using every experience that your personage undergoes to achieve that.*

— And what about you?

— *You enter one dream after another all the time, but you keep a vigil. You are constantly aware of yourself entering these dreams. It seems to me that one should constantly remember that one is not a personage.*

— What does it mean to remember? How can I remember that?

— *You observe your every manifestation: thoughts, feelings, and actions.*

— How can I observe that when I enter a dream? I get submerged in it. What do I do? What is it that allows me to constantly maintain the state of awareness?

— *You observe your personage.*

— I use something that prevents me from losing my ability to be aware.

— *You accept any side of a duality you encounter.*

— **I use verbalization. I always verbalize the state I happen to be in. I pick up a state, and I start to verbalize it. That's how I de-identify with the state and the dream I happen to get in. I enter my negative sides, and I investigate them. A normal sleeping human being does not want to see or hear about these states. I, on the other hand, use them to become self-aware.**

— *Do you verbalize these states in front of someone?*

— Yes.

— *What if you don't have people around you?*

— If I don't have people around me, it means I don't need them. If I need something, I will have it. If I don't need something, I will not have it.

— *What happens when you don't verbalize your state? Can you still see that you are not this role?*

— When I verbalize my state, I start to see the state I am in as an illusion. My personage contains as many illusions as any other personage here. Every one of us is submerged in the old matrix of one-sided perception. All of us are influenced by it. There are no exceptions here. My personage is equally subjected to this influence.

— *I have to ask my fellow students a question. Do any of you remember this mandatory requirement to verbalize your states?*

— Good question. Moreover, how many of you know that you need to verbalize your states? And if you know that you need to verbalize them, do you do it? If you do, do you do it constantly? Until you see yourself as the subject of self-investigation, you will remain asleep. We have started to discuss betrayal, and you suddenly became silent. If I were to see my betrayer side, I would start exploring and verbalizing it right away. If I were to see that I am the dirtiest pig on this planet, I would start talking about it immediately.

— *I think I can see it without verbalizing it. I can see images of me without identifying with them. I don't need to verbalize anything. It's important for me not to identify with them. These images are built on one side of duality and they change all the time. There might be millions of them.*

— When you discuss the role you play, understanding its dual nature, i.e. seeing the role opposite to it, you de-identify with that duality. If you don't discuss it, you don't see the dual nature of your role—you continue to identify with it.

— *So, by verbalizing and discussing the situation you are in, you shed fear.*

— Exactly. I share multiple stories about my personage with you. Some of these stories are horrific. In the process, I start to see these stories as fairytales, and my personage as a player in the world of illusions. I use my personage to investigate the old, one-sided matrix of perception in all its manifestations. That allows me to see every mechanism of its functioning. If you are identified with something, you cannot see it holistically. When you de-identify with your personage, you can talk about him as your experience. You de-identify with the experience acquired by your personality. Thus, you de-identify with your personality. Personality is your experience.

— *I am not sure why, but the states I experience do not require verbalization. The state of de-identification simply appears.*

— How do you know you are not identified with this state?

— *I can easily see dualities when I am in this state.*

— Are you constantly in this state?

— *No.*

— What part of your day are you in this state, percentage wise?

— *Very small. Perhaps one tenth of a percent.*

— Great. So, where are you during the rest of your day?

— *I am asleep.*

— We have discussed how to de-identify with a state of sleep by using my technique. I discuss my personage as an experience. Do you discuss your personage as an experience? Do you consider the experience that your personage has acquired to be your experience? Do you accept your entire experience? No. That's what slows you down on your way to becoming aware of yourself holistically.

— *Who is it that decides to accept experience or not to accept it?*

— Only you can decide that.

— *I want to accept it, but something prevents me from doing it.*

Do you see the experience of your betrayal?

— Who is this you? For example, you are a betrayer. You receive the experience of betrayal. Who decides to discuss this

46

experience here or not? Who does it? You say you want to accept yourself. I say, "Tell us about your experience of betrayal." And what happens?

— *I don't see this experience.*

— Have you ever been betrayed by a friend?

— *Yes.*

— That was you. The experience that your friend had is your own experience, but you don't see it. You see your friend betraying you, and you condemn him. But if you were to see yourself doing what your friend did, you would not be able to condemn your friend any longer. **The habitual system on which the old matrix of consciousness operates is to condemn other people for what you don't see in yourself.** When you start to see your own experience, you will not be able to condemn others for it.

— *Can you slow down please.*

— Your mind is getting stuck. Your habitual mode of perception starts to break. It is habitual for you to condemn someone and to feel pride for not being a betrayer. You condemn other people who you think have betrayed you. I, on the other hand, tell you that you are this betrayer, and the experience of this betrayal is yours. When you start to see your inner betrayer, you will not be able to condemn those who, as it presently appears to you, have betrayed you. We are observing what happens to a creature called a human being when it is shown two sides of itself. What is happening to you now?

— *I feel this* betrayer *in me, but I don't want to be him. I cannot accept him.*

— Great. If you accept him in yourself, you will not be able to condemn others for their betrayal. You will also not be able to experience pride of superiority. People run around full of pride. I just showed you the mechanism of pride's action.

— *What will we be left with then?*

47

— You will be left with nothing. You will not be able to say, "How proud the word man rings!" anymore. This phrase is a proclamation of the pride of the ego. For your ego to be full of pride, you need to humiliate other people. In that case, you can appear white on their background. I am speaking as simply as I can. Do you understand the simple language I use? Your understanding will depend on your acceptance of your own opposite sides. Do you accept them or not? You need to accept every negative side of your personality. In that case, you will not be able to condemn others for their wrongdoings or experience self-pity for being wronged. When you are betrayed, you wallow in self-pity and swell with pride from condemning the man who betrayed you.

— How are we to manifest ourselves in that case? Will it not lead to full inactivity?

— You need to change the old system of perception of yourself and other people. You cannot do that yet. Your gut feeling tells you that Pint is speaking the Truth, but you are not willing to do what he suggests. Pint talks and talks. You listen to him, but you continue to do nothing. When you start to do what he asks you to do, your pride and exclusivity will end. Your ego doesn't want to experience such an end. In that case, it needs to condemn me: "He wants my death. Therefore, he is bad." You come here for this, but the end never comes. It is close. Your state can be described as the near end. You are running after this end, but as soon as you see it, you hide or run away. I describe things the way they are, and it makes a certain impression on you. Your gut feeling is that I am right, but your ego says, "No! We are not going to do that."

— But we need to do something ...

— Correct. I am calling you to action, but you are afraid to act because that will be the end of your one-sided ego and of the state of conflict connected to it.

— It will be the end of my authority and prestige.

48

— Why are you trying to hold on to your authority and prestige so tightly? For example, you can say that you will not respect me for doing something you don't want me to do. I will tell you that you don't have to respect me. I will agree with everything you say about me. But your mind has created a notion that in this case, Pint will lose his authority. He will not be an authority for you, and your mind needs an authority. These are different forms of hallucinations. Everyone here is hallucinating in a different way. Someone is afraid to lose his authority through me losing my authority; another one is afraid to lose me as a source of knowledge. This is the atmosphere in which we are working. I am describing a situation the way I see it. I do what I do, and I continue to do it. I also show you where what I do leads us to. What do you suggest I do? I am asking for your advice.

I invite you to investigate your fear, but you run away from it

— *The only thing I know is that fear is not something we need to run away from. It is a signal we need in order to verbalize what we feel. It is a pointer and a helper. Fear is always here; one doesn't need to invent anything.*

— Exactly. You either start to investigate your fear, or you get afraid and try to run away from it. I am not sure where you want to run, but you are trying to run away from it. The fear of fear and the investigation of fear are two totally different positions. I exacerbate fear in you. You become afraid of your fear, and you run. I invite you to investigate fear, but you continue to run from it.

— *You are right, there is nowhere to run to.*

— I ask you, "How do you feel?" You say you are scared. I ask you to look at your fear. You say you are afraid, and you continue to run away from it.

— *That's how we can see our fear...*

— You don't see your fear. You get scared. You must stop, turn around, and look your fear in the eye. Instead, you run away

49

from it. I run next to you screaming that this is just an illusion. You agree that this is an illusion, tell me you see it, and run even faster. I ask, "Why do you run?" You reply you are afraid of it. That means you don't see it.

— *This illusion is our life.*

— "This illusion is my life, and I run through my life." I am telling you that this is not life. You insist you don't have another life, and you ask me to run next to you. You say you like to talk to me, but you tell me you will continue to run away from your fear because you are afraid of it. I run after you during a seminar while you are running away from your fear. Then I disappear, and you say that you are terribly scared because you don't see Pint who would remind you that fear is an illusion. While Pint is next to you, reminding you that this is an illusion, you continue to run from fear. "He helps me to sort out what I am afraid of, but I am still afraid and I continue to run," you say. I describe things the way they are. And what can we do with this?

— *When you talked about us not understanding anything, I experienced fear. It seems to me, that in the case of my personage, awareness is identification of the personage with the part of my personality that is aware and comes to the seminars. Prior to this seminar, I spent three days in the country. I experienced a state of total meaninglessness and aimlessness. I saw many of my identifications. When one is in the personage, one always has an aim. One always either wants something or doesn't want something. While in the country, I could care less. Mom was calling me in the morning to go somewhere, but I felt indifferent: "Okay, I will come with you." I would spend hours doing nothing. I was not drawn to anything. TV used to irritate me a lot. Now, I can watch it.*

— I can dig a ditch or sit by a ditch.

— *I experience a state of meaninglesness, but I don't feel bad. I don't feel depressed. I just see my total emptiness. I used to see it in other people, but I thought I was different. I used to read a lot. I used to be very active. Now, I feel tranquility. I don't want to read. I don't need to do anything.*

— Why did you pursue the new books? You were reinforcing the pride of your smart side. Suddenly, you saw it was a bluff. To see the paradox clearly is to remove the buffer that blocks energy from moving freely between the opposite poles of a duality. Energy forms in a personage in a form of voltage that accumulates between the opposite sides of duality. It seems to you that the stronger the voltage, the more energy you have. A personage thinks that if he is to become aware of duality, he would lose energy. Actually, energy will not disappear. It will run freely from one side of a duality to another without resistance. A personage connects his excitation, i.e. stress, with the level of energy he has, while excitation is an indicator of a block that obstructs the free flow of this energy.

— *I would not say there is no energy there. The situation is reversed—I don't even get tired.*

— You aquire energy of a totally different quality.

— *Yes, something entirely different happens. We come home and realize that we forgot to buy milk. The grocery store is far away. Everyone wants milk. People ask me, "Do you want milk?" I scan myself—I don't care. I can do with or without milk, but I offer to go to the store. I walk for thirty minutes, feeling like a robot. Mom thinks I am a hero, but I don't care. I am submerged in this robotic state.*

Programmer—a master of the game of duality

— The meaning of your life is determined by you. What I do can be considered as meaningless or very important. The same can be said about every one of you. Take any role you know and play it. That will allow you to acquire a certain experience. Your personage is holding on to the roles in which he experiences the state of fear, but if you were to become aware of your fear, you would start to feed on a different, higher quality energy. We call this energy Unconditional Love.

— *How can one live in a state of meaninglessness?*

— It's one thing when you get into certain meanings and play a role of a mechanism that rotates in these meanings, and another when you choose the meaning of your game yourself. A human being who lives mechanically cannot do that. He gets into the system of meanings inculcated into him and simply realizes them. The awakened one can choose. A human being who lives mechanically will get born again and again into the new roles and play out these roles mechanically without a choice. The work we do here creates an opportunity for us to have a choice. A man who lives mechanically doesn't have this choice.

— *By making a choice, you become fully responsible for this choice.*

— By itself, responsibility is the result of me being aware of myself. The reality of the dual matrix of perception is based on the game populated by a multitude of typical roles that have commonly accepted meanings, roles such as mother, father, lover, businessman, etc. This is just a game. Personages that get into these roles identify with them mechanically. They acquire experience. In the process of my work, I get in touch with every experience available here. I approach these experiences from the point of view of Awareness, i.e. from the point of view of seeing the mechanisms of their functioning. I am a specialist. My specialty is the game of duality.

— *You are also an organizer of this game.*

— Yes. Imagine a programmer who has created a computer game and entered it as one of the players. He turns into a participant of the game created by him. Every personage in the game is a part of the program created by him. For them, the Programmer is God who can change the game, take some personages out of the game, or introduce new personages. You, as a personage, enter the game and acquire a certain experience. But the game itself can only be transformed by the programmer who has created this game. This game will last for as long as the programmer needs it to last. But this programmer has his own programmer who programs the game of the programmer who has created the game of three-dimensional reality. Do you understand?

— *Can the programmer that plays the game of three-dimensional reality end this game?*

— To become aware of yourself is to get to the level of consciousness of the programmer. If you are just a personage in this game; you cannot get out of it. You can only exit the game when you have done what was expected of your personage by the programmer and die. Later, you will reenter the game, but in some other role. That will allow you to receive a different experience. I play a role of a programmer now. I am giving you the speech of a programmer. I explain to you the rules of this game. I talk about them and about the game as a mechanism. This program has been downloaded as a base of the game of the dual three-dimensional reality. I invite you to get to the level of the consciousness of a programmer. Some personages of this game start to catch up to the basic principles of the game. When you start to do that, you cannot play this game solely on the mechanical level anymore. You can become a programmer or remain a personage in the game of a programmer. This is the illustration of the problem that developed in our group. When you transfer to the state of the programmer, you will not be able to play your roles the way you have played them before.

— *We would lose interest in this game.*

— There are two interests here: the interest of a personage of the game and the interest of the programmer who has created the game. Those are two different interests. Take any computer game. Every actor in any given game has his interest. When two actors fight, they are both interested in winning the fight. The players themselves have a very limited understanding of the essence of the game. They have their own, personal interests. For example, to win a fight with an opponent. They don't have common interests. Only the programmer is aware of these interests.

53

— *They cannot even imagine these other interests.*

— When a player's interest is taken away from him, he sees it as the end—his life is over. And this is true. His life, as the life of a player who is fighting another player, is over. On the other hand, his life as a programmer who can change the game is just starting. A player, who has started to become aware of himself as a programmer, sees a much broader meaning of the game. His old role is not being taken away from him. He can continue to participate in combat, but it doesn't interest him any longer. He starts to become more interested in the mechanisms of the game and to discuss these mechanisms with other players. That's what I do. Many players don't want to hear that. They are only interested in the game they play at the level of their personages. They are identified with the roles they play, and thus, they do not want to hear anything that does not fit their conditioned notions. If they start to listen to what Pint says and to understand it, they will have to part with the player's role. But to do that, to part with this role, is to part with life as they know it.

— *I am scared now. You always say that you reflect our Supreme "I". You say this Supreme "I" is in us.*

— You can say that your Supreme "I" is a Programmer.

— *Okay. You are a Programmer. I am a player. I play my part. You say you reflect the fact that a similar Programmer is present in me. I experienced this during the last seminar. I suddenly saw myself as both a Programmer and a player in the physical body. I project this super master, this Programmer, or God onto you. My personage knows something, but fear prevents me from discussing it. I am afraid to be misunderstood and condemned. I am afraid to appear stupid.*

— This is part of the role your personage is playing.

— *Yes. When I got into this unusual state, I disassociated. I am God. I am the Programmer who creates this game. It was interesting to experience this state, but I was afraid to say that I can be that. My second part was in the opposite side. It has also dissociated from me. It had entered this game to receive the experience of separation.*

— I conduct an experiment. **The goal of this experiment is to transform the game of the three-dimensional reality. I discuss the rules of this game with you. When the players start to absorb this information, the habitual game begins to transform. You cannot play the old game the way you have played it before once you come to know the mechanisms of the game. This is an experiment. I don't know how it will end either.**

— *You show us the conditions that made players out of us.*

— I see that the players do not want to understand the rules of the game because they became identified with their roles. Is total de-identification possible? I don't know. This is one part of my experiment. I discuss everything that I, as a Programmer, know with you. I transfer this knowledge to you, the players, and by doing that, I transform this game.

— *Yes, you are a good example for us. This experiment can come to fruition only when the players start to investigate the game they play and the rules by which they play.*

— I invite you to become the Programmers of your game. Start to see how your game is programmed. I observe how the players react when they are provided with the rules of the game. The appearance of someone who possesses such knowledge in the game indicates that the program is about to be changed. Otherwise, this knowledge would not have been revealed to the players. The players, who receive this knowledge, stop playing the game the way they played.

— *Presently, we are far from stopping the game.*

— I keep sharing what I *see* with you. This causes you to experience a certain resonance. I ask you to discuss what you feel.

— *It's important for my personage to feel that it understands more than others.*

— I can conclude that the player with whom I discuss this knowledge is not capable of absorbing it; he is just showing off, the way he always did, playing his part of the game.

— *Yes, that's what he always did. He continues to do that.*

— He just records what he hears and replies from the matrix of perception he is in.

— *I feel as if something was taken away from me. I feel very uncomfortable now. The meaning of my life was taken away from me.*

— Every player in this game has his own meaning that allows him to play this game, but he plays it mechanically. When he is told that, he experiences rejection.

— *On one side, I want to exit the game. On the other side, this knowledge overwhelms me. I start to think, "What else can be here?" Everything becomes meaningless. I don't understand anything anymore.*

— Let's finish for today.

— *Wow! You hit us very hard, and you want to finish now?*

Duality of a tough personage

— Let's start.

— *Everyone is silent, so I will start.*

— She will talk because all of you are silent.

— *She cannot shut up for five minutes.*

— *Yes, I will speak up. I experienced a heavy chest pain coming here. My chest felt constricted. I asked myself, "What is it that constricts me and makes me short of breath? Where is this fear coming from? What am I afraid of?" It turned out that my personage is scared. It is afraid to show its face. It lives in hallucinations, fantasies, and illusions. I started to investigate. One side of my personage is afraid to manifest itself. It is afraid to live. It is totally inactive.*

— Wait a minute. We can have an impression that your personage is something small, miserable, and invisible that wants to get under the table and stay there. But your personage is different. All of us see that clearly.

— *Yes, it is different.*

— Okay. You are talking out of the part that wants to hide under a table and be invisible, but another part is present in you, too.

— *Yes. The other part knows and understand everything. It knows more than anyone here.*

— It doesn't just knows everything. It experiences kaif* because it knows everything and can condemn everyone. It experiences kaif of condemnation.

— *I don't think its kaif is in condemnation. This part of the personage doesn't love anyone.*

— Wait a minute. You are beating around the bush now. There are two ways to experience kaif: condemnation and self-pity.

— *I start to condemn someone or myself as soon as I wake up in the morning.*

— Correct. **And the stronger the condemnation, the more kaif a personage experiences. But it does it mechanically, not understanding that it condemns itself.**

— *The second part of the personage experiences pain when the first part condemns it.*

— Yes. But in order not to see the second part of the personage that wants to hide under the table, the first part has to condemn the second part strongly. As it condemns, the first part feels how tough it is.

— *Vadim showed me this toughness of my personage during our last seminar. He knows everything. He is smarter than anyone.*

— He knows everything, and he walks around silently. If your ego knows that two times two is four, it will brag about it all the time. It will condemn anyone who thinks it is five. This is the pride of the ego, and it is not a trifle. Otherwise, it appears that the ego doesn't experience kaif. It appears that the ego, as a small mouse, got under the table. No. This small mouse will grow into a huge elephant and break everything in its way. It condemns everything, and that's where its kaif lies.

57

— *It looks like the other part is very weak.*

— It pities itself. That's where its kaif lies.

— *Yes. It does pity itself.*

— Please pay attention here. Every personage has two sides. One side manifests itself stronger than the other. The other side sits there quietly, like a mouse in a hole. It is afraid of everything and it pities itself. One side of the personage condemns the other side and experiences the kaif of condemnation. When it condemns, it feels like Truth itself.

— *My boy used to play with a toy that had two buttons and two soldiers. He would press one button, and one soldier would pop up. He would press the other button, and the second soldier would appear. We cannot press both buttons at once. When I enter one part, the second part suppresses itself.*

— When the ego condemns, it experiences kaif. However, as soon as you condemn someone, you experience the feeling of guilt. The feeling of guilt always accompanies condemnation. You just don't see it. Submerged in a sleep, you can't see it. You don't understand that condemnation and guilt are two sides of one coin. A personage needs to enter a state of condemnation. He feels tough there. Otherwise, he feels like a victim.

— *I will demonstrate my ego to you. One part of it constantly condemns the other part for being smart and active. The other part doesn't want to study. It doesn't want to do anything. This smart part oppresses the lazy part. It says, "Why are you lying on the couch? Who is going to work and become aware?" These parts are fighting inside. One part wants to become aware. The other wants to sleep.*

— Great. You can investigate any duality, but in essence the mechanism of interaction of the opposite sides of any duality is the same. You need to see that. While submerged into the hallucination of this reality, which acts like a sleeping gas, a human being raves, unable to understand himself. What we explore now allows us to clearly see how it happens.

Everything here boils down to condemnation and guilt. Condemnation is great. It offers you a surge of energy. Let's look at the *Dancing with the Stars* show. What do these young, ambitious people do? They compete while trying to prove which one of them is tougher, prettier, and a better dancer. This is a popular show. Young people watch it. Why do they watch it? They watch it because they want to be like them. What we call a winner or a leader usually appears out of condemnation. Where does the energy of the life of the so called "winner" come from?

— *It comes out of the conflict between a winner and a loser.*

— The energy of a personage is voltage that apears between two opposite sides of multiple dual parts of his personality. But this energy cannot flow freely through a figure eight. It is blocked in the middle. The result is that it circulates on one side only.

— *I don's see my structure as very energetic. I see condemnation, but I don't have much energy. Does it mean I don't condemn strongly enough?*

— You?

— *Yes. From the standpoint of the quantity of energy, it appears that I don't condemn strongly enough.*

— You are such a quiet mouse. Can we say that Anna is tough? You will have to get her pretty angry to see certain manifestations of her energy. The voltage between your inner dualities is low. Your inner dualities are not strongly charged. Look at Zhirinovsky*. *(Notorious politician frequently featured on Russian TV whose political style is aggressive condemnation of his opponents). He manifests great excitation. He condemns everyone. He is always right. What does he do, and why is he so popular? What are people envious of?

— *They envy his toughness.*

— What is toughness? Now we know what it is. Zhirinovsky is full of condemnation. He has built a very successful political career out of it.

— *Every politician builds his career on condemnation. They might differ in the form and expression of their condemnation, but all of them condemn each other.*

— *Yes, but the way* Zhirinovsky *does it is unique.*

— He doesn't hide his condemnation. Most of them do not manifest their condemnation so openly. Putin, for example, doesn't manifest his condemnation so openly in public. In the case of Zhirinovsky, public display of condemnation is essential. That's why he is so popular.

What exactly do you want, Anna?

— *I want to have more energy.*

— Did you say you want energy? You should start watching Steven Segal movies. Their plots are all the same. A man is living quietly in a nice suburban house surrounded by his wife and loving children. Suddenly, an oppressor appears who rapes his wife and kills his children, breaking the ideal picture. Tremendous condemnation awakens in Steven, multiplied by his aikido and killer talents. We see him killing every bad guy he sees. He would have never done it if they did not touch his family. But they did. Now we have to watch for two hours how he kills everyone in sight. We watch him kill people, and we empathize with him.

— *But there are many opressors here.*

— That's right. There are many oppressors here. I just described the fight between a "peace loving" Steven and seventy-five oppressors. This is a typical action movie plot.

— *Well, looks like this oppressor was siting inside him. He just manifested his inner oppressor now.*

— You don't say. He is the nicest man around. He is a proper family man who loves his wife and children. He strives for the American dream: a nice house, kids laughing in the backyard, two cars in the garage, and barbeque on Sunday afternoon. But suddenly an oppressor appears who breaks his lifestyle. He fights him while we watch. This topic, Anna, deals with the question of how to elevate your energy. What would happen to you if an oppressor were to appear and kill your dog in front of you?

— *She would be iinstantly filled with energy.*

— You don't have many attachments. Your dog is your main attachment. Suddenly, we see a guy wearing a black mask. He enters your house and grabs your dog. He ties the dog to the stove and you to a table. He starts to kill your dog. Anger and hatred fill you up. You start to condemn him. First, quietly and politely: "This is my dog. What are you doing to my dog? This is my apartment? What are you doing here?" He laughs you in the face and says, "I came to kill your dog." You try to reach for a knife, but you can't. At this point, the voltage of your duality rises. He leaves your home, and you spend the night with a dead dog. Morning comes, and you have changed. Have you seen how avengers equip themselves before they start on the war path? It can be compared to a woman who is geting ready for a ballroom party. I can see that you still don't understand how this relates to you, Anna.

— *What happens when the vector of condemnation turns inwards? What happens when I condemn myself?*

— Condemnation directed inside causes disease. You can direct condemnation outside and insult someone, for example, by calling him an idiot. This is an external manifestation of condemnation. But what happens when you direct condemnation inside yourself? How do you do that?

Condemnation as a source of energy

— *I start to condemn myself for something. Let me share a specific situation with you. I came to pick up my daughter from kindergarten yesterday. I thought her teacher was inappropriately strict with her. I positioned myself between them to protect my kid. Suddenly, I was filled with energy. Then, I realized that I should not do that. I should not enforce my rules there. I should not tell them what to do. I should not tell them how to behave.*

— They will tell you that it is you who should behave according to the rules established there. This would be opposite to what you say.

— *I tried to say that.*

— You tell a teacher she should get out of the kindergarten. She looks at you and says that it is you who should get out of the kindergarten.

— *Yes, that's right. The feeling of guilt appears. It is directed inside. I think, "Why should I go against my desire?" I know my daughter feels bad in kindergarten, but I still take her there every morning. I can't understand why I do that.*

— You don't understand why you do that, but I do. What do I understand?

— *Will you tell us?*

— I will tell you when you answer my question. Why does she take her daughter to kindergarten which is being run by this horrible teacher?

— *She does it to turn on her daughter's program.*

— She does it to increase her energy level by condemning and blaming the teacher. She expresses her condemnation externally. Each one of you performs many such actions throughout the day. Your ego doesn't understand why this is happening, but it creates these scenes constantly.

— *I stopped taking her to the kindergarten.*

— So, you have lost. If you were a good fighter, you would have forced this damn teacher to be fired. But no, she won; she kicked you and your daughter out.

— *That's fine. My daughter feels good now.*

— Correct. That means your aggression has turned inward; it is directed inside now. That's what I want you to see.

— *I got it. Thank you.*

— You realize the second option—the option of self-condemnation. I ask you, "How do you realize it?" The first option is to condemn the external world. This option gets inculcated into a child at a very young age to make a good fighter out of him. He is being brought up on certain literary and movie images such as Robin Hood, Braveheart, etc. While fighting the "enemies", ego elevates its voltage and energy. But Russians are notorious for their intelligentsia class, which has a habit of condemning itself. Lenin used to call these people "rotten, good for nothing intelligentsia." Revolutions need fighters, not "rotten intelligentsia". Dictators don't need people who doubt. Every totalitarian state kills intelligentsia fast because intelligentsia sows confusion. The ideology of dictatorship is simple: "We don't need thinkers. We need fighters who will hate and kill the enemy without questions." To do that, you need to have an external enemy you can hate. Such hatred sublimates into multiple manifestations. If a country is at war, it is physically killing the enemy. If it is cold war, it is in one country proving its superiority over another. Recall the surge of energy we experienced during the cold war between USSR and USA.

The idea of the external enemy is a strong stimulus that has been used by every dictator since Nero's time. Mao Dze Dun once declared war on sparrows. Where does the energy to perform such ridiculous things come from? Why do people commit these crazy acts? It happens because people, submerged in a sleep of consciousness, are hypnotized. They are told who their enemy is, given a rifle, and sent to the battlefields. They don't need to think. They need to act. I am discussing this in connection to the question you have asked and in terms of the sources of energy of the personality of a human being.

— *It seems to me that energy is needed to support a personage.*

— **Some personages are full of energy, and some lack it. Where does energy come from? Where is it going? I assert that every personage that happens to be in a sleep of**

63

consciousness is always in a state of condemnation or self-pity.

— Does it happen because of pride?

— Yes. Maintanance and reinforcement of pride is the aim of a country that wants to be better than its neighbor. This is the side that manifests condemnation. But at the same time, another side always exists. It is the feeling of guilt that eventually leads to self-pity. These two sides exist simultaneously. One of them we are conscious of—it is brought to consciousness. The other side is submerged deep into the sub-consciousness. We are starting to discuss the other side now—the feeling of guilt. How do you realize your feeling of guilt?

— There are many ways to realize it: disease, accidents.

— I was riding a bus yesterday. It was full. Suddenly, a homeless man squeezed through the crowd and sat next to me. He was dirty, unkept, and covered in bruises. I was trying to observe my inner states. I didn't see irritation or condemnation. I was sitting there quietly, patiently observing the situation. He fell asleep and started to lean on my shoulder. I was observing my emotions. Suddenly, I felt that whether I stayed or moved to another chair, I would be hooked on the hook of my mind anyway. If I stayed, I would force myself to put up with it. If I moved, I would display my squeamishness toward him. I was sitting there thinking that this human being is also me. He is also in me. I spaced out for a while, and when I woke up, he was sitting five feet away from me.

— Take a look at the way the mind works. It can only come up with several associations. I, on the other hand, push you to see the dual mechanism of its functioning. You bring up certain situations here without a full understanding of what they mean. Why did you bring this situation to the table?

— My mind offered me only two options: to sit next to this homeless man or to move away. I didn't have any other choice.

— Okay. Let's recall Zhirinovsky again. Consciously, he manifests only one side of his ego—the condemning side. Let's review his opposite side. What is it?

— According to a documentary I watched about him, he is still crying over his mother. He continues to reminisce about his cold and hungry childhood years. He cries when he talks about his childhood. He behaves like a little boy.

— He is a weak boy that everyone insults. He pities himself. We discuss these well-known personages in order to investigate something in us. You have asked the question, "What happens when one directs his aggression inward?"

What happens? A human being experiences guilt. How does guilt develop, and what does it lead to?

— When in a state of guilt, a human being creates situations that force others to do something.

My husband got drunk

— Yesterday, you told us about your husband who you condemn. You have wondered why he upsets you so much. Let's return to your question.

— It is hard for me to return to this situation now. Many things have happened since yesterday. Last night, while I was here, he managed to get very drunk. I almost threw him out of my life two months ago for this behavior.

— You cannot throw him out of your life because he is you.

— Well, yes.

— What does your "Well, yes" mean? Does it mean, "Don't interrupt me. I am going to tell you how he got drunk and what he did when he got home. I will tell you how much I hate him"? I point your attention to something very basic here. I ask you, "How did this man wind up next to you? Why does he irritate you? Why do you get nauseated when he does what he does? Why do you want to dump him? Why?"

— I feel the states he is in: guilt and despondency.

— Yes. He is in a state of guilt and despondency. He gets drunk because he cannot withstand this constant and total feeling of guilt. It is extremely difficult to tolerate these states. Who here knows what it is to feel guilty?

— *I know what it feels like.*

— *I know that too.*

— Okay. Looks like many of you know this feeling. This is a horrible state. What do you do when you feel guilty? What do you do when this feeling is very strong?

— *I usually beg for forgiveness.*

— Yes. Some people get on their knees and kiss the feet of people they feel guilty around. I am not exaggerating. That is what happens when the feeling of guilt gets very strong.

— *One will do anything to get rid of it.*

— Yes. People will do anything to rid themselves of this feeling.

— *Some look for punishment.*

— Yes. You can get into an accident. That's how accidents happen. In any crime, there is a victim and an oppressor. It is common for people to say that an oppressor is looking for a victim. But I will tell you that a victim is also looking for an oppressor. You can be hit by a car, but it will be driven by an oppressor. You attracted him to get rid of the feeling of guilt. You can fall and hurt yourself. You can get sick. You can lose consciousness.

— *What if you are young and don't understand that you are experiencing a feeling of guilt. Where does an oppressor show up in such a case?*

— What do you mean you don't understand? You don't understand much about yourself now either. A personage spends his days in a rave of one-sided perception. What kind of understanding can we talk about when we discuss a sleeping human being? A man is in a state of guilt and victimhood. These states attract the opposite side—an oppressor. We frequently hear phrases like, "innocent bystanders were killed" or "an innocent victim was hurt". Are these people really innocent?

— *What I meant was that even without pronouncing the words* victim *and* oppressor, *people, just based on their inner qualities—one being a victim, another an oppressor—will attract each other. It follows that meetings only occur between opposite people.*

— Yes. Take a look at the dating columns: "A beautiful, intelligent woman is looking for a man who will make her happy." Read between the lines—an oppressor is looking for a victim. Anywhere you look, whether it is dating business or a car dealership, a victim is looking for an oppressor. People talk and write about many different things, but we can see the same mechanism at work here. When you start to understand the essence of things, you will see what's really happening here. So, what do you do in a state of victimhood, when you feel guilty?

— *Usually, I want to justify myself.*

— *I try to lower and humiliate myself.*

— I will ask you to review some work-related situations or situations with friends and lovers that you have experienced. What do you do in these cases?

Now, let's return to your husband. Here he is. He is sitting here unhappy and drunk, nauseating you. You see your own part in him that experiences a state of guilt, and you condemn this part. You feel righteous. Look at this. Your husband provides you with an opportunity to get out of the state of guilt and victimhood and to experience the state of an oppressor. It's a much more pleasant state than the state of a victim.

— *I feel guilty coming to a seminar, and he usually gets drunk when I do that.*

— Exactly.

— *As soon as I leave him with kids, I immediately submerge into a state of guilt.*

67

— Observe and speak out about when and how you feel guilty. **This is the most effective method of spiritual development. Start tracking the states of guilt and your actions at the time. Start tracking the states of condemnation and your actions at the time.**

You will become aware that you experience the feeling of guilt for the things for which you condemn others. You can start with guilt or you can start with condemnation. You feel guilty for the same things for which you condemn others, i.e. yourself. You condemn a man onto whom you project your own feeling of guilt. You condemn yourself for your own feeling of guilt. The mechanism of duality "condemnation—guilt" works in every sphere of life. It works at every age and in every social role. When you become aware of something, you cannot forget it. It is a difficult work, but it is our ability to become aware of something that drives us to do the work of self-investigation. Pay attention to the way your mind works. It comes up with stories. It doesn't want to understand what I discuss. **Your spiritual development will start once your mind starts to investigate your life from the position of the dualities "condemnation—guilt" and "victim—oppressor".**

— *I got it. In order not to feel guilty, I have to condemn someone, onto whom I project the idea that he condemns me.*

— Exactly. That's how this mechanism works. It is extremely difficult for us to experience the feeling of guilt. The feeling of guilt is a horrible feeling. It's hell. As soon as we start to feel guilty, the mechanism of condemnation gets triggered—our ego starts to look for a scapegoat. The ego is always looking for a scapegoat. Who will play the role of the scapegoat? It's going to be someone onto whom you will project your guilt and condemn. That will allow you to shift to a state of condemnation. Guilt, however, will not leave you—you will have to suppress it constantly. How do you suppress the state of guilt?

— I start to defend myself.

— I defend myself too. I wiggle my way out of it, one way or another.

— I can't talk to anyone when I feel guilty. I sit in the bathroom and cry.

— I get angry, and I condemn myself.

— I attack. That's the best way.

— I want you to pay attention here. We keep returning to this topic again and again. No one can tolerate the state of guilt for a long time. The only way out of it is to attack. To do that, you need a scapegoat. Since I experience the state of guilt all the time, I always need to have a scapegoat next to me to dump this difficult state of guilt onto. There are plenty of professional scapegoats around us: homeless and other unprotected marginal people who we call "neither meat nor fish". They are abused by society, but they cannot protect themselves. They are silent most of the time. As you can see now, we need these people.

— We need them to balance all these Zhirinovskies.

— You need them so you can condemn them. The business of alms giving is built on the feeling of guilt. You see an old woman standing on a street corner begging for alms. What do you feel when you give her a coin? You project your helpless, unhappy part onto her.

— God forbid I find myself in her shoes.

Of those who stepped outside the norms

— Gauss's law of normal distribution shows that a small part of a distribution curve of any given parameter happens to be on top or on the bottom while its largest part is inside the borders of a norm. We consider a human being who doesn't express something very strongly to be normal. Let's look at someone who steps outside the norms. Who shall we pick?

— A dictator.

— A killer. A serial killer.

— A judge.

69

— The position of a judge is a very interesting position. A judge can condemn other people without being judged—a complete break of Jesus's commandment, "Don't judge and you will not be judged." A judge judges, but no one judges him. This is society's way to legalize condemnation and to view it as normal behavior.

— *I used to work as a court secretary. This is a paradox. Many family members of judges and lawyers have spent time behind bars, some of them for brutal crimes.*

— Let's take a look at the opposite category of people who also happen to be outside of the norm. Who are they?

— *Disabled people.*

— *Poor, homeless people.*

— Whacky people. There were plenty of those throughout the history of Russia. Many of them occupied themselves with self-flagellation—aggression directed inside. They oppress their bodies. Ascetic practice is a way to punish oneself and one's body by depriving it of something.

— *Rejection of the material world in the name of the spiritual world.*

— How about those vegetarians who abstain from meat?

— *Can't one just abstain from meat for no reason?*

— The ego never does anything without a reason. Why does the ego do what it does? Most vegetarians proclaim they don't eat meat because they don't want to oppress animals. But vegetarians frequently oppress other people with their beliefs. They condemn other people for eating meat. Forcing one's point of view on someone in the form of a diet is another form of oppression.

— *You are right. They frequently condemn meat eaters.*

— If you explore different spiritual, religious, and esoteric traditions, you will find that most of them are full of condemnation.

— *Gurdgieff is a good example. He pressures you very hard. Do this, and that's it.*

— You can play being angry or be angry.

— *When one plays the role of being angry, one experiences energy of a different quality. When one is angry, one loses energy; one feels the energy of very low vibrations.*

I gave birth to you, and I will kill you

— I will ask every one of you to talk about what we have just discussed.

— *I feel guilty for being in debt. I am living with my kids now. I am totally dependent on them. One part of me tries to please them. I cook and clean for them. Another part of me cannot accept the fact that I owe something to my children. This part behaves aggressively toward them. Yes, I owe you, but you owe me too. I gave birth to you. You live in my house. The first dependent part is patient for a while, but if something is off, the second part gets to the scene: "You owe me everything!"*

— "I feel guilty because I live off my kids". Then another part comes out, "You would not even exist without me. You owe me everything." That's how these two parts work.

— *My daughter screams that her husband does everything in the house. I tell her my husband built it, and now it's her husband's turn to maintain it.*

— "If it was not for me, you would not even have a father, not to mention a husband."

— *Exactly.*

— That's exactly what happens, but your ego doesn't see it.

— *I have noticed that I don't react to small problems. I swallow them. Guilt accumulates. Eventually, I blow up.*

— The feeling of guilt accumulates and eventually spills out as condemnation.

— *Yes. It gets to be so powerful, I cannot contain it.*

— The feeling of guilt squeezes you like a spring. It stores and accumulates energy. Finally, it straightens up and fires condemnation all around you—everyone runs for cover.

— *It's a tsunami.*

71

— "You bastards. You would not even be here if it was not for me. You say I owe you? I don't owe you anything!" They retaliate: "Take everything, but stop screaming." They shake with fear. You take everything you want, but suddenly you feel guilty: "What did I do? How could I take something from my own kids?" Now, they get up and scream at you: "How could you take our money?" Now you are scared, and you hide from them. Then, the situation reverses again: "If it wasn't for me...!" They run for cover again.

— *Yes, that's how we live.*

— Yes, that's what happens everywhere all the time.

— *I feel guilty, and I stuff everything inside, pain on top of pain. Then it blows up. I scream at everyone, and I feel good for a while.*

— The part that happens to be in a state of guilt wants to reinforce itself. The second part also wants to get stronger. To reinforce the guilt, you need an oppressor. "This victim is looking for an oppressor" is written all over your face.

— *As soon as I get up in the morning, the oppressor is there: "This is not in the right place. That should not be here." One of my parts immediately feels guilty and starts to defend itself. But the second part hits back full force, and the oppressor runs for cover.*

— Yes. You don't have to spend a lot of time looking for an oppressor—kids, parents, husband, coworkers—whoever is close will do. That's how it works. One side attacks. The second side retreats. For example, kids attack: "Why are you home all the time, mom? Why don't you find a job?" And this side starts to feel guilty, to defend itself, and apologize for its behavior.

— *You have not be working for a long time. You have to do this and that. Why don't you do something?*

— "Please, forgive me, kids. I am old. I am sick." Then, the second part comes to the stage: "What did you say? Did you say I have to do something? Get lost bastards!" And the kids run away scared.

— Some of them are laughing. Others don't understand anything: "Mom, what's wrong with you? Why are you screaming?"

— They start to feel guilty. That's what they need. They start to fill up with guilt, and they become more and more obedient. They get on their defensive side. Then they flip and start to attack. I describe the common mechanism to you, which plays out in different contexts. A man who is asleep cannot see it. He gets satisfied by superficial explanations that do not even get close to the essence of conflicts that happen in his life. His thinking is one sided. He doesn't understand the duality that gives birth to these conflicts. You do it all the time, but you don't see it.

How personality gets charged and how it discharges

I invite you to track this mechanism of interchanging condemnation and guilt throughout your life history. I will repeat. The guilty part demands an escalation of punishment. It needs to be reinforced. To do that, it will reinforce oppression, pressuring you with its victimhood. The condemning part will reinforce itself by condemning and oppressing you. They work in unison like a seesaw, swinging from the highest point to the lowest and back again. Every pendulum has its own amplitude of oscillations, and so does every ego. The movement of mental, emotional, and physical processes proceeds from one side to the other. As the feeling of guilt escalates, you reach the maximum point of patience and flip to condemnation. Condemnation gets stronger and stronger, reaches its maximum point, and swings toward guilt. This happens continuously. The moment when you spill condemnation out transfers you from the state of condemnation to the state of guilt. When you reach the highest point of feeling guilty, you move to the state of condemnation. Review these fluctuations in your life. The amplitude of these fluctuations differs from one ego to another. Someone can be

73

patient for a very long time, storing the feeling of guilt, but at a certain point, the swing will occur, and a long, heavy outburst of aggressive condemnation will follow. Other egos have smaller amplitudes. You may experience a mild feeling of guilt in the morning, and by evening, you are in mild condemnation. Mild guilt and mild condemnation. This depends on the energy capacity of the ego. Energy of the personality is a voltage that appears between two polar sides. If your ego structure is very energetic, you will strongly condemn and experience an equally strong feeling of guilt. If your ego structure is less powerful, you will not condemn strongly, and you will not experience heavy guilt.

— *My boss screams loudly when she is in a state of condemnation, but I know that I only need to wait for a couple of minutes for her to flip and to start to feel guilty. She starts to appologize for her behavior. I have figured her out by now, and I don't react to her angry outbursts. I just need to be patient for a couple of minutes. She always feels guilty after she has condemned someone.*

— **Who were you talking about now?**

— *I was talking about myself.*

— **Don't forget that.**

— *Yes, I understand that. Hmmm, this is interesting. I can recall a few instances when I experienced condemnation, but I cannot recall the last time I felt guilty.*

— Correct. As we can see, the feeling of guilt is hard to experience. This is a very heavy, painful state.

— *Do we erase it from our memory?*

— Yes.

— *In my case, it is different. The feeling of guilt gets recorded, but condemnation does not.*

— Tell us more about that.

— *I have felt guilty all morning. I reached my limit. On one hand, I am being oppressed by my husband who asks me to do something for him. On the other hand, I am being oppressed at work. I also had to ask for time off to come to the seminar. I reached a point when I started to scream at my coworkers.*

— It looks like you have two oppressors to deal with: your work and your husband.

— I also have my mom.

— You have three oppressors. This is a great way to accumulate energy.

— I felt crazy before this seminar. I thought I was losing my mind. At work, I screamed at everyone. I told them I was irreplaceable. I made my boss pay me earlier than my paycheck was due. I screamed at my husband, too. I told him that I had had enough, that he should do everything by himself now. That's how I flipped from victim into oppressor.

— Your pendulum swung back.

— I feel better now.

— You have accumulated a lot of guilt. While in this state, you felt worse and worse. But all of this was done in order to enter the state of condemnation and to oppress everyone around you. That's when you started to feel better.

— It was very bad. I was close to being fired. I almost separated from my husband. But I feel much better since I entered the condemnation mode.

— Will you be able to withstand the state of condemnation for long? Soon you will face your mom, husband, and colleagues at work. They will start to oppress you. You will be compressed more and more, accumulating the feeling of guilt. Then, you will burst and start to scream and yell at them again. This is the cycle of the work of the ego. This is how our ego gets charged and how it discharges. It is similar to the way an accumulator gets charged and discharged. Such cyclic nature of the functioning of the ego is normal and habitual for it. It doesn't want to part with it because the state of guilt is followed by the outburst of the energy of condemnation, which is kaif for the ego. When we are in a state of guilt, we accumulate energy. Later, we spill this energy in a form of condemnation. We find great kaif in this up and down process.

75

— Do I accumulate the feeling of guilt in order to be higher than them?

The booth that exchanges guilt to condemnation

— Yes. It's as if you save up tokens. When you have accumulated enough of them, you want to exchange them for some type of "product". For example, your husband is cheating on you with another woman. You endure it for a while, and then you invite your prettiest girlfriend to a party. He hits on her, and you reach your zenith. That's when you throw everything you have saved at him—every token you've saved will be used for condemnation. There is great kaif in it. You have found this girlfriend yourself. You have arranged everything to accumulate many tokens of guilt with only one aim in mind: to exchange them for tokens of condemnation.

— I have experienced many similar situations with my husband. I easily create them by being cold to him. He would come home drunk and angry, knowing very well that he would soon feel guilty for that. He used to say that the best defense is an offense. He would scream and break chairs. I had to hide in the bathroom.

— "Have fun boy! Let us accumulate our tokens. We will exchange them pretty soon."

— I speak calmly to him. My voice is hard and cold. I condemn him so severely that sometimes I lose consciousness.

— Kaif.

— Perhaps I experienced pleasure and kaif, but to lose consciousness ...

— Look. This is super kaif.

— I don't know how I was able to go to work after these scenes.

— This is kaif! You have been accumulating tokens for a very long time and now you can exchange them for one token that would allow you to "kill a bear"— "That's it, honey! You are done!"

— I was pushing him into a state of guilt.

— "Because I was in a similar state. But now, I am going to give it all back to you!" That's how revolutions are made: "Who had nothing will get everything! Let's kill the rich!" That's how poor peasants and factory workers got the permission to express their condemnation and saved up aggression. They had also received society's approved tokens in the form of rifles. That allowed them to distribute their aggression right and left, killing the elite.

— *What's interesting is that these tokens are accumulated with the best of intentions, under the slogans "I am going to help you. I will do everything for you. I will endure everything."*

— *I will be irreplaceble.*

— *Tokens are saved and exchanged.*

— "I endured, and I will endure more. I will do everything you need." That's how I accumulate these tokens. Nobody knows about it, including me. But when I've saved enough of them, I will recoup. This is kaif of the ego, and it doesn't want to part with this kaif.

— *One part is ready to endure poverty in a shabby apartment on the edge of town only to accumulate the tokens.*

— That's how you prove your sainthood. "I do everything for you, but you don't appreciate me! Just you wait until I get enough tokens to condemn you. Then I will recoup everything."

— *From my side, it was a desire to help a man who needed help. He was raised without a father. His dream was to get into a good school. I thought I should wait, and I gave him everything I had.*

— "I will endure and persevere. I will tighten my belt. I am sick and tired of it, but I will continue to suffer. I will bear it all. Then one day, you will do something, and you will fall into my trap. That's when I will blast you to pieces." Am I right?

— *Was I enduring all this suffering and building these plans for revenge at the same time?*

— Of course. "I have endured all of this to accumulate energy and to start a counter attack of condemnation." In some cases, it may take people a lifetime to flip to the other side. Many marriages end after twenty years with one of the spouses screaming, "I knew you were a bastard all along!" That's the apotheosis of fifteen years of married life. "You have destroyed my life! I don't want to see you again." The "bastard" in question feels, "Yes, I am a bastard. I ruined her life," and starts to look for punishment. Prior to that, he acted as a judge. He used to condemn and abuse her. He used to scream at her and chase her around the house feeling righteous wrath. But the one who was nobody suddenly became everything and decided to occupy the whole place. This is kaif.

— *This is sad and funny at the same time.*

— I emphasize again that this is the kaif that the ego doesn't want to part with.

— *What else does the ego have except this kaif?*

— People say they are suffering and have problems, but in reality, they don't want to part with this mechanism. To understand this mechanism is to decipher the game of the ego. But in that case, you will stop receiving the kaif you receive when you condemn and pity yourself.

At the level of energy of the ego, this is the best kaif. It is better than sex.

— *Why? Is it because the preparation phase, i.e the foreplay is longer?*

— Yes, the preparation is long, and it must be successful. When I talk to you about the new matrix of perception, your mind reviews the number of tokens you have accumulated and says, "I am expecting apotheosis soon. What does he want me to do? Do I have to burn every token I have saved? No, I am not going to do that. I am going to use my tokens."

— *I feel interest now. My ego experiences kaif by tracking down which part said what twenty-four hours a day. It is doing its best. This is kaif, too. You reprimanded me: "Can you stop thinking and not ask any questions for a minute?" This is kaif, too—to see all of this.*

— Tomorrow you will chastise me for not teaching you the right thing. Only one step separates praise from crucifixion.

— *This is not praise. This is something else. This is not from the sphere of conflict. It's kaif to sort out and to be able to see something clearly.*

— Okay. But behind this kaif stands the feelings of guilt and condemnation. They are very subtle, and it is difficult to see them. I repeat, "Everything that the ego does, and the "sleeping" man doesn't have anything aside from the ego, boils down to condemnation and guilt." Irrespective of the context, the mechanism is the same. **To see the mechanism of the ego at work is to become aware of yourself.** When you start to see the mechanism of the ego, you cannot function the old way. But your ego wants something else. It wants to think that it is becoming aware. It wants to collect points, pretending to be "aware and enlightened". To be aware is better than to be smart. He is smart, but I am aware—the mechanism of the trap is the same. The ego doesn't want to part with the illusions because it gets kaif there.

— *It seems to me, the personage will never be able to escape this seesaw.*

— Yes, the personage, or the ego, or the personality, will never do that.

— *Nothing else is available here. I either judge someone or I judge myself. Then comes the feeling of guilt.*

Reprograming the fear game

— Condemnation and guilt work on the energy of fear. Fear, which has billions of covers, manifests itself through condemnation and guilt. Fear is the result of the conflict that occurs between two sides of a duality. Have you noticed that I boil everything down to duality? Everything! The character of the interaction that occurs between the opposite sides of dualities shows everything that happens in this reality. But the ego cannot see the fight of its opposite sides. It is built in such a way that one of its sides always fights the other side, not even seeing this. This is the harshest prison I know. One cannot exit it on the horizontal plane. To exit it, you need to transfer to the vertical plane.

A while back, I asked you what a human being is. You started to discuss your notions. Neither of you could explain what a human being was, but each one of you tried to compare himself to someone, concluding that he is either better or worst in comparison to the one he was comparing himself with. This is not a definition of a human being. I define a human being as cosmic energy. When you hear this, your mind gets stunned. It gets bored. You start to yawn and you lose attention because you cannot understand what I am talking about. Why do I return to this topic? I have told you that to understand what a human being is, we need to understand what humanity is. However, we can only understand what humanity is when we understand what kind of a role humanity plays in the Grand Design of the Creation.

Humanity is a part of the organic life that covers the Earth. Organic life performs a certain function. It transfers energy from the Sun and planets to the Earth. For a long time, we, Humanity, transmitted vibrations that were set in a certain diapason of frequency. I call this diapason of vibration—fear. A few years ago, an opportunity appeared to transmit vibrations of a different quality. I call this Unconditional Love. Presently, both energies are present on Earth: the energy of the old quality and the energy of the new quality. But they are not compatible. To transfer to the energy of the new high-quality vibrations, you need to get out of the old vibrations of fear. That's what we do here. We are getting out of the vibrations of fear.

Who is the programmer of this game? We have compared the script of the three-dimensional reality with a certain game that was created by a certain computer programmer. The appearance and distribution of the new knowledge on Earth tells us that the Master programmer started to reprogram the game.

When we review the last few thousand years of human history, we see tribal relationships change to feudalism, and then to capitalism. The game develops. People call this development evolution. People used to ride horses. Now they drive cars. They call it scientific revolution, and they compare it to biological evolution. But in my opinion, the marker of evolution is the transformation of the essence of the game people play. Up to now, all we did was to play the game that I call fear.

— *Change in the essence of the game points to the fact that the programmer has started to transmit new information to the beings whose egoes used to generate the energy of fear.*

— The programmer programs everything in a way that is necessary for the game he plays. But as a programmer, our Sun is a sub-program of the next programmer. I want you to pay attention to this. The next programmer is also under the influence of the higher-level programmer. That's how we move to God, who is the Master programmer of Everything that exists.

— *We also create.*

— Yes, but the "sleeping" man, submerged in the energy of fear, creates without awareness.

— *I don't understand. Are we speaking of the ego or a human being? It seems to me that the ego is inside the structure of a human being. If it is possible to exit the borders of the ego, a human being is not just the ego.*

— Exactly, but try to explain this to a "sleeping" man.

— *What do you mean when you say the word "man"?*

— What kind of a human being are you? Are you the ego and nothing else, or is there something else there? If there is something else there, what is it?

— *I am someone who observes the ego.*

— And what does this someone see when he observes the ego?

— *He understands that this is just the mechanism.*

— *You teach us to do that. You show us how it is done.*

— Are you doing this work?

— *Sometimes we can do that, and sometimes we can't.*

— What can you do now? I want to see the results. Please, share with us what you have observed in pertaining to the

81

mechanisms of work of your ego. I urge you to perform your own self-investigation.

— *I had two parts in me that would not let me rest for a minute. I still have them in me. One says, "You are bad." Another retorts, "Why do you say that? I am good." — "You say you are good, therefore you are bad. This is pride talking." That's how they chew each other out. I have spread them apart and started to investigate them. One part is dark, slimy, and wavering. It can betray at any minute. You cannot rely on it. It is totally dark. Another part is like Joan of Arc. It is ready to burn for everyone. It loves everyone. It is always right. They are fighting all the time. They cannot agree on anything. I submerge into one side, and I see I cannot be only in it. When I get into the white part, I turn into a stone statue that cannot move. Life in the dark part has some movement. Recently, I discovered that I like the dark part better. If I were to use an analogy, I'd rather be Tom than Jerry.*

— Who is it that loves the dark part better? This is your dark side talking. It says it loves itself. "I don't love the light part. It is too heavy." If you move to the light side, it will say that the dark side is a villain. You swing between two parts of this duality, and in the process, you say — "i". But who are you? Who is talking to me now? Is it the dark part or the light part? Moreover, it is not clear what the "dark" and the "light" parts are at all. You frequently use phrases such as "I am good" or "I am positive". These phrases are related to the light part, but they also point to the presence of two opposite parts in you or two terminals of the accumulator that you cannot connect. The cartoon series *Tom and Jerry* which you brought up is a great illustration of how two opposite parts interact. A dark housecat is running after a light grey colored mouse. That's exactly how the interaction between these two parts occur. When you are in the cat, you look for a mouse to catch and destroy. When you are in the mouse, you look for a cat to run away from. This is what happens to you while you consider yourself to be a unified human being. This is the grand illusion. A human being talks about himself as if he is "one", while he is actually "two". Moreover, those "two" are manifested in every personality in the form of multiple dual pairs. These pairs interact in such a complicated way that it is very difficult to figure out the structure and character of their interactions. You have asked, what is a human being? I am returning your question to you. I am asking you, what are you?

— You have described the structure of the ego. Our work at school, the way I see it, is to see how the fight between our notions about ourselves occur.

You are an assignment—solve it

— Our work creates an opportunity for you *to see*, but do you recognize this opportunity? This is the question. It's not a fact that by gathering here at the school where people occupy themselves with Seeing or Awareness, we are already Aware. When we hear something about awareness, we give birth to two parts in our personality: a part which is aware and a part which is not aware. And based on the conflict that occurs between these two parts, we say that we are aware. We say that the aware part is better than the smart, beautiful, and successful part. We pretend to rise to the top of the hill.

— Why? We begin to understand that the notions we had about ourselves as good or bad are just our notions. It is the conflict between two illusions. One illusion is fighting the other.

— Do you just say this, or do you understand this? Your tongue can say many different things, but do you really understand what you are saying? There is a huge difference here. I share the results of my self-investigation with you, and I keep asking you to describe the results of your self-investigation.

— Should we talk about the external changes we experience?

— If you start to talk about your awareness of yourself as a personage, I will say, "Yes, you are more than the ego." Until you start to discuss your structure, I will not say that you are more than the ego. You hear what I say, and then you restate it from your ego. You have the illusion that you are not only ego anymore. Do you see your own duality?

— *Yes. I have spoken about my relationship with my husbands and about the feelings of guilt and condemnation I have experienced. I see these states clearly.*

— If you see these states, talk about them—describe them.

— *Shall I talk about the feeling of guilt I feel, and how it makes me go crazy?*

— Yes. That's exactly what I am asking you to do.

— *You share the results of your self-investigation with us.*

— How do I do that?

— *You discuss your own life. You act as an example to us.*

— Why don't you do the same?

— *So, it is not enough to describe what I went through, you want me to describe the mechanism that triggered it.*

— I don't want you to repeat my words. I want to hear the results of your self-investigation. When I hear that, I will say that you are more than your ego. Until I hear that from you, I will not say that you are more than your ego. Therefore, the question you have asked, "What is a human being?" remains open. A human being is a question mark for now. How you will answer this question depends on you. If you fill this answer with the results of your self-investigation, you will describe the structure of your ego-personality.

— *Let me clarify this. Do I have to loudly verbalize what we have discussed?*

— You *don't have to* do anything here. This is an experiment. We got together based on our interest in this experiment. I am a part of this experiment. I am grateful to every one of you for being here because without you, this experiment would not be possible. Your contribution to the experiment is as important as mine. Perhaps this experiment presupposes the presence of those who are not aware, so some of us can become aware. Perhaps this is the case.

— In that case, those who are not aware play their role very well.

— I get an opportunity to see my personage from the side thanks to you. Seeing one personage clearly allows us to understand the structure of the whole group, like seeing one molecule of a certain substance allows us to understand the structure of the entire substance. Our experiment is necessary to describe the matrix of separated, dual perception in minute detail. Moreover, while in the dual reality, the mind is also dual. Therefore, the language created by it is dual. Thus, everything that is expressed through words is just half-truth. I have to use this dual language to create a system of pointers that can take us to experience the whole Truth inside ourselves. In expressing something using dual words, I create a system of pointers.

— Will this system lead us to enlightenment?

— Our school is not a stove through which everyone becomes enlightened. We conduct an experiment, and it is quite possible that according to the conditions of this experiment you don't need to become enlightened. Perhaps you don't even need to become aware.

— Then what are we doing here? Are we here for personal change?

Personal change is the opportunity for transformation

— Personal development seminars aim to strengthen one part of the personality in order to change it. Changes in the personality occur when a man gets into situations that are unusual for him. These situations are unfamiliar to his conscious part, but his subconscious part needs them and seeks them out. When you start to enter and to accept these situations, your subconscious part will come to consciousness. In the process, the conflict of the opposite sides of your personality—conscious and subconscious—will get exacerbated. The process of personality change is very painful. It deals with the conscious transfer from one side of inner polarity to the other. During our seminars, we work with personal changes and the transformation of the personality. For transformation to occur, changes are necessary. These changes are related to personality. To transform is to exit out of personality. When we talk about transformation, we start with changing the personality. That's what happens to most personages. You cannot become aware of your inner parts without seeing their dual nature. In the process, you consider one part of the duality to be good and the opposite part to be bad—you don't want to see yourself, as your changes are connected to you, allowing yourself to see your "bad" part. You start to understand that this so-called "bad" part is as necessary for you as the so-called "good" part. The opportunity to become aware appears when changes appear. In the absence of change, there is no opportunity for awareness or transformation. Do you understand what I mean when I speak of changes and transformation?

— *I am not sure I do.*

— *To change is to transfer to the oposite side. Transformation is …*

— The difference between transformation and change is similar to the difference between intention and desire. Do you see the difference?

— *To desire is to want, while to intend is to be.*

— The word "intention" comes out of *to be*, and it is not dual. A desire appears out of *to have*, and it is dual. Therefore, every desire is accompanied by a conflict. The intention is never conflicting. Awareness is never conflicting either. Personality cannot understand that because it exists amidst the conflict of inner desires without any understanding of them. Personality is conscious of only one of its desires. It's not conscious of its opposite desire. I constantly show you that. Do you get it?

— *In one of your books, you said that "If you cannot allow yourself to experience something in your mind, you will experience it in the external world." I thought I could imagine myself being a whore. I thought I had experienced this role internally. Do I have to experience this role in the*

86

external world? I don't understand what I need to experience. What is my notion of a whore? I don't even understand why I need to experience it inside.

— You need to do that in order to not condemn yourself. Presently, you condemn yourself for manifesting your "whore" side. But do you see this condemnation? We are back where we started. If you don't accept your inner whore, you will condemn other women for manifesting their whore part; in other words, you will condemn yourself. You condemn, but you condemn so slyly that you don't even see your condemnation. Do you understand?

— *I don't condemn myself for flirting on a bus. I have the same whore in me as other whores that cheat with married men. I don't think I condemn them.*

— That tells us that you have entered this particular duality and have started to investigate it. But for some reason, even though you have barely started this work, you already declare that you are done with it. I doubt you are finished. I know how long it takes to experience basic dualities.

— *Do I understand you correctly, I need to go to bed with someone's husband?*

— I don't know what you need to do to investigate this side of your duality.

— *I have a notion of what a whore is. I don't know what to do with it. I am totally mixed up now. I have just learned that I can experience all of this in my mind.*

— Earlier during this seminar, you discussed a guru in whose presence you can sit and experience physical kaif, or to feel love as you call it. You feel kaif in your body. What kind of an experience is that?

— *I used to consider myself to be a dry, senseless log that cannot feel anything. While with that group, I understood that I can feel. I am very happy I felt it. I started to feel my physical body, too.*

— You are just getting to know your physical and emotional bodies, but your ego behaves like the first grader who, after spending three days in the first grade, declares his readiness for the second grade.

— *I don't understand. Should I find a man and go to bed with him?*

— What do you ask from me? Are you asking me for recommendations? I don't know what you should do. I am clarifying the duality you are working with for you.

— *I don't understand what it means to experience something physically.*

— I want you to pay attention here. I don't tell anyone what to do. You keep asking, "What is this? What do I do with this?" My task is to point you in the right direction. It's your job to figure out what to do and how to do it.

— *I am getting angry because I don't understand anything.*

— Of course. You have just started here, and you are already saying that you are done.

— *I know I am not done yet, but it appears to me that if I accept this thought and can behave this way, I don't have to do anything anymore.*

— "It appeared to me that if I accept this thought, I have finished already." Please, pay attention to what you are saying.

"I am afraid to experience being a whore…"

— *I still don't undertsand. Do I really have to experience the physical process of being a whore?*

— Why are you so afraid to experience it? If you have to experience it, you will experience it. What are you so afraid of? Why don't you say, "Yes, I will have to experience it" and smile?

— *I think a whore is a woman who takes a man away from his family. So, I need to experience this. I don't want to experience it, because I know…*

— You are discussing your fears now. There are many ways to experiences this role. For example, you may find a man who you will not need to take away from anyone; you may simply have a good time with him.

— *But in that case, the woman is not a whore.*

— You have used this word yourself. Then you started to explain to us how you see the role of a whore. And as I understand it, you see a whore as a woman who seduces a married man. You are describing your notion to us, and you get upset: "Do I really have to do that?"

— *That's exactly what I asked you: "Do I have to experience my own notion in order to accept it?"*

— Who else should experience it?

— *I don't want to do that. I can see my resistance now. I feel it. Why do I resist so hard? I don't accept this! I can't accept this!*

— You do not see it. When you see something clearly, you do not experience resistance. When you experience resistance, you start to see resistance.

— *I know. I undersand that I don't accept this part of me. I don't want to experience this notion. It is horror for me. I don't want to experience that.*

— Why do you find it so horrible? Speak up please. Have you seduced a married man before?

— *Yes, I had this experience. He had a wife and two kids.*

— And what did you do to him?

— *I didn't do anything to him. I fell in love with him. I did not care about his wife. I didn't care about his family. My defense was that he had a bad relationship with his wife and his kids.*

— There you go. This is the second side of duality.

— *I did not think I was doing anything wrong.*

— The notions of a woman-mother, whose provider can be taken away from her family, are totally different. Look, you have a mother sitting in front of you, and we see her indignation. It is written all over her face. And here we have a happy woman who does not care whether this man has a wife and ten kids to feed: "I love you. Let's go to my place."

— *I am upset that I have to break into a fully formed family. "Screw the kids! Let me satisfy my desires."*

— That's what the second part of your duality thinks. A woman-mother says to her husband, "You are a scoundrel, of course, but those are your kids, and you are going to live with us."

— *No, I don't need him to live with us.*

— Wait a minute. What do you mean?

— *I mean, you don't need to live with us. You can separate and live on your own.*

— Then, why are you upset? You allow him to live separately from you. Suddenly, Natasha shows up and takes him away.

— *Let me tell you what pisses me off. Our last fight. He has not been living with us for over a year. Suddenly, he comes home and uses my home to meet someone.*

— He is using you the same way you are using him, but you don't want to see that.

— *He brought some photographs with him.*

— What kind of photographs?

— *He brought photographs of him being intimate with another woman.*

— What happened then? Did he show these photographs to you?

— *He was getting dressed, and he dropped them on the floor. I saw them accidentally.*

— You have said that it does not bother you. Does it bother you or not?

— *No, but I've asked him why he brought those photographs.*

— What difference does it make to you?

— *He came because he could not have gone to her place. I have thrown him out.*

— So, what bothers you, exactly? You don't know what it is, but you are telling us you understand everything and everything is fine with you.

— *I am confused. What is a family? How do I live from now on? I am told that when I live with someone, I should only take care of my own needs. What kind of family is it if everyone only cares for himself? If I care for myself and only for myself, how can I care for another human being?*

90

— Hey, aunty! This is your situation. Your ex-husband comes to you with a bunch of photographs of a woman with whom he is currently living. Does it irritate you? **I want to remind you that you created this situation yourself!**

— *I don't understand what you are talkng about.*

— That's great. And how are we to work with this?

— *I want to know exactly what each one of you means when you use the word "whore". I have a feeling that we are talking about different things. For me, this word means something else. I had a dream last night. I was at some sky resort. I knew I was married, but somehow I found myself at this sky resort all alone. I was totally free. Suddenly, out of nowhere, this handsome ski instructor shows up. I pick him up out of pure vanity. I don't really need him. I pick him up, and we go to my room. We have sex, but it is boring. I woke up nauseated.*

— *What about your husband? How did you feel about him?*

— *When I awoke, I felt the sense of reality. I felt disgusted with myself.*

— *To experience a sense of reality, you had to experience a sense of unreality.*

— *That was a dream.*

— *That's a very convinient position. When you have sex with him, you are asleep. When you wake up, you don't need him. That's the real you, and that's you asleep.*

— *That was a dream. I was disgusted with the fact that I didn't feel anything. I would not be upset with myself if I had been swept away by passion, if I could not resist the guy: "I want you and I want you now!" kind of scenario. The hell with everything, including my husband. But I was just dragging. That was disgusting. If you ask me what I don't accept in myself, then this is it. If you ask me what a whore is, I would say it is a woman who can have sex with a man without any desire. Why do I talk about this? Because you think that a whore is a woman who snatches a man from his family.*

— A whore is a woman who experiences pleasure when she has sex.

91

— I see what it is. I am sitting here calm and quiet. I am not crying. I feel like I am about to get upset. I see that I want to feel pity for myself. I detach and observe my state. There are certain states I cannot overcome because I don't have this experience. I don't understand how to do this work differently.

— In order to receive a certain experience, you need to enter it, not detach from it. You need to experience everything this experience carries. Otherwise, you are playing into awareness, while in reality, you detach from receiving an experience.

— I see certain things as a sign of promiscuity. I cannot allow myself to ...

— That's dumb. You will not get enlightened this way. What kind of transformation can we talk about here? We cannot even talk about change.

— I am afraid to move to another part of myself.

— From my personage to your personage: "Yes, this work is very difficult." But from my Aware part, I will say that you will not experience enlightenment unless you enter your shadow parts.

— I am afraid to think about it. I am afraid to imagine it. I attended a training once where people were shifting to another side. They would dim the light and scream at each other, "Don't be afraid! Do it!" One gets energized and one turns into something else.

— This looks like some kind of energizing dance before the war, when people become euphoric in order to not feel pain and fear. Afterwards, they would get back to their life, and everything would be back to normal. Occasionally, they would recall these episodes when they screamed something and did something. We are dealing with something else here. I know that this work is difficult and painful. At the same time, I am telling you out of my aware side, "You will not be able to do anything here without experiencing it." You are afraid of promiscuity. Okay. Find this promiscuous part inside yourself. It loves something that, from the point of view of the opposite part, is horror and nightmare.

From the point of view of the promiscuous part it is kaif. Can you manifest something out of your promiscuous part now?

The bonfire of debauchery

— *I cannot do it verbally.*

— What do you mean? How else can you do it?

— *I can use body language.*

— It is in you. You are just afraid to talk about it.

— *Yes, it is in me.*

— It is in you, but you don't accept it. You cannot even talk about this part, not to mention allowing it to manifest itself. What's going to happen then?

— *Nothing will happen. I'll keep doing what I am doing.*

— Okay. Keep doing what you are doing. However, this part creates situations in your life, and you manifest it but do not accept it in yourself; you project it onto other people and condemn them. It did not leave you. It created, creates, and will create problems in your life. If it were to disappear because of your not seeing, not feeling, and not talking about it, it would be great. But it exists, and it does what it does. Okay. Let's try something else. Find someone here who you consider to be promiscuous and condemn her. What? You can't even do that?

— *Last night, I went to Natasha's room. She was sitting on her bed with Alex. She was quite unrestrained in her behavior. I don't consider her to be a slut, but...*

— Tell us about her slutty behavior.

— *She was lying on her bed. Alex was fondling her. A thought passed through my head: "Do you have to do it in front of everyone?"*

— She should have resisted. She should have screamed, "Get your hands off me!"

— *You asked me for an example, and I recalled this incident.*

— Condemn her. Here she is sitting in front of you.

— *I told you that I didn't like it.*

— Condemn her.

93

— *Natasha, was it necesary for you to do that in front of me? On one hand, I don't like it. On the other hand, I understand that people in our group are free to manifest themselves the way they want. We can use foul language. We can go to a bath house together.*

— You are a part of the group.

— *Then this is something I don't accept.*

— So, condemn her.

— *Alex is married. He has kids. How could you do that?*

— She is also married, and she has children.

— *That's exactly what I am saying. I see it as part of a lesson.*

— They have whored here. They have done it right under the roof of the School of Holistic Psychology.

— *That's why we come here.*

— That's why they are here. Do you understand?

— *Are you serious?*

— Yes.

— *You have not seen what Anton did. You have not seen the real stuff.*

— *You have not seen how he mounted Anna during the seminar.*

— The whores are laughing.

— *I told Anton to get lost right away.*

— Great! So, condemn these whores. They are sitting here happy. They are full of themselves. Do they need any transformation? They want to whore around. They don't want to do anything else. Their husbands hold them tight, but here, at the seminar, they get totally wild.

— *I expected some conditioned patterns of behavior to be removed, but...*

— *We only remove our underwear here.*

— What conditioned patterns of behavior are you talking about? This is just a ploy. They use me and my school to whore around.

— *I am confused.*

— *I don't understand anything. I should dig the books.*

— What are you talking about? What books do you want to dig? You must condemn those damn whores!

— *What is there to condemn? They are free of complexes.*

— What? Who is free of complexes here? They are all whores. As soon as I leave, they start to screw around. They just talk about transformation with their husbands at home. They are here for a totally different reason. Condemn them. Otherwise, they are going to keep doing what they are doing.

— *Let them do what they do. It is their choice.*

— Oh, come on. This is an unacceptable behavior. Will our school condone debauchery?

— *You break every rule...*

— They are whores. You are the only decent woman here. You are our last hope—condemn them!

— *I can start by condemning you for your foul language. How many times should I tell you not to use profanities in my presence? I got it! I got it! If I don't accept foul language, it's a lesson I should work on.*

— *So, why don't you pass this lesson?*

— *I have used this language quite a few times here. This is not a problem for me anymore.*

— *So, say it! Give it to them!*

— *I have done it already. I don't need to use this type of language anymore.*

— We have not sorted out one duality, but another one is popping up already.

— *My God, how many of them are there?*

— *I know. I see that this is a duality. I just don't want to do anything about it.*

— *Come on. You condemn this woman. Why don't you express your feelings?*

— *How should I express it? I explained everything. I told you, "I don't like it!" What else should I do?*

— *Who doesn't like it?*

— *Talk to Natasha. Tell her you don't like the way she behaves around men.*

— I can't say I don't like it. I thought we were supposed to get rid of our stereotypes here.

— What if this was to happen outside the school? What if she were to get involved with your husband? How would you react?

— I have experienced that. I have shed my tears.

— You are holding tight to your limitations.

— I see these limitations. I understand that, but I don't know how to get out of this situation. I don't see how I can experience this situation now in reality. I can imagine something in my head, but how can I combine it with my notion of decency?

— Tell us how you understand decency.

— As I have told you already, I cannot do what they do. Yes, this is how I see "the whore". I cannot behave this way.

— But you want to do what they do very much.

---

* Kaif or Kif - from Arabic kayf pleasure. Any drug or agent that when smoked can produce a euphoric condition. The euphoric condition produced by smoking marijuana

CHAPTER 2
GUILT AND CONDEMNATION—
INSPIRATION AND EXPIRATION OF THE
EGO

What is an aware change?

— *I am investigating a duality that I define as "initiative—not initiative". It manifests itself in my inability to approach a stranger and to strike up a conversation. I was unable to do that for a long time. When I understood what was going on, I started to consciously manifest my shy, not initiative part. I noticed that when the shy part acts and manifests itself, people see me. They relate well to me. A man who identifies with being shy thinks that people do not notice him. I used to turn away when I manifested my shy part. I used to look down and move away from people.*

As in every duality, the opposite side is always present. It was very difficult for me to move in the opposite, initiative side. This side was observing what was going on and preparing itself mentally for a very long time. Slowly, it started to act and to manifest itself. I drive the same bus to work every day. A good-looking girl rides this bus with me. We have never said a word to each other. Yesterday, I decided to do something different.

— So, what did you do? Did you kiss her?

— *No, not right away. I have to talk to her first.*

— **Okay. As we have discussed already, the only option we have while in the dual personality is to transfer from one side of personality to its other, opposite side. This transfer usually happens without our awareness, and thus, we don't get to see both sides of duality as one whole. The transfer from one part of duality to the other part usually occurs**

97

because of some dramatic and shocking event. **A sleeping man is never aware of this transfer. Our work is to move to the opposite sides of our dualities while being fully aware of both sides and comparing them. This is an opportunity to transform. Have you experienced such an awareness?**

— *When I moved into the opposite part, the initiative part, I noticed that it was full of energy. It was talking nonstop.*

— Okay. One part of the duality is "shy". This is the part of the duality that is habitual for you. How would you define the second part?

— I have defined them as "initiative" and "not initiative". One part may stand for hours looking, thinking, and not doing anything. The opposite part acts swiftly. As I was driving here this morning, I saw a girl who I know. I approached her in a totally different fashion: "Hello! What's up?! How you are doing?"

— What happens when you are in the "shy, not initiative" part? Do you want to approach and talk to a girl when you are in this part? Do you allow yourself to do that?

— *Quite frequently I want to approach a girl. There are many beautiful girls around here, but I have not done that.*

— You want to approach a girl, but you don't allow yourself to do that.

— *Yes. At some point, when I noticed this, I started to avoid girls.*

— Okay. Why do you want to approach a girl? Why do you need to do that?

— *I don't know. I am interested in girls.*

— What exactly are you interested in?

— *There might be more that one interest there. Sometimes, it is a sexual impulse. But most often, I just want to talk to a girl.*

— What do you want to talk about? Are you looking for information?

— *No.*

— Then, what are you going to discuss? Do you separate sexual impulse from a simple conversation?

— *I don't know. First, you look at a girl. Then you approach her and strike up a conversation. Eventually, everything leads to sex.*

— Everything leads to sex. What's the name of this duality? Every contact here leads to sex. The need to discuss things appears only if the sexual interest is present. If there is no sexual interest there, what is there to talk about?

— *I experience something very similar to what Eugene is experiencing. There is this guy at work who I like. When I asked myself, "What do you want from him?" I realized I just want to talk to him.*

— And why do you want to talk to him?

— *It took me a week to see that I was sexualy interested in him. There are many smart people around me, but for some reason I don't want to talk to them.*

— You are not sexualy interested in them. That's why you don't want to talk to them. So, what do you want?

— *Something doesn't allow me to perceive what you are discussing. I can see that energy is always present when two extreme points of a duality are spread apart. Is this energy always connected to condemnation? Sometimes these highly charged energy states appear during inspiration, excitation, and impatience. A personage strives to receive what he consciously wants and feels he is getting close. Some other type of energy appears. When one condemns, the energy that comes out is very self-assured, strong, and deep. It comes from the inside. Energy states that appear during inspiration, excitation, and impatience are different.*

The breathing pattern of the Ego

— I will ask you to pay attention to a very interesting sign. We are sitting in a room called "Centaurus". Centaurus is a creature from Greek mythology. It is a hybrid of a human and a horse. Let's look at the way every animal functions. Let us take the simplest organism. What kind of a life cycle does the simplest organism follow? It is constriction and release. Inspiration and

99

expiration. The heart works the same way: systole-diastole, accumulation and release of blood. Our organism uses the same principle. A human being is a long tube: food gets absorbed from one side, and its remnants come out the opposite side. Accumulation—release, accumulation—release, while part of the energy remains with us. The amount of energy that the body processes depends on this cyclic pattern. There is no condemnation in our body. Condemnation is a mental notion. Unicellular and many multicellular organisms do not possess mental constructs. It is only human beings who have them.

Let's review the way personality functions. As I have mentioned already, the personality functions by utilizing the states of guilt and condemnation, a cycle that is similar to the cycle of constriction and release. This cycle is present in every action of a social animal called human being. I am not talking about the physical body now. I am reviewing a social superstructure: guilt acts as a constriction, condemnation acts as a release.

The energy of a sleeping human being is spent to maintain sleep. People call it life here. I call it the sleeping mode or a mode of survival. A sleeping human being survives. He survives from birth to death. The energy on which a human being feeds is fear.

— *If we were to talk about a sleeping man and a man who woke up ...*

— Right now, we are discusing a sleeping man.

— *How did we wind up here? Did we just fall asleep?*

— Why do you need to know that? Is it important for you?

— *Yes.*

— Why do you want to awaken? Are not you happy with the dream you are in?

— *I am not.*

— What's the problem? What is it exactly that doesn't satisfy you?

— *I don't like the fact that my body is subjected to some kind of laws.*

I want freedom, but I don't know what freedom is

— You are striving for freedom. You connect the notion of "freedom" with the notion of "enlightenment".

— *Yes. I want to free myself from certain laws.*

— The history of humanity represents a fight for freedom. Let's take a look at the Russian Revolution of 1917. A Russian proletariat disposed of the aristocracy and declared freedom, or in other words, the dictatorship of the proletariat. The proletariat was not fighting for total freedom; it was fighting only for its own freedom. But your enlightenment, the way I understand you, deals with total freedom.

— *Does total freedom exist?*

— I don't know. I am trying to discern between these two notions: "freedom" and "enlightenment". Are they the same to you?

— *I think they are different.*

— In that case, what is "freedom"?

— *Freedom is a sensation.*

— What kind of a sensation is it? There are two different freedoms that I know of: freedom *from* something and freedom *for* something. People usually strive to be free from something they don't like.

— *I have read Gurdjieff and Ouspensky, and I think real freedom is freedom from habits.*

— Imagine yourself free from every habit. You would not even be able to get dressed.

— *Is one's ability to get dressed a habit?*

— Of course. Everything here is a habit. Our entire life is a set of habits.

— *Perhaps you are right.*

— Perhaps I am wrong. Don't take my words for granted. We are trying to sort something out here.

— Perhaps you are right, and our entire life is just a collection of habits.

— We wake up, brush our teeth, get dressed, have breakfast, etc. Imagine you suddenly find yourself without a single habit.

— I would not even exist.

— Yes. You would not exist.

— What kind of me would not exist?

— The habitual you would not exist.

— Would a different me, not a habitual me, show up?

— What is not a habitual you?

— I don't know this me, but I would like to know her.

— How can you get to know her if you cannot say anything about her?

— Perhaps I can feel her?

— Feeling is also a habit. A human being has three bodies: a physical body, an emotional or a feeling body, and an intellectual or a mental body. Each one of these bodies has its own habits. Take a heartbeat, for example. What is it? It is a certain habit to which we pay no attention. We walk a certain way, and we sleep a certain way. We eat a certain way. Those are physical habits that you don't even pay attention to. You start to feel a habit only when you don't realize it. For example, if you skip breakfast, the habit of having breakfast at nine o'clock in the morning will remind you about it.

— That's how I can see a habit.

— Yes. You will be able to see a habit and to understand that you are dealing with a habit, or you may not understand that. The same principle works in the sphere of feelings. You have a habitual set of feelings. That's a good way to look at survival. You have certain habitual states that make up the structure of your emotional body. You have mental habits. For example, I say, "A rabbit." What's a rabbit?

— It's an animal.

102

— It's an animal. You have just applied a certain mental habit. Someone says that he loves to hunt rabbits. Another man says that rabbits run very fast.

— *I love a well-cooked rabbit.*

— This is a mental approach that uses preformed habits to see something. Personality is a structure that consists of such habits: physical, emotional, and mental. Do you say you want to get rid of these habits?

— *Yes.*

— Do you understand that if you are to succeed in doing that, you would free yourself completely from what you are now. You would turn into a newborn baby.

— *Perhaps I didn't make myself clear. I want to free myself from the habits that bring uncomfortable sensations and those that slow down my development, whether they are physical, mental, or emotional. Laziness slows me down.*

Personality turns on two forces: one force is directed toward achieving an aim, the other resists this aim

— Is laziness a bad habit?

— *Of course, it is a bad habit.*

— From which point of view is it a bad habit?

— *It is a bad habit from the point of view of achieving your aims.*

— The notion "good—bad" appears when you have an aim. If you don't have an aim, the notion "good—bad" doesn't appear. It is necessary to have an aim. In that case, whatever helps you to achieve your aim is good, and whatever prevents you from achieving it is bad. Let me describe an example from high school physics. Let's say we have a powerful automobile that happens to be on a road devoid of traction. You press the gas pedal hard. The wheels are rotating at a very high speed, but the car is not moving. There is no traction. Without traction, there is no movement.

— *So, effort is necesary.*

— A strong effort is being applied. The engine is working at the maximum speed. The wheels are turning very fast. What else do we need for the car to move?

— *Traction.*

— The road may not have enough traction. In that case, your car will not move. In order for this car to drive, you need to have at least two components. What are they?

— *The force of traction and the force of resistance.*

— Correct. The engine speeds up the wheels, but we also need the force of road traction for the vehicle to move. If the engine doesn't work, while the road has traction, the automobile would not move either. For it to move, we must have two forces acting in opposite directions. We have reviewed the physics of movement. Now, let us apply this to our daily life. You have an aim that you want to achieve. Imagine you could achieve it instantly. Would you strive for it in that case? No. You would search for another aim. To achieve an aim that you have set up for yourself, you need to have a force of traction. You have a force that is directed toward achieving your aim. The force of resistance is directed in the opposite direction. It might be laziness, for example. In that case, laziness is a force that resists the force that is trying to achieve your goal. But without resistance, movement is impossible. Is laziness an unnecessary force, in that case? No. It is a "bad" but necessary condition needed to achieve a goal. It represents a force of resistance. It seems to people that there is something out there that prohibits them from reaching their goal and that removing this something will set them free. Let's say you have arrived where you wanted to go instantly, without any resistance. What would you do next?

— *I would search for something else.*

— Yes. You would search for another aim, and you would achieve it instantly too. What's next?

— *I would seach for something that cannot be achieved instantly.*

— Then you understand that the force of resistance is necessary. That's how this reality is built. It is built dually. That presupposes the presence of two, oppositely directed forces. In a dual universe, a human being is a dual creature whose perception is also dual. Therefore, for you to achieve your goal, you need to have resistance. Being in a dual reality and having a dual perception, you reject resistance. You call it "bad" or "negative". Different words can be used here. For example, "ill-tempered— good-natured". You say you are good natured, and you reject yourself as being ill-tempered. "Ill-tempered" is the force of resistance here. If you are "positive", you reject yourself being "negative", which is also a force of resistance. If you are good, you are not bad. You are rejecting "bad" again, i.e. the force of resistance. You do not accept the law of duality upon which this reality operates. Did my explanation influence your notion of what you want in any way?

— *Yes.*

— In what way?

— *I think I have to apply effort to achieve my aim.*

— Yes, you had that thought before. You thought laziness was preventing you from achieving your aim. You considered laziness to be bad. You didn't understand that to achieve your goal you had to have the force of resistance. Without resistance, there cannot be any movement, or it would be an instantaneous transfer into a certain aim with the following search for the next aim, which you would instantly achieve.

— *Why? This is not a fact. I may not instantly achieve another aim. I may encounter some resistance.*

— This is a fact if you deny the presence of the force of resistance. Let's assume that nothing prevents you from

105

achieving the aim you want to achieve. In that case, you would instantly achieve your aim. That's the story you started with.

— *What did I start with?*

— Here you go! You forget where you started already. This is normal. The thinking pattern of a man submerged in dual perception is similar to the thinking pattern of a lunatic. Actually, he is a lunatic who does not even remember what he says. When asked what he was talking about, he does not remember. He cannot remember. Here, we have an opportunity to discern a lunatic who doesn't remember anything from the one who is whole, the one who remembers and knows everything.

— *We talked about freedom. Then, we moved on to discuss freedom from something.*

— Then, we figured out that you want to be free from resistance.

— *Yes.*

— I have said already that without the force of resistance no movement is possible. You would experience instantaneous transfer to your aim. You would find yourself in a situation where you don't need what you want anymore. You want something, and *boom*—you have it instantly. You cannot want something that you already have. If you want something, you must move toward it, and to move, you need to overcome resistance. Imagine you want to become an Olympic champion, and you instantly became one.

— *It would not be interesting.*

— In order for something to be interesting, you have to overcome many obstacles, i.e. you have to overcome the force of resistance.

— *This is interesting.*

You need laziness to play the game of achieving your aim

— *Is resistance just a part of this game?*

106

— Yes.

— *Then, what is laziness? Is it also a part of the game?*

— Laziness is resistance. There are two types of resistance: external and internal. Let's say you encountered a fence on your way. This is external resistance. You may try to break it or to climb over it. You may also encounter inner resistance: no fence in front of you, but you don't want to go anywhere. You can walk easily, but you just don't want to go anywhere. Your laziness is inner resistance.

— *When I have to, I just do it. That's it.*

— What does it mean, "I just do it"?

— *I don't know. I just do it.*

— This is a premature conclusion. We have returned to the spot where we started. You say that you just need to do it and that's it, but then you find yourself in a state of laziness. You will talk about what needs to be done, but you will feel lazy about doing it.

— *One does not have to pay atention to laziness.*

— It is impossible to not pay attention to it. You have been here for a few years already. Did you try to not pay attention to laziness?

— *Yes.*

— Were you successful? Did it disappear?

— *I do what I plan to do. I plan in the evening to do something in the morning. I wake up in the morning and I find myself with the thought of not doing it. I reject this thought, get up, and do what I planned to do.*

— But you didn't ignore it. You are discussing laziness as if it didn't exist: "Laziness came, and I didn't pay any attention to it." Did laziness just go away? Did you do what you planned to do? Did you overcome this laziness?

— *I don't know what to call it. I probably didn't pay attention to this lazy thought. Otherwise, it could have gotten bigger. I'll try to do it tomorrow.*

— What happens if you don't pay attention to it? Does it disappear?

— *Yes, it does.*

— In that case, you don't have inner resistance.

— *In the morning, I feel very unpleasant.*

— You feel unpleasant because you are overcoming laziness.

— *Yes.*

— So, do you overcome laziness, or does it simply disappear? Those are two totally different things.

— *Why?*

— Let's imagine that you are a mountain climber. You want to conquer a mountain, but at the same time you are lazy about it. Will you conquer it or not? If you plan to do it, you will need to overcome your laziness.

— *Mountain? I don't understand…*

— How clearly do you see what is happening to you? Do you see what is happening to you now, as we have this conversation?

— *Not really.*

What does Pint transmit? The peculiarities of your perception

— What specific intentions have brought you here?

— *I had many reasons to come here, but I cannot define the main one.*

— Some kind of a reason brought you here. How did you find out about this seminar?

— *A few weeks ago I bought one of your books. I read it. On the back cover I found your website. It led me here.*

— Have you experienced some kind of a resonance while reading my books?

— *When something bad happens to me or when I am disappointed with myself, I read your books and my inner, emotional state changes. I don't know what exactly changes, but something changes. That's how I became interested in coming here.*

— This interest brought you here, but you cannot define your intention.

— *I came to experience certain sensations.*

— When we speak of sensations, we speak of the physical body. Sensations are related to certain parts or organs of the body. For example, you may sense itch or pain in your foot or in some other part of your body.

— *When I overcome something, I experience certain sensations. Is it only about the body?*

— We have already discussed that a human being has at least three bodies: physical, emotional, and mental. One of them prevails over the other two in every human being. One man's attention concentrates primarily on the physical body and its sensations, while another man's attention concentrates primarily on his feelings. The attention of the third man concentrates predominantly on his thoughts. This doesn't mean that these men are enlightened, whole, and not dual. No, this is not the case. Everything here is dual, but every one of us has a prevailing body through which he perceives the world. For example, if your prevailing body is your physical body, you would have difficult time understanding what I say if I were to talk to you mentally.

— *I would be bored.*

— You are used to the language of the body, right?

— *Yes, you are right.*

— Okay. How can I transmit what I transmit mentally and emotionally using body language? You might have some kind of a notion about it since you have read my books.

— *I am not sure I understand you. How can you transmit what?*

— How can I transmit the knowledge I transmit using the physical body?

— *The knowledge?*

— What do you think I transmit?

— *I thought you create certain conditions here.*

109

— Every one of you will perceive the information I transmit differently. Those of you who are oriented toward the physical body need to experience physical sensations. Others, who are oriented toward the mental body, needs thoughts. The third group, oriented toward the emotional body, needs feelings. Every one of these bodies is seen by a "sleeping" man dually. The physical body experiences both negative and positive sensations. We can categorize disease states as negative sensations, and the opposite sensations as positive, healthy states. From the point of view of the emotional body, we are dealing with positive and negative feelings. For example, the state of satisfaction and the state of dissatisfaction. From the point of view of the mental body, we are dealing with "correct" and "incorrect" thoughts. If you are oriented toward your physical body, your body wants to experience positive sensations. When you experience them, you are happy. If, on the other hand, you experience negative sensations, you are not happy. I want you to pay attention to the fact that I am leading a mental conversation now. What's your perception of what I transmit to you now?

— *I am confused.*

— Okay. Next.

— *I felt again that the personage feels that he exists when he desires, when he desires to desire, and when he is identified with one side. On my way here today, I clearly saw that everything here is dual, and that every state I have ever experienced gets immediately transformed by my personage into an image, which has the opposite image. And from this opposite image, it condemns the prior image. Identification—de-identification is another image, i.e. a certain behavior. The so-called de-identified part is condemning the identified part.*

— Okay. Let's express what you brought up using the analogy of a moving automobile.

— *We can say that the automobile condemns traction, i.e. resistance.*

110

The force generated by your subconsciousness resists the force of your consciousness

— The presence of two opposite sides in the personality always leads to the resistance between the subconscious and conscious sides. This resistance allows the conscious side to move toward its aim. Without this resistance of the subconscious side, the conscious side would instantly achieve its aim. In that case, we would not receive the experience we need to receive here. Let's take a look at the space ships that move not in the three-dimensional but in higher dimensions. They are attuned with a pilot. When a pilot imagines the place where he wants to arrive, his spaceship moves there instantly. I am describing how it happens in other, less dense realities. The reality in which we presently exist is very dense, inert, and material. The lower the frequency of vibrations, the denser the matter and the stronger the resistance. Why do I bring this up? Your subconscious side prevents your conscious side from playing the game it wants to play by creating a force that resists its desires. I am not talking about your desires now. Whether you want to get married or get a divorce, to give birth to a child, or to go to Hawaii, those are your desires. To achieve them, you will have to overcome the resistance of your subconscious side. While in the vibrations of the third dimension, you cannot receive what you want right away, as this reality is dense and dual. Simultaneously, with the appearance of the desire in you, a force appears that is opposite to your desire, i.e. the force of resistance. This is the inner force, but it will manifest itself through the external situations.

— *It looks like it is impossible to reach one's goal here at all.*

— I did not say it was impossible. I said it was difficult.

— *We fight the resistance, and we don't have any energy left to get what we want.*

— You cannot do it any other way here. We can say that an automobile driving on the road fights the resistance of the road. When a heavily loaded truck drives over a steep hill, it struggles against the resistance of the road. It needs to have a powerful engine to overcome this resistance. Not every automobile will be able to get over this hill. One's engine may not be powerful enough to create the force necessary to overcome the resistance.

— *What does this mean? Are you saying that without resistance, there would …?*

— Let's say, your vehicle has a very powerful engine but old, worn out tires. You try to drive up a steep hill. It is winter time, and the road is covered with ice, and it is slippery. Your automobile keeps sliding back, even though its engine is very powerful. If the road was not slippery, you would have easily mastered this hill, but presently you are sliding back. A powerful engine does not guarantee that the aim will be reached. You have to have good traction, i.e. good resistance.

— *But it should not be too strong.*

— *I am confused. Wouldn't our desire to achieve a certain aim presuppose the absence of resistance?*

— I would say that overly strong resistance would dig your automobile into the ground. Where am I leading you? I am explaining to you that dual parts of the personality are necessary for each other. Every one of us has certain goals we want to achieve, but something always interferes with our achieving these goals: laziness, external obstacles, our own notions, people, etc. If this resistance were removed, you would not have to apply any effort to achieve your goals. But those are conditions of another, not three-dimensional reality. We can move in this reality only by overcoming the resistance, i.e. by applying some effort.

— *I saw two of my parts fighting each other today. I want to discuss something very important now, and at the same time, I see the opposite part that doesn't want to discuss anything. I am in a vacuum. What can I do?*

112

— This is what happens when you don't have an aim. If you have an aim, you have to have resistance to move toward it, and therefore, you need to apply a certain effort. The higher your aim, the stronger the inner resistance to which it gives birth. If the force of your drive is stronger than the force of your resistance, you move toward your aim. If, on the other hand, the force of the resistance is stronger than the force of your drive, you move in the direction opposite to the direction of your aim. We have already discussed that the energy of the personality is the result of the stretch between its dualities. When your duality is widely stretched, you are consciously in one of its sides. But at the same time, the opposite side of duality creates a resistance necessary for such a movement. This is the essence of the game played in the three-dimensional reality we inhabit. Do you understand?

— *One cannot exist without the other.*

— *This state of emptiness in which I found myself is very confusing.*

— The state of emptiness is a state where you don't want anything, i.e. your inner dualities are not active.

— *Are you telling us that we need to have desires? We need to be identified with one side of duality. If we are not in one side, we don't have a desire.*

— If you don't have a desire, your inner battery gets low on energy. You start to feel nauseated because you are getting discharged. But this is not enlightenment. This is fear of action. From the energy standpoint, a personage gets discharged. You are talking about the fact that your personage has been discharged.

— *It was important for me to know that. I feel some other type of energy. I cannot say that this is just a discharged state of my accumulator.*

— The game of three-dimensional reality presupposes the realization of certain aims. Do you agree?

— *What if we were to concentrate not on the aim but on becoming an intention?*

113

— I want you to remember that we need "to be in this world, but not of this world." Your personage is in this world, and as long as it is here, it exists. You cannot do anything about that. But there is something in you that is not of this world, something that observes the play of your personage in this dual world.

I can say that I am enlightened and I don't need anything at all, but why do I need to work with you? I am tired of your not understanding and of your resistance. This is one side of the game, but there is also another side to it. I am interested in producing a show of a different quality here. That's why I accept your resistance as a given of this game.

What is evil for a "sleeping" man is a subject of investigation for an aware man

— I invite you to look at this reality like a prison. Imagine you were thrown into a jail for some reason. What would you do?

— *I would start to plan an escape.*

— *I would try to run away too.*

— Where would you run? This prison has no exit. You need to occupy yourself with something. You look around and you see prisoners who are doing different things. But let's say you are not interested in anything they do. You are interested in escape. In that case, you would try to figure out how this prison works. You would learn the mechanisms on which this prison operates. That's what my personage does. I don't just figure out these mechanisms, I become an expert in this investigation. This is the aim of my game here, and this aim provides me with the energy necessary to do this work. Two forces operate in every game in this prison: one force allows you to move toward your goal, another force, the force of resistance, prevents you from achieving it. I speak as a self-investigator now.

Let's say I need to get to a bus station. This action would be accompanied by a certain resistance, if nothing else, by the

114

resistance of the road I walk upon. Without resistance, I will not be able to move. The question is whether you accept both sides—walking movement and resistance—or do you get irritated by the resistance that appears and call it evil? Do you want to remove evil from your life? Do you want to cleanse yourself from it? You cannot do that as this is part of the game of this reality. When my resistance increases, I, as investigator, start to become aware of the reasons why it is happening. I am interested in what's going on, and I use both sides of a duality to understand it. The "sleeping" man gets irritated by every force of resistance that appears in his way. The forces of resistance appear constantly; nobody can free you from their actions. You can keep whining about it, or you can start to accept and investigate these forces. This is the difference between the approaches a "sleeping" man and an aware man take.

— *I am not interested in the old approach anymore, but I don't see the new aim yet.*

— The meaning of your life is in what you believe it to be. Nobody will bring meaning into your life but you. Meanings can differ, but you are the only one who can introduce meaning into your life. You can pick up one of the meanings available here. That's what people who are "asleep" do. For many people, the meaning of life is to give birth to children and for these children to live a life that is better than the life their parents had. Others find meaning in building a house and planting a tree. As a rule, people do not choose the meaning of life; it gets inculcated into them the same way a program gets downloaded into a computer. The meaning of the life of a self-investigator is to sort out the mechanisms on which these programs are operating. A self-investigator is not of this world. For the self-investigator to investigate what is in this world, i.e. the personality, this personality has to be formed. The impulse to self-investigate appears when the personality has been fully formed. You start to investigate your personality, and in the process of this

115

investigation, your personality empties out. That's what you come to.

— *I have been diligently investigating my personality over the last two years. I didn't try to suppress my fears.*

— And what did you come to? Did you come to a sore throat and depression?

— *No. I will tell you what I came to.*

— You appear to be in a strange state. Are you catching a cold?

— *I am crying. It is very important for me to sort this out. I came to the point that nothing that happens around me bothers me.*

— Your resistance has gotten stronger. That's why nothing bothers you.

— *But there is also another side. It is bothered by everything.*

— Great. You believe that nothing bothers you, and you keep whining. Stop and take a look at the side of you that is bothered by everything.

— *Yes, certain things still* bother *me.*

— Tell us about these things. What bothers you?

— *The duality "understanding—not understanding" bothers me, but if we were to look really deep, I don't think it bothers me either.*

— What bothers you emotionally? Let's get to the level of the feelings: who, what, and why bother you?

— *There is this man at my work. He is a CPA. He bothers me. When I see him, I feel something in my heart. Fear appears. I feel warm. I have a desire to see him, but I am also afraid of seeing him.*

— Great! Is this how you feel the duality "understanding—not understanding"?

— *As soon as he leaves, those feelings disappear. I cannot dream of him.*

— What do you mean, you can't dream of him?

— *I cannot dream of him. He doesn't stir anything in my body. He doesn't stir up any feelings either.*

116

— What do you want? Do you want to call him? Do you want to see him?

— *I want to get close to him. I want to sit next to him.*

— This is an aim. As we can see, you already have an aim: to sit on a CPA's lap. How can you get there? You can call him, for example, and ask him out. To do that, you will need to find his phone number.

— *Out of the state I am in now, I can do things that I could not do before when things used to upset me greatly. For example, I can congratulate him on his birthday. I can tell him that I admire him.*

— You are intellectualizing now. Let's get a bit more real. You want to sit on his lap. How can you get there? You need to set a goal and start to work toward reaching it. When you start to do that, resistance will appear. For example, it may turn out that his lap is already occupied by a woman. He might have two women sitting on his lap. Therefore, you will have to catch a moment when his lap is free of women. This is getting interesting. We are in the game already.

— *Yes. I can wait for a New Year's party, or I can organize one.*

— You can organize a party, get him drunk, get on his lap, and experience butterflies in your stomach. Then, you may find that you are not interested in him anymore but are interested in the CEO who works next door. Another goal will appear, and you will have to reach it. A new force of resistance will appear.

— *I would like to organize a seminar.*

— Then why are you sitting here in your "understanding—not understanding"? Why don't you organize a seminar? We have plenty of work to do in school.

— *Yes, this is a goal I can work on.*

— Great. The School of Holistic Psychology salutes your goal. Do it! In order "to be in this world, but not of this world" you have to at least be in this world. And it will be good if you find it interesting. Otherwise, how can you investigate anything?

— *I will observe what I am interested in.*

117

— Exactly. Determine what exactly your personage is interested in. Allow your personage to do what it is interested in doing and investigate. There is one caveat here: when resistance appears, don't consider it to be bad; investigate it. It is not bad. We investigate both sides of ourselves. This is our game.

You have a choice: you can be afraid of your duality or you can investigate it.

— *What can I do with fear? What should I do when I am scared?*

— **Fear is the interaction between two dual sides of the personality.** The personality of a human being consists of qualities which carry opposite signs. Let's get practical here. Tell us about one feature of your personality.

— *I am responsible.*

— You are responsible, but you also have the irresponsible part in you. For the responsible part, the irresponsible part is unacceptable; it is afraid of it. This can be said about all opposite parts of every dual personality. One part of the personality is always afraid of the part that is opposite to it. For example, you consider yourself to be a decent woman. You are afraid of being indecent. You experience terrible fear to appear indecent. The interrelationship of two parts of the dual personality of a human being is always characterized by fear. To exit this fear, you have to see that these two sides complement each other. They are two sides of one coin. You cannot learn what responsibility is if you don't understand irresponsibility. **Pay attention to the fact that when you are responsible, you have many irresponsible people around you who you condemn for being irresponsible.** In condemning them, you condemn yourself because you don't see your own irresponsible part. You project your own irresponsible part onto other people and fight it in them. I am describing the dual mechanism of the personality. For example, you are afraid that the irresponsible part will not fulfill its responsibilities. I invite you to see another point of view—a point of view from another world. Don't be afraid of those you

118

condemn, and don't condemn them. In reality, they are you. Understand that they show you your opposite side. To be responsible, you have to be amongst irresponsible people. That's the only way you can be conscious of yourself as a responsible human being. If someone more responsible than you were to show up, you would become irresponsible on their background.

— *This is the interaction. What if we were to talk about the results?*

— Why are you in such a hurry? We must figure out the mechanism first. Every dual part of yours has its own goals, and it tries to achieve these goals. I am discussing the ways these goals get blocked, i.e. the resistance that the opposite part renders. As we discovered earlier, resistance is a force that must be present in order for you to achieve any one of your goals. Therefore, we should not look at resistance as something bad and unnecessary. **Resistance is a force necessary to achieve our goals.** We need to understand that. We are beginning to become aware that our opposite sides complement each other. Don't forget that any goal of yours is just a goal in your game— you can always change it.

— *The game, eh? What if I feel responsible for my life and, while playing this game, I do certain things that are horrible, dangerous, and risky?*

— What kind of horrible things?

— *Let's say I decided to investigate what it means to betray another human being or to speed up the freeway and get into an accident. I can even be killed.*

— Do you want to investigate betrayal and death?

— *No, I don't.*

— If you want to get into an accident or to get killed, you do. Or perhaps you want to investigate multiple fractures and a state of coma.

— *No.*

— Why do you say no? You are talking about these situations. That means you have these tendencies.

119

— *This is horrible.*

— What's so horrible about it? While in the physical universe, we realize our fears. If you are not aware of your fears, you realize them physically. In that case, you will have to investigate them physically. You can investigate them differently, but to do that, you need to accept the fact that these fears, i.e. these subconscious desires, are in you and investigate them. But you see your fears as horrible. You don't want to see them.

— *Yes, I am scared.*

— Having these fears, i.e. subconscious desires, you realize them in the physical reality.

— *How?*

— You do it the way you just described: you betray your friend, for example. You have done it many times.

— *Are you serious? I am scared.*

Let's investigate the mechanism of betrayal and irresponsibility

— Every human being on this planet betrays. What is betrayal?

— *Betrayal is loss of a realtionship.*

— Okay. Have you betrayed anyone before? You don't remember that you did it because you reject your betraying part. You erase from your memory what this part did. Moreover, it continues to do that. You don't remember it, and it appears to you that it is not in you. To see the mechanism of betrayal, you must accept your own betraying part and start to see what it does and how it does it. Let's take a look at the people you betrayed.

— *I can only recall one case. It happened in high school. There was this boy and this girl. They were dating. They were my friends. He had slept with someone else, and I told her. This was an act of betrayal on my part.*

— These kids experienced pleasure, and you spoke about their pleasure. You consider it to be a betrayal.

— *Yes.*

— Okay. That's what you remember. Different people understand betrayal differently. You have described a situation that you have experienced many times since you graduated from high school. I am sure of that.

— *I ratted on this boy. I did it out of good intentions.*

— We do everything out of good intentions.

— *I cannot recall another instance when I betrayed anyone.*

— This is a block. This is a typical state of a "sleeping" human being. A "sleeping" man doesn't remember what he rejects in himself. You don't accept your betraying part, and you don't accept your irresponsible part. What else don't you accept in yourself? What else do you project onto other people and condemn them for?

— *Sloppiness.*

— Okay. Do you understand that this sloppiness is in you?

— *No!*

— Do you see what happens here?

— *I feel nauseous.*

— Who feels nauseous? Your responsible part feels nauseous now, the part that condemns the irresponsible part. The responsible part cannot see itself as responsible unless it has the irresponsible part next to it. And it is always next to you in the shape of other people who you condemn for their irresponsibility. I present to you another point of view. Look at these people and start seeing yourself in them.

— *If this is a part of me, does it mean I can behave irresponsibly too?*

— Not only you can you behave irresponsibly, you *do* behave irresponsibly. You just don't remember that. That's the reason you cannot conduct self-investigation. Pay attention to what self-investigation is, everyone. **To self-investigate is to become aware of your wholeness, i.e. of your positive and negative sides, like two sides of one coin. You cannot investigate something you don't see or don't accept in yourself.** You can only self-investigate yourself. If you don't see something in

121

yourself, you are deep asleep. That's how a "sleeping" man lives, indignant of everyone and condemning everyone who opposes his one-sided notion of himself. He doesn't understand that the people he condemns reflect him. There are no other people here; just you and your projections on them. When you start to understand that, you start to accept these parts in yourself and to become aware of how they work in you. They work in you your entire life.

— *Do I have to accept them first or to see them first?*

— First, you have to accept the parts you consider to be negative. Let's take a look at the duality "responsible— irresponsible." If I were to tell you that you are irresponsible, you would immediately develop a fear that you are irresponsible. This is bad from your point of view, and you don't want to be bad.

— *I start thinking of where I behave irresponsibly right away.*

— **You are approaching the point of accepting this part. That means you are not totally asleep. The "sleeping" man just feels fear. He will become indignant and scream that it is Pint who is irresponsible. You, on the other hand, are starting to accept this part and search for it inside yourself. How do you search for it? Are you interested or full or fear?**

— *The fear appears when I feel that it relates to me. I feel ashamed to appear "bad" in front of other people.*

— We will review one more mechanism now. You have said that it is bad from the point of view of other people, but you didn't say that it was bad from your point of view. You project the appraisal of your irresponsibility onto other people, expecting them to condemn you.

— *Well, my irresponsible behavior can lead to negative consequences.*

— Everything that happens in dual reality has consequences. No one will be able to avoid these consequences. The question is whether we understand ourselves or not.

Are you ready to accept both sides of this duality in yourself?

— *I am ready.*

— Now, when you have accepted your irresponsibility, you will start to search for situations where you behave irresponsibly. What state are you in when you search for it?

— *I am interested.*

— Now you are interested. Great. Do tell us when and where have you been irresponsible.

— *Do I need to recall the situations in which I behaved irresponsibly?*

— Yes. Moreover, I will tell you that you have behaved the same way as the people you have condemned for their irresponsible behavior. Recall the latest example of such condemnation.

Anna and emptiness

— *Can I say something while she is thinking? During these three days of the seminar, I felt very irritated with Anna and this emptiness of hers. I am sitting here now wondering why I react to her this way. I don't see this emptiness in myself.*

— You don't accept your own emptiness. The story you have told us about a girl who was fed cupcakes just to vomit them back up speaks about your inability to accept emptiness. The feeling of hunger appears because the stomach gets empty. Food fills the emptiness of the stomach. The stories people tell us reflect their lives. In using these stories, one can decipher the entire scenario of a man's life.

— *Perhaps it is not my emptiness that you don't accept. Perhaps you think I am too pretentious.*

— *No. You were talking about your emptiness, and I got caught in it.*

— You are afraid of emptiness. You have the opposite side in which you consider yourself full, but you also have an empty side that you are afraid of.

— *Looks like I am afraid of inactivity.*

— You are afraid of emptiness. "Activity and inactivity" is another duality. Emptiness is a state of the absence of everything.

123

Mom, I am a thief and a drug addict …

— *The last thing that irritated me was my friend not keeping his word and my colleague lying to me. I think both of these things are in me.*

— Good. Now, search for the incidents when you didn't keep your word and when you lied.

— *I can recall few of these cases.*

— Are you ready to talk about them?

— *I think I am.*

— When you talk about your personage, you de-identify with your personage. If you are not aware of your personage, you will not discuss your personage as a personage because this is your personage's horrible secret. If you can discuss everything your personage has done, you are not your personage anymore.

— *Who are you, then?*

— You are someone who is "not of this world", but at the same time you are still a personage. When you look at the situation this way, you can review your personage with some detachment. The more you discuss and describe your personage from both the negative and the positive sides, the more you deidentify with him. This is the road to enlightenment.

— *But this is unpleasant.*

— It is very unpleasant, especially if you think you have to be pleasant all the time. It is very unpleasant, if you believe that the unpleasant part is not you. In that case, you are afraid of being unpleasant. You deal with people who are "asleep", and that is what happens in their world. What exactly are you afraid to say to people who are close to you—to people who are "asleep"?

— *What am I afraid to say to my friends, parents, and relatives?*

— Yes, what are you afraid of saying to those people, who see you only as a personage?

— *I cannot tell my mom that I am a thief. I cannot tell her I am a drug dealer.*

— *I cannot tell her that I was condemned for a prison term. She would not survive it.*

— Great. Your mom is part of your personage. That's why it is so difficult for you to tell her something that would make her upset.

— *I cannot do that.*

— Imagine you have been thrown into jail for three years. What did you do? Why were you punished? Imagine this situation. Describe it to us.

— *I was sent to jail for selling drugs.*

— Who were you selling drugs to?

— *I was selling drugs to minors.*

— Tell us more.

— *I was selling drugs at the clubs.*

— Where were you getting the drugs?

— *I found a distributor, and I started to make a good profit selling stuff at a higher price.*

— Are you making good money?

— *Yes, I do.*

— You are making money off minors. Do you like what you do?

— *On one hand, it is great. But on the other hand, it is horrible.*

— On one hand it is great, but on the other hand it is horrible. That's what we are talking about now. We are talking about the horrible side of the duality. Unless you accept it, you cannot investigate yourself. You need to see both of your sides. The "sleeping" man experiences irritation and indignation in relationship to the side he considers to be negative. It is so horrible that he cannot even think of it let alone talk about it. But at the same time, this side creates what it creates.

— **To accept means to accept that I can do it, right?**

— **To accept is to accept that it is in you. Every human being contains everything in him.**

— *So, it is in me. And what do I do with it? Do I have to accept the fact that everything can manifest itself in action any minute?*

— You have to start to investigate it.

— Let me get it straight. If I accept it, I can investigate it. Am I right?

— Yes. We can say that you are occupied with defilement of minors.

— No! No! No!

— I say, yes! Now, let's look at how you defile minors. Everyone here is occupied with the defilement of minors. The original function of parents is to inculcate a program of illusions into their child. An illusion is a narcotic. We can say that parents transmit narcotics to their children in the form of illusions. Later, children transmit it to their children. The question is how you look at what you do.

Your personality is a set of notions from a second-hand store

— How can I see these illusions? How can I determine whether they are even mine?

— There is nothing here that is yours.

— Why?

— What do you consider to be yours?

— It is something that comes from the heart.

— Wait a minute. You think it is responsibility and honesty. But where did you get the notion of responsibility and honesty?

— Perhaps I had experienced it before.

— As soon as you are born, you get inculcated with the notion that you should be responsible and honest. Your parents talk about it daily. Moreover, this is not only done through words. They hold you responsible for wetting the bed. They insist you eat the food they feed you. They reprimand you for screaming loudly.

— Yes, our parents and school system start to work on us as soon as we are born.

— Exactly. You parents and teachers transmit these notions to you. Are these notions yours?

— No. However, if I accept them they turn into my notions.

126

— You consider them yours, but they are not yours. They have been transmitted to you. Your personage does not have anything of his own; he absorbs the notions transmitted to him by the people who surround him and starts to consider them to be his.

— *Can a personage choose which notions to take and which to reject?*

— A child gets born at a certain time, in a certain country, and in a certain family. That's where the transmission process and inculcation of notions occur.

— *Can the child change these notions later on?*

— He cannot change them because he is these notions now. I am offering changes to you, but you can see how difficult it is for you to change anything. At the present time, I only invite you to investigate these notions. Let's not talk about changing them yet. Presently, you need to investigate and to get to know your notions about yourself. To do that, you need to start seeing them. To see them, you need to accept your opposite side.

I cannot get close to someone to whom I want to be close

— What is the most incredible thing that you've done in your life?

— *Do you mean bad and horrible when you say incredible?*

— Yes, let's discuss something bad and horrible that you did.

— *The most horrible thing I did was to not follow my desires.*

— What do you mean?

— *When I want something badly, I experience strong resistance or fear, and I succumb to it. I am talking about my personal relationship with a man. I don't know whether it is horrible or not.*

— It depends on how *you* look at it.

— *Sometimes I go crazy not knowing what to do. I think I should take the first step, then I think I should not do it. I find good reason not to do it. Time goes by, but this desire to see him remains in me. This is horrible.*

127

— So, the most horrible thing for you consists of your inability to get close to someone to whom you want to be close. Am I right?

— *Yes.*

— And you continue to recreate this horrible thing.

— *Yes.*

— This is horrible. However, you continue to do this horrible thing and to experience kaif from doing it. Am I right? You create horror by not doing what you want to do. Thus, we can say that you want to experience this horror. Am I correct?

— *Yes, I think I want to experience that horror.*

— That means you do what you want to do. One side of you wants to experience this horror, and it creates the situation where you don't get to know the man that you want to get to know. Your other side wants to get to know this man. We are dealing with the duality "action—inaction." For you, horror is the side that is opposite to the action side, the side that wants to get to know this man. The mechanism we have explored previously works everywhere.

— *Fear and resistance.*

— Yes. You want to experience this fear, and you experience it. You say, "This is horrible. I wanted to approach this man, but I didn't." You experience this horrible state. What would happen if you were to approach him?

— *To approach him would not be enough.*

— Let's say you have aproached him. What happens then?

— *Why don't I do that? Is it because of the fear? Is it because the opposite side…?*

— Wait a minute. I am not talking about fear now. **Fear is the interrelationship of two opposite sides of a duality.** I am trying to sort out what exactly each of these two opposite parts of yours wants. One part does not want what the part that is opposite to it wants. What would happen if you were to approach this guy?

128

— *Is the opposite part the good part?*

— The opposite part is the part that wants to approach this guy and to connect with him.

— *This part wants to be with this man.*

— What do you mean when you say, "I want to be with this man"?

— *I just want to be with him.*

— What does it mean to be with him? You can climb on his back. You can have dinner with him. You can get into his car and have him drive you around. What exactly do you want?

— *I want everything. This part wants to be with him all the time.*

— You can slap each other and scream profanities at each other. Some people call it "being together".

— *No, this is not about that.*

— What is it about?

— *It's about her meeting him ...*

— Okay. They are on a street. They meet each other. She comes up to him and says, "Hi, it's me." He says, "Ah, I've been waiting for you for so long." What happens next?

— *I don't know. I am scared.*

— You don't have a script, and as a result, you don't have anything to realize. It turns out you don't know what to do after you have said, "Hi, it's me." You don't even know what to say to him. You stay there for three hours. It's getting dark. You still don't know what to say. That's the reason the part that does not want to approach this man is being realized. It happens because you don't have anything to say to him or do with him after you approach him.

— *There will be some kind of action afterwards.*

— What kind of action? You don't even know what to do. If you don't know what to do, then who knows? He definitely does not know what to do.

— *Why?*

— Because this is your script, not his.

— *At least I know what to do with my CPA.*

— Yes, you get a report from your CPA on a monthly basis. You know what to do. Here, on the other hand, we are dealing with a totally different situation. Nothing will happen without a script, and as a result, we see a freeze-frame in this show of yours. You approach him, but you don't know what to do next. That's why your second part tells you not to get close to him. You have not thought about what is going to happen next. You have some vague expectations. You are waiting for a prince on a white horse, but here he comes, and you don't know what to do with him.

— *Perhaps nothing will happen afterwards.*

— If you don't know what will happen next, nothing will happen next. Therefore, the best thing you can do is to not approach him and to stew in your own uncertain expectations.

— *She can dream about their next meeting.*

— She doesn't dream. If she dreamt about anything, she would have told us about one of her dreams. For example, they could have gone to the beach or to the movies. She doesn't say anything about it.

— *She doesn't say anything, but she has a dream.*

— No, she doesn't have a dream.

— *This prince on the white horse ... I don't see him as a husband.*

— *Forget the husband ...*

— Think a little bit ahead. What can happen after this initial meeting? As they write at the end of the fairytales, "They lived happily ever after and died on the same day." Such a great script about their happiness. But why were they so happy? When exactly did they die and where? This information stays behind the screen. You're your scenario; you need to go to City Hall and die right after you meet him. Whatever is downloaded into your script will realize itself in your life. I am digging out the stuff that was downloaded there. This is a revelation to you.

Why do freeze-frames occur in the script of your life?

— *Can everything we fantasize about be realized?*

— Of course.

— *Wait a minute. If I fantasize that I already have what I want, it is fiction. It's another illusion. Will you explain this to me, please?*

— How do you live? You have to live until the moment of your death. How many more years do you expect to live? This time should be filled somehow.

— *But my personage never receives what it wants. As soon as it receives something, it stops desiring it.*

— If you don't know what you want, you will not receive anything but depression and boredom.

— *Can a personage receive what it wants?*

— **A personage cannot receive what it wants, but a force of resistance develops in a personage while it desires something.** I will ask you to pay very close attention to what we are reviewing now. We are reviewing your life scenario from the point of view of your personage. I have said that a personage will never receive what it doesn't want to receive, but when I said that, I was out of this reality. The context of our conversation is very important.

— *This has to do with the timing of when this information gets into the system of notions of the personage, as new dualities appear in the personage in connection with this information. It's impossible for them not to appear.*

— We are coming to the conclusion that self-investigation is only possible in the presence of the personage, or the personality. The energy of the personage manifests itself in its desires. Therefore, in order for you to interact with your Supreme I, i.e. with your own part that is not of "this world", you need to be aware of what is happening in "this world", i.e. of your personage. Your personage's life is based on its desires. When you start to investigate your desires, you have the material for self-investigation. To investigate, you have to conduct a revision of the half-dead desires that your personages have. I am talking about the personages present here. Your personage must come to life. The life of the personage is survival. You have to start to survive, i.e. to desire something. We have just opened one of your half-dead desires, which consists of meeting a man and having him express a miniscule reaction to you. You don't know what to do next. Nothing is written in your script. It is as if you went to a movie theater to see a movie about a woman who thinks she wants to get acquainted with a man. Then she thinks, "No, I cannot do this. I am afraid. I cannot approach him." Five minutes later, she finally decides to approach him. She walks toward him and tells him she likes him. He smiles and replies, "I like you too." The movie stops. We have seen five minutes of action, and now we face the black screen. We wait for two hours. The screen remains black. Everyone is upset. It turns out the screenwriter didn't finish the script.

— *I see how my desires get supressed. What happened with this CPA guy? At first, I was afraid of him. Then, I experienced a strong desire to see him. While trying to overcome my fear, I found myself desiring him more and more. When he was in the lunch room, I would run to the cafeteria and buy lunch, hoping to get close to him and to spend some time with him. But by the time I would get there, he would leave. I started to realize that I cannot get what I want when my desire is very strong. When I was afraid of seeing him, he would show up. When I experienced a very strong desire to see him, he could not be found.*

— Your script is unfinished. A freeze-frame appears on the screen. You have to work on increasing the forces that develop the plot of further action. You got stuck in the freeze-frame. Your life is at standstill. Sit down and think about how it could have happened differently. Invent different scenarios and start to invest energy in the scene you like the best. That will allow your script to evolve. You have to allow yourself to experience this desire, to laugh, to be merry, and to cry. You will become aware of all these emotions later, but please don't cry over one freeze-frame for the rest of your life—continue on with the show. Create new scripts and stage them. You are both actors and script writers. You came to this drama theater called Earth. So, create the scripts of your survival, but remember that you have two directors. With this memory in mind, you will understand what I am talking about. Presently, you cannot even understand what I say because you are stuck. Where is your freeze-frame? You have become frozen saying that it can never happen. It is horrible and it can't happen. Make peace with this part by saying that everything is possible. Then drink a shot of vodka and fantasize about what you see as horrible. Bring all these horrors to consciousness.

— *I have entered my horror. It is my family and kids. It is the maintenance of the apartment, doing the work around the house, etc. I am horrified of mundane routine.*

— Okay. Allow yourself to experience mundane routine now.

— *I got it. I felt this yesterday after the seminar. I felt this desire to live, to make mistakes, to do something…*

— I salute you.

— *I came here with a bunch of complexes. I could not accept many things. Then my mind created another trap. I thought I could investigate things that I didn't accept.*

— That's right. You cannot investigate things you don't accept.

— *I didn't know that.*

— Now you do.

— *I have one more question. What do you mean when you say we need to accept the second side?*

— Try to be more specific.

— *For example, a man calls me and says, "Let's go to the movies." I feel I want to go with him.*

— To simply say that you want to go to the movies with him is not enough. You must make it more specific. You must

133

arrange your desire into a story line. For example, "We want to get into a car and have a nice drive along the ocean, or we want to go bungee jumping, or I want to get on top of him."

— I will get to the bottom of this today! Why should I desire this? I will build up this part just to be disappointed later. I will create a different plot and will not get it either. I will move to the part that can explain why I don't want this to happen. I will find hundreds of reasons why I don't want this to happen.

— Take a look where this pseudo spirituality brought you. Your personage is totally blocked. You don't even want to come to the seminar. You don't have any desires.

— That's true. I didn't want to come here this time. Before, I used to count days to seminar…

The script of your life scenario is downloaded into your personality.

— Our seminar is an opportunity for you to realize your every desire. Your desires are your potential to become Aware. If you put a lid on them, you cannot become aware of anything. Your personage is the subject of your investigation. You have to allow your personage to realize its every desire. As we have already discussed, a personage contains desires and anti-desires. Both the driving force and the force of resistance are necessary for movement. Do not be afraid of resistance. You have to move toward what you want by overcoming the resistance. The program of movement is downloaded into your personage. It has been downloaded already. Your personage must complete his journey from birth to death. You have a long way to go, but you don't want to walk. You have to activate your desires and to start moving. Later, you will become aware of what is happening to you.

— Let's say, I have written a script of what is about to happen tonight. According to this script, I have certain expectations. I expect to receive something. What if my expectations are not met?

— Aha. Now turn on the Observer and start to investigate the desires of your personage.

— *I used to see my personage as something negative that I need to get rid of, but it turns out I have to investigate him.*

— You have to investigate your personage because he is inculcated with every tendency that you need to experience, understand, and become aware of during this incarnation. The script of your life scenario is downloaded into your personality. You don't need to search for it anywhere else. You can only find it in your personality.

— *It looks like the script represents a set of rules and convictions downloaded into our personalities. We have taken these rules and convictions from the people around us and consider them to be ours.*

— Exactly. You are this personage. Don't look at your personage with such malice. This personage is you in this world.

— *But you have said that it is the duality of the personage that leads to suffering. You have said that suffering is produced by one side fighting the other side.*

— So, suffer. Suffer and laugh! Why are you so afraid of suffering?

— *I got it. I have to continue to suffer and to observe my suffering to see the mechanism of how this suffering gets created. Am I right?*

— *I will suffer. I will experience pain and disappointment. But at the same time, someone in me will experience pleasure. Isn't it a great idea?*

— As the old Russian proverb goes, "Don't stroll through the woods if you are afraid of wolves." You are so afraid of the wolves, you don't even leave your apartment. We are investigating the woods, but you don't even get close to the woods. How can I discuss self-investigation with you if you don't even enter it?

— *I had no idea what we were doing here.*

— I live and I investigate every experience through which I live. I always have material for self-investigation.

— You don't do anything without a reason. You do everything based on your investigation needs. It always leads you somewhere.

— I keep spinning dualities of my personality further and deeper, and I investigate them using awareness.

— Do you really feel everything? Do you experience irritation?

— Of course I feel everything. Of course I *experience irritation*.

— I have tried to self-investigate in order to feel it less.

— No, that's not the way to do it.

— I am reading Osho. He says that this flutter is superficial—it doesn't touch our core. I thought that was the place we were going. I thought the idea was not to be bothered on a deeper level.

— Osho writes what Osho writes. I occupy myself with self-investigation. As I said, there is an investigator in us who has a certain subject to investigate. The subject of our investigation is our dual personality. If the personality is frozen, there is nothing to investigate. We need a subject to investigate, and we need to spin it hard enough for it to express itself fully. Then and only then we can become aware of it.

— You describe what you see very well. Oleg describes things very well too. He manifests good mental understanding, but the way I see it, he doesn't feel that Real World that you feel. You get to experience certain states. I have felt these states myself but not to the extend you feel them.

— I realize what I choose to realize. For example, I write books. This is one of the ways my personage realizes himself. This work is done by my personage, not by the one who is "not of this world". The one who is "not of this world" is not here. He cannot write books, talk to the agencies, etc. My personage has chosen to do this, and in connection with work, my personage experiences some pleasant and unpleasant emotional states. But thanks to the fact that I observe my personage, his actions, and the unpleasant states associated with these actions as part of the process of his realization, I receive the results of my self-investigation and discuss them with you, but my personage lives a full life.

136

— *Let me ask you a question then. By investigating the personage the way we do, we become aware of who we are. Will we also become aware of what is Real?*

— Your personage is a necessary but not the only required ingredient our Process needs. To become aware, the one who is "not of this world" must be present here too. We have come to the point where, in order to continue the process of self-investigation, you will need a boost of energy to develop your personage.

— *Does the investigator who investigates the personage influence the personage? Does the investigator influence what is to become of the personage?*

— Of course, he does. **Observation by itself influences the personage. To change something in the personage, you must see what needs to be changed. And in order to see that, you need to do something. For you to stretch the duality of your personage, you have to move to the point of view of your personage's subconscious side, i.e. to overcome the force of the personage's resistance. In the process of doing that, you observe the conflict that occurs between the opposite sides of your personality.**

— *This approach differs from the one you have described in* The Butterfly, *where you advised us to "get rid of dependencies, illusions, and old notions." Now you are inviting my personage to act again, but it can only act in accordance with his notions and illusions.*

— I will ask you to pay attention to something very important. What I say and how I say it always differs depending on the context of my own transformation. My earlier books differ from my latest books, and they will continue to change. Every one of my books reflects one of the stages of my self-investigation. This process is eternal.

— *I have the feeling that by freeing yourself from multiple attachments and dependencies, you arrived at some kind of emptiness. It filled you up, and now, out of this state, you investigate your personage.*

— You can trace the entire dynamic of my self-investigation by listening to the recordings of my seminars and reading my books. Many seminars have not been published in book format yet. The new books will be of a different quality. They will reflect the changes my personage experiences. My personage did what it did the way it would have done it back then. It could not have done it differently. Now it can be done differently, and the quality of my books is changing. This is my answer to your question: the personage can only change in the process of self-investigation.

— *Can we say that to become aware is to accept?*

— To become aware is to see the personage fully. To accept is to start seeing the personage the way it is. To start to investigate your personage, you need to accept the opposite parts of your personality. This is the most difficult part of our work. When you start to accept the dualities of your personality, you start to become aware of their manifestation in you. I track down how this process occurs in you step by step. I do it myself, and I know how to do it. I don't know how it is going to happen in your case. This is a difficult and painful process. Perhaps you will leave. I don't know who will stay and who will leave. I don't know a riskier or more intriguing gamble than the process of self-investigation.

Can I self-investigate on my own?

— *Can I self-investigate on my own?*

— You need mirrors that will reflect your parts and a guide who knows the intricate details of this process. The path of self-investigation is different for everyone. The knowledge of the principles of this movement helps us to proceed. You will become aware gradually, step by step. That's why you have to be in the Process constantly. This is not a dependency. This is co-creativity of self-investigators. I just happen to be a step ahead of you. I know what each one of you will face. I undergo transformation, and I know what is about to happen to you.

— *You were brought up to be a decent man. You were not supposed to be wild.*

— I have been different. I was plenty wild.

— *Will the group come to know all the mechanisms in due time?*

— Yes, of course. You move the way you move, but I am always ahead of you. I know your every step, and I can point you in the right direction. My task is to provide pointers for the group and for each one of you in particular. I provide you with a system of pointers so you can use them without suppressing your personage. The game that we play here at the School of Holistic Psychology is a very interesting game. Everything is possible here.

— *Can we manifest ourselves any way we want on the physical plane?*

— Yes. Your physical manifestation is of utmost importance here. We can start with where and how we are to conduct our next seminar and finish by exploring its script. Every personality receives what it is supposed to receive during the seminar. Later, we sort out and become aware of the gifts of awareness you have received. Our Process doesn't block the development of the personality. On the contrary, your personage gets stimulated, as it is the subject of our investigation. That's what I offer you here.

— *One can do something if one sees this process as a game.*

— That's right. This is the game we are playing. What kind of a game it is going to be depends on us. I invite you to make this game more interesting.

— *What are you offering? Give us an example, please.*

— How do you see our meetings? Self-investigation is a lifelong process, not something you can do episodically. We conduct seminars. We go to different countries.

— *All of you, together?*

— Yes, the whole group goes on a trip. We experience something very important during each seminar. Every one of us experiences exactly what his or her personality needs to experience. It can be done differently. We can do whatever we decide to do.

— *The group is suddenly alive.*

— *Yes. I feel the surge of energy.*

— *I am tired of pretending to be interested in something that ceased to interest me long time ago.*

— Awareness is not a low-grade depression.

— *Condemnation, guilt, condemnation ... I am tired of it.*

— Okay. Please, condemn and experience guilt. Do what you want to do, because you will do it anyway. These states are inculcated in your personality. I invite you to become aware of them.

— *I have noticed this morning that the time periods between me condemning someone and experiencing guilt become shorter. As soon as I condemn someone, I immediately flip into guilt.*

Your life is a river that got tired of running and turned into a wetland

— Let's take a look at what your personality wants.

— *What are the desires of my personality? I want to quit my job. I am bored with it. I am sitting in front of a computer all day long. It is so boring ...*

— Great. What do you want?

— *I want to stop this process. I am getting sick of it.*

— Do you want to die?

— *No.*

— Which process do you want to stop?

— *I want to stop working. I want to stop doing the work I have been doing for the last ten years.*

— Do you want to stop working, or do you want to find another job?

— *I want to try to find another job, of course.*

— What do you mean to try? To try and to find are two totally different things. To try to get up from a chair is to sit on a chair and to try to get up from it. To get up from a chair is a different thing.

— *In order to do that, I have to quit the work I do.*

— So, say it. Say that you are planning to quit your old job and to find a new job that interests you.

— *But I also have another side, and it opposes this decision. It prefers to act based on the principle, "One can endure anything for a good paycheck. You are working for a big corporation. You are safe."*

— This is the force of resistance. The force of your resistance is stronger than your moving force. The whole group is in a similar situation. You have to allow your moving force to develop. You should move forward.

— *My mind says it will be stupid to quit this job.*

— Your mind has two opposite points of view. You started this conversation talking from your mental center. You started off well, but look at how you've ended it. Your resistance is very strong. Your life is a river which, tired of running, stopped and turned into a wetland. You must start running again.

— *Fear, fear, and one more time, fear.*

— If you are scared, then sit here in fear. If you want to move, move.

— *Wouldn't I oppress myself in trying to overcome this fear?*

— Fear is an illusion.

— *You want to quit this job. That means you don't accept the part that wants to work there. You need to accept this work and the part that wants to work there. What kind of a job is it? It is boring. It is horribly boring. So, accept the part that is not interested in being there. In that case, with this horribly boring job on the background, you will be able to feel, compare, and find what is interesting.*

— You liked this job up to a certain point, but now you don't like it. You can indignantly walk through this garbage: "What disgusting garbage. But I need to accept it. I don't want to

141

fall in it, but I have to do that. I don't want to eat it, but I have to." You keep eating it and eating it.

— *That's what I used to say before. When my shoes get old, I go and buy a new pair of shoes, but I see this work situation as something that I need to accept.*

— You have been exploring one side, and I'm not saying that it was not necessary. I am pushing you to get to the next level. You have been marching in one spot for a long time. Allow the force of action to manifest itself.

The privileges of our Process

— *My aim is to organize a seminar in my city.*

— Great! Where are we going?

— *We are going to Kazan.*

— You will receive many gifts of awareness when you organize a seminar in the city of your birth.

— *I have already experienced the force of resistance.*

— Resistance will escalate as the energy necessary to achieve your aim increases. The more energy of the aim you feel, the stronger the resistance is going to be. There are two sides to every coin. Don't be afraid of the resistance. By becoming aware of both sides of the duality simultaneously, you will become aware of yourself. This is what wholeness is about. You cannot become aware of anything if you don't do anything. The bigger the aim that you set up from the point of view of our Process, the more awareness you will get. Otherwise, you will not get anything. That's why I call it a privilege. To transcribe a seminar is a privilege. To organize a seminar is a privilege. Everything you do at the School is part of this Process. When you perform these tasks, you stay awake and receive your profit of awareness.

I will ask you to feel your most important aims now. I will also ask you to feel the resistance that appears in connection with these aims. Feel these aims as something that causes excitation and high voltage in your personage, and become Aware of the aim and of the resistance that this aim produces.

— *A few months ago, I decided to go to Europe with my girlfriend. For some reason, I thought of Germany. I thought about organizing a seminar there. I also thought of gathering a group of people to study Holistic Psychology there. I don't know why, but I have been contemplating this idea for a while now.*

— Feel the energy of this idea. If this is something that is important for you, it will be filled with energy. This aim will burn in you.

— *I also feel the resistance. It manifests itself as laziness, fear of dealing with people I will have to deal with. These forces are in me. There are no external reasons to prevent me from doing what I want to do.*

— Exactly. You will have to work with these two opposite forces.

— *If I really want something, it will happen. That's it.*

— You will have to work with laziness. You will have to investigate it. As you prepare the seminar, you will face the necessary context, which will help you to investigate laziness. Every human being who does something for the Process receives an opportunity to become aware of many things. Just by sitting here, you receive these opportunities. You must have an aim that will burn in you. You will receive many presents of awareness when you follow your aim. The name of the place in which we conduct this seminar is "Centaur". This is our second seminar here. Take a closer look at this sign, and you will see something very important. This centaurus has a bow in his hands. He is shooting an arrow. During our last seminar, we investigated the duality "Animal—Human being". Now, we have come to the second attribute of this sign, "Bow and arrow." Aim. This is a very important sign. Sagittarius. This sign is about achieving the aim.

143

— I have received something very important here. I have been stuck for a while. I have three kids. I need to learn how to love my husband. I need to learn how to love my kids. I have discovered many of my dependencies.

You cannot learn to love your husband. You can only learn to love yourself.

— You cannot learn to love your husband. You can only learn to love yourself. We are discussing movement toward this Love. What kind of love can we talk about if you don't accept your own half?

— I am grateful to you for what I learned about myself. I dug up many of my dependencies and plenty of guilt and condemnation. I have enough material to start seeing. I saw some of it before, but now I see more.

— No. You didn't see anything, and you still don't see anything. You are using these words without any understanding of what they mean.

— I have to master what I have not mastered yet.

— In order to do that, you need to be among the people who are not "asleep". If you think you understand everything, you are asleep. You sort out things for a day, and you know everything. The next morning, you are totally asleep again.

— It seems to me that even when I come to one seminar a year, the process occurs anyway.

— If you don't come to the seminars regularly and don't do anything for the Process, you are asleep.

— What if I prepare people to participate in our Process?

— Where are these so-called prepared by you people? The mind will always try to defend the state it is in, i.e. sleep.

— So, if one doesn't attend every seminar, one is asleep?

— You don't have to come to every seminar, but if you miss three months, you are asleep. You can say anything you want, but those are the hallucinations of a "sleeping" man.

— What about you paying your school dues? You have not paid your share, and you said yesterday that you are not going to pay at all.

144

— This is a manifestation of your resistance, but you don't see it. You justify your resistance without even seeing it.

— *This is also a necessary excitation ...*

— What are you trying to say now? Are you saying you can stay home, not attend the seminars, and not be asleep?

— *No. I am trying to say that if I were to come to every seminar, the level of my excitation would get very high. I will have to lower it somehow. I will do it by allowing myself to fall asleep.*

Your personality is a tea kettle that boils on a high flame

— Your excitation gets higher and higher, but you don't express it. Then you start to yawn and you fall asleep. You have been silent for three days. You will develop such a strong excitation that you will have to sleep for the rest of your life. We are dealing with fire here. Your personages are like tea kettles that boil over on a high flame. I keep telling you, "Speak up and express everything that tries to get out," but you keep your silence.

— *I talk when my excitation goes overboard.*

— Okay. Then you need very high excitation. Everyone here is different, but certain things are common for all of us. Someone who missed three seminars and does not work with the School materials is asleep.

— *Every one of us brings something of his own here.*

— What are you trying to say?

— *I come here and I ask what I need to ask when I am concerned enough about it.*

— Today you are concerned, but tomorrow comes and you are not concerned. You are on the border of sleep. A tiny push and you will fall asleep completely, forgetting what you have heard here. Your mind will explain everything. You will always be right. I am clarifying your position for you. This is not a condemnation. This is a fact.

145

— *I remember what happened when I left. I thought I would not forget anything, but I quickly forgot everything. Do you know what woke me up? I fell off a ladder. I figured out that I did not fall without a reason. Something was wrong with me. That's when I decided to come back.*

— Take a look at how something that we consider to be an unpleasant mishap turns into success. This is a miracle. Only the one who tries to awaken can see these miracles. For other people, they are ephemeral. Miracles for them are water turned into wine.

— *I came back here after attending a seminar where I had to manifest only one of my sides.*

— We don't reject anything here. While here, you don't have to suppress your personage. You can manifest everything you have in you. Everything that happens to you is great. Whatever you feel and experience is great. Become aware of everything. You will enter different situations to accumulate fragments of the experiences you need to become aware of. Here, at the seminar, we integrate the experiences you have accumulated prior to coming here.

— *My aim is to think the way you think, to feel the way you feel, and to act the way you act.*

— This is nonsense. Why do you want to copy someone?

— *I knew you would say that.*

— Why did you ask this question if you knew what my reply would be? Don't do anything the way I do. Why do you have to make an idol out of me?

— *I didn't make an idol out of you. I want to do what you do. I was thinking about doing it for many years.*

— In that case, you will have to learn a lot. You will have to develop your intellectual center. You are taking a big aim.

— *I know I am.*

— How do you plan to develop your intellectual, emotional, and physical bodies? I do it constantly. I have been involved with different sports since I was thirteen. I develop my emotional body by listening to music, watching movies, and participating in different arts. I develop my intellectual body. I work on all three of my centers. Do you understand what kind of a task you are setting for yourself? How will you go about it? It's not so simple. I have been working on my personage for forty-nine years. Your assignment should correspond to the reality of your personality. You should not try to copy anyone.

— *Why not?*

— Here you go. You have just erased everything I said. You say you want to be like me, but you cannot be like me. You have created a certain ideal, and you resist it. You have just showed this very clearly. I am not saying it in a condemning tone of voice. The aim that you have to pick up should come from your personality.

— *When I went to my first seminar, I knew I had found what I was looking for.*

— Great. Then, don't talk about me, talk about yourself. What kind of steps are you planning to make to achieve your aim?

— *I will see these steps soon. I feel them.*

— Okay. I think we have had enough for today. Thank you. I'll see you tomorrow.

CHAPTER 3
BETRAYAL OF THE MIND

How someone who is being rescued becomes a rescuer

— I felt many of my desires yesterday. I reviewed my life, and it turned out that I have always realized my desires. If I were to want something really badly, I would always get it. However, by the time I would get it, I already wanted something else. I finished college and got a degree. Then I gave birth to two kids. The kids grew up. I went to college and got a second degree. As soon I started to work in the new field, I got pregnant. I always had a very low self-esteem. I could never overcome this problem. I was constantly dissatisfied with myself as a kid. It is killing me. I am constantly thrown from one side to another. I was thinking about my husbands, i.e. the men I attract. Both had very low self-esteem, too. I wanted to talk to you about these two energies you spoke of: the energies of condemnation and guilt. I have one more energy in me: the energy of a rescuer.

— Many psychologists work with sub-personalities. What we discuss here sheds some light on the way these sub-personalities interact. They interact as opposite sides of dualities. Where a rescuer is present, another opposite sub-personality is also present. One part begs—rescue me, another screams—I will rescue you. The presence of such opposites in a personality is its essence. It is very important to understand that. Unless you understand that, you will not understand anything I say.

A human being consists of a multitude of sub-personalities, which, in turn, consist of dual pairs. Every part of a personality of a human being has an opposite part. Psychologists, not understanding the dual nature of these sub-personalities, just

148

increase their numbers. That prevents them from seeing these sub-personalities clearly. The only way for us to clarify this situation is to understand duality.

— *I understand. The part that I accept in myself helps, saves, and rescues other people. Both of my husbands were attracted by me when they were insecure and unsure of themselves. I saw them differently. I saw them the way they really were, and I wanted them to get up. I kept saying, "You can do it! You can do it!"*

— By having someone who cannot do something in the background, you turn into someone who *can* do it. Look, you need men like them.

— *Yes. Every man I attract has these qualities.*

Self-esteem is another name for pride

— These men will be drawn into your life. For you to bring up your low self-esteem, you need to have those whose self-esteem is less than yours. You choose a man and you see that his self-esteem is low, but it is precisely because of his low self-esteem that you can transfer to the side of higher self-esteem. Self-esteem is an abstract notion. We need to sort out why your self-esteem is low.

For example, you can have high self-esteem because you can spit further than anybody else. Why is your self-esteem low? We are entering the structure of duality again. Self-esteem is analogous to pride. Pride is a subject that religious and esoteric systems discuss at great length. They fight pride without understanding the origins and mechanisms of its appearance. The mechanism of pride originates in duality. One side of a duality ascends over the other, as one side of a seesaw ascends over another. This is a mechanism of action of the opposite sides of every duality present in the structure of personality. The question of self-esteem is the question of which part of a duality you are conscious of now as being *you*. **Pride is a consequence of the conflict that occurs between the opposite sides of a certain**

149

duality. To understand the mechanism of pride's appearance, we need to see it.

— *There is energy there. As you spoke about the need to stretch duality yesterday, I realized that this process of transferring from one state to another was infusing me with energy. I used to hold on to it for a very long time.*

— What do you mean when you say, "I used to hold on to it for a very long time"? Are not you holding to it now? A personage cannot build his survival on anything else.

— *Is there something else here except the personage?*

— No. Ego. Personality. Personage. All these terms describe a psychological structure or a social construct that separates a human being from an animal. A human being, the way he is now, is a social animal. A human being as a social animal is body-mind. Society conditions the structure of our personality.

— *I have a question. My brakes prevent me from realizing my desires and potential scenarios. The moment I have to take a step forward, some mechanism turns on. Someone inside me says, "You don't look good. You can't speak properly. You can't do anything." My desires wither right away.*

— Define the duality. You are new here, and you don't see your dualities yet. I keep talking about duality all the time, and I will remind you about it again and again because that's what we are dealing with. You have listed certain situations connected to the inner conflicts you experience. My role is to show you how to see and deal with these situations.

— *Presently, I just see both states and myself in them.*

— Define these two states.

— *The state of confidence, haughtiness, and pride.*

— You are describing the upper level of one side of a duality. However, we need to descend to the causal level of duality. I am talking about the mechanism of pride's origination while you say you are feeling it. I just explained to you that pride appears because of the inner game of the ego that consists of the rising and lowering of its opposite, dual sides. The next question we should ask is which duality of your personality gives birth to pride in you? Many dualities give birth to pride, making the process of self-investigation very difficult. **The entire life of a self-investigator is dedicated to the clarification of the mechanisms that give birth to pride in his structure.** You have said you see pride in your personage. Great. Anyone here can say that.

— *But I also see the opposite side of this pride.*

— Do you see the mechanism that maintains this pride? Which specific duality has been activated in you? What is it that allows you to feel pride?

— *What makes me proud? My intellectual center works very well. I can easily sort out difficult logical constructs.*

— So, you are smart.

— *I am very smart.*

— And they are stupid.

— *They are ... different.*

— What do you mean different? If they are different, some of them might be smarter than you. You are saying that they are different, but you are always smarter than them.

— *The level of their smartness may differ. They are given to me for comparison.*

— If you are always smarter, they cannot be smarter than you. So, they are not only different, they are not as smart as you.

— *When I meet someone who I think might be smarter than me, I either start to build up a part that from my point of view appears to be low, or I say I don't need that, and I dump that person.*

— Correct. You run away because you are afraid to be with someone who is smarter than you. Am I smarter than you?

— *Yes.*

— How do you feel about that?

— *I feel good.*

— What about your pride?

— *I came here thinking I would learn from you.*

151

— What about your pride? You have met someone who is smarter than you.

— I am happy there are people who are smarter than me. I have places to climb up to.

— Your pride says, "We have an ideal, and we will climb up to it. We will get to be smarter than him." This is what Olga was saying yesterday, "I want to be the way you are." No. She wants to be better than me.

— Yes, you got me right.

Fighting for exclusivity, a human being excludes himself from a society of other people

— The mind you are so proud of works on comparison. Your mind constantly compares. How do you come up with judgement? Your mind does it. Let's hear one of your judgements.

— I appraise a situation somehow. For example, "We are studying in school now."

— Okay. So, there is some kind of a difference between a school and the rest of the world. For example, we are not studying in the park. We are not studying at the beach. We are at a school. This is a judgement produced by your mind. What if I were to say that we are not sitting in a room, but in a lake. What will your mind say?

— I will look for an opportunity…

— Why can't you say that I am imagining things? I mean, really, this is a room, not a lake.

— The word lake can be used to describe many different things. It's one thing when we talk about water, but it might be a "lake of hope."

— Take your clothes off. Let's go for a swim.

— One can swim in a lake of feelings.

— Okay. Undress. Let's go for a swim.

152

— Why do we need to undress? These are your fantasies.

— I show you how the mind works. You grabbed my fantasy, and you immediately started to develop it. I invited you to undress and go for a swim, and you immediately retorted that this is a lake of feelings and we don't need to undress here. I am not saying that this is meaningless, but if we follow this road, we will, at best, turn into poets, not self-investigators. You say you are smart. I, on the other side, don't say that I am smart. I say I know the mechanisms on which the mind operates. This is a different level of seeing this situation. This is not just an intellectual point of view.

— I cannot brag that I know how the mind works.

— You can't brag, but you want to.

— I would like to come to know how the mind works.

— Then you will see that smart and stupid are two sides of one coin. When you see that, you will not be able to be proud for being smart anymore. Your personage will be dissatisfied with losing its pride. The personage is always proud of something. It's pride that creates a personage's exclusivity. Everyone here wants to be exclusive and tries to find which area in which he is exclusive.

— I am trying to do it in many boards at once.

— What is exclusivity?

— I am better than other people. If I am not better than them, I am different from them.

— If we were to dig further, exclusivity is exclusion.

— That's how we separate ourselves from other people.

— In fighting for exclusivity, people exclude themselves and then become indignant that nobody understands them. But look how paradoxical that is; nobody understands them because they are so exclusive.

— We exclude ourselves.

— In fighting for exclusivity, you exclude yourself from the group and become indignant that no one understands you. We have discussed how pride appears. You consciously consider yourself to be smart. Therefore, you have to surround yourself with stupid people against whose background you will appear to be smart and experience pride. Isn't that so?

— *How can I put it? I like to be in the company of people.*

— Other people are you mirrors. You are surrounded by mirrors that reflect you. You project both sides of your personality onto other people—consciously and subconsciously.

— *Based on what you have just said, activated pride constantly surrounds itself with "Draculas".*

— In order for you to feel pride connected to your notion of being a smart woman, you need to be surrounded by stupid people. Okay. Do you think I am smarter than you? Do you feel pride when you deal with me?

— *I don't know whether it is pride or not, but I feel satisfied that I came here.*

— Okay. You feel satisfaction. You feel we are equal. I am smart, but your replies and questions are also smart. You have found a partner with whom you can have an intelligent conversation, and you experience pleasure from it.

— *I don't think about my answers as being smart or stupid. I am at risk of saying something stupid. That's why I am frequently silent.*

— Okay. What would happen if you were to say something stupid?

— *I would be open to your attack.*

— Did you just do that?

— *I am lost now. I want to talk. I feel restrained when I am silent. I feel powerless.*

— Our dialogue shows that you don't understand how your own mind works.

— *I am trying to understand. When you speak, I understand everything.*

— I understand that you are trying, but our conversation shows that PRESENTLY you DO NOT understand what's going on. I am not saying that you will *never* understand.

— *Tell me please, what exactly don't I understand?*

— You don't even understand that you don't understand anything.

— *If I were to understand what I don't understand, I would have understood.*

— Do you agree that you don't understand? You cannot understand something if you don't understand that you don't understand it at the present time. Why would you want to understand something that you already understand?

— *You say you know how the mind works, and I don't. I agree, I don't know how the mind works to the degree you know it.*

— Great. And how do you feel about that?

— *I am interested.*

— What about your pride? What happened to it? Is it your main pride or not? When we touch upon someone's basic pride, something happens.

— *But that's what I think it was.*

— Perhaps this is not your main pride.

How to upset an older woman who tries to look younger

— *I have one more pride. I have been active in sports all my life. I run. I go to the gym. I play volleyball. Is there pride in that?*

— What affects you the most about these activities?

— *I am upset that I am getting older. I cannot perform at the level I used to perform.*

— Why does aging bother you? Are you upset you are not as energetic as you used to be?

— *My body cannot endure the activities that it used to endure easily.*

— What makes you upset? How can we upset you? Let's try to get her upset.

155

— *You are not a good mother. You don't care about your kids.*

— Listen to what people are saying. Do not reply. Observe your reactions.

— *First of all, you don't understand anything, but you keep up the appearance that you understand everything. You are a dummy. You just pretend to be smart. You don't allow the thought that you don't understand anything to enter your head. Secondly, you pretend to be younger than you are. Your age doesn't allow you to run and play volleyball, but you push yourself. You are an old woman, but you try to look younger. You make us laugh.*

— *You should not be dating younger men. Find a man your own age.*

— *Your hair looks ugly. You could have at least had your hair done before coming here.*

— *Your happiness is fake.*

— *You are too much. Your capabilities are lower than your ambitions.*

— This is way too smart. Please, simplify.

— *She said she was smart. Looks like she is not that smart.*

— Okay. Which comment upset you the most?

— It was, *"The older woman who tries to look younger."*

— Does it have to do with your appearance?

— *It deals with my desire to not get old. It's fear.*

— What does it mean "to not get old"?

— *I think it is the fear of the changes that occur in my body and in my physical appearance. There is a fear of death behind it, too.*

— You will not get a new husband if you are old. You will not be able to run or go to the gym anymore. No one will even talk to you.

— *Your attractiveness is very childish: "I am very active in sports." Your age does not allow you to use this activity to attract men. This is not working anymore.*

— *Yes, I saw it already. I see how I do it. I condemn myself for it afterwards. I feel nauseated thinking how this older woman is trying to attract younger men.*

156

— Good. We are approaching something very important. What do you need? Why are you trying to attract younger men? How do you attract them? Are you trying to prove something to them? What are you trying to prove? What is it that you find more and more difficult to prove as you grow older?

— *I think it is my sexuality.*

— What is your sexual appeal based upon?

— *It is based on my appearance. It is based on my state of …*

— Is it the state of motherhood?

— *No. I don't want to give birth anymore.*

Sexual pride

— What about your sexual pride. If we are to talk about sexual appeal, you must be number one in this competition. What criteria do you base your sexual pride on?

— *When I was young, I always had three or four guys around me. I like to flirt. This is not about sex. This is just a game.*

— Do you consider yourself to be an interesting woman?

— *From which point of view?*

— From the point of view of the flirt.

— *From the point of view of the flirt, I need to be complimented and talked to.*

— Do you communicate as a man or a woman?

— *Do I look like a man?*

— There is a man and a woman in every human being, and quite frequently, it is not obvious which one of them a human being manifests. One can be in a woman's body but be controlled by an inner man. Is it your inner man who flirts with women in men's bodies? Who is flirting in you—a man or a woman?

— *One day it is a man, and the next day it is a woman. I know how my woman flirts, and I know how my man flirts.*

— Okay. Let's ask our group for help. Does she flirt as a man or as a woman?

157

— *To me, she flirts as a man.*

— *Based on her clothes and her appearance, she definitely flirts as a man.*

— *The state she manifests is the state of a man.*

— *Her inner man is very strong.*

— *Based on the fact that she only flirts and does not have sex with men, it's a flirt of a man.*

— The flirt of a woman is totally different. Let's ask our men. Who can tell us how women flirt?

— *For me, this is clearly defined. I can clearly see it in me. The way I see it, the flirt of a woman is not just a flirt; it always leads to the continuation of a relationship.*

— Your relationship with a man can also progress further. When a man flirts with a woman, after a while they start to move in unison. How does your woman flirt, and how is your man's flirt different?

— *When I am in the role of a woman, I use slow, revolving motions. I move very sensually. I send eye signals. It's important for me to be seen in the proper light.*

— What kind of a light?

— *In the winning-for-me light.*

— What does it mean to be in the winning light from a woman's point of view?

— *I am well-dressed. My hair is well-done. My makeup is impeccable.*

— Is that what we see now?

— *What you see now is not even close. I am comfortable now.*

— *Are you comfortable wearing these high heels?*

— *There was time when I would not leave the house without a makeup and a pair of high heels.*

— Is that time gone?

— *I got tired of it. I will not break my legs for men anymore.*

— This flirt is still very important for you. We can clearly see the attributes of your flirting woman. You have presented them very well. What about your inner man? How does he flirt?

158

— *I did not come here to flirt.*

— Your personality will manifest itself everywhere.

— *We have discussed the way a woman flirts. She attracts attention to herself.*

— First of all, it is the appearance. A woman manifests herself by using her appearance. That's why her appearance is extremely important to her. She can be stupid, but she should look good. So, how should your woman look?

— *She should always look sexy.*

— What does that mean?

— *She sends a signal that she desires sex. She can only be desired when she desires sex herself.*

— So, her appearance is not very important. What's more important is her desire to have sex.

— *She has to demonstrate this desire; a desire to have sex is attractive by itself.*

Flirt à la man and flirt à la woman

— *What does it mean to flirt as a man, and what does it mean to flirt as a woman? I don't understand that. I am trying to apply it to myself. I don't know how I do that.*

— We need to discern this. The duality "man—woman" is physically manifested. Let's investigate it. You don't know your inner man, and you don't know your inner woman. That's why you cannot discern between them. You don't know what to do with a guy after you approach him. Continue with your script. You have met him on the street. What's next?

— *What is the background of this meeting? If I want to have sex with him, I can skip the formalities. I can drop the movies or other romantic bullshit and take him straight to bed.*

— Great. What type of behavior does she demonstrate now?

— *This is the masculine type of behavior.*

— Yes, this is her inner man talking.

— Yes. This is a masculine type of behavior. To have sex, a man needs a woman. By the way, this is related to lesbians and gays, too. Irrespective of the physical body people inhabit, they always manifest polar types of behavior.

— *When I try to attract a man using my feminine side, I demonstrate my appearance. I let him see certain parts of my body. I smile provocatively and activate physical contact.*

— What does a woman do? A woman stimulates activity of her man. It's a man who manifests activity. A woman stimulates him to be active. Whenever someone manifests activity, it is a man. A woman manifests her activity by stimulating the activity of her man.

— *She does it in a very subtle way that is liked by both of them.*

— *Oh my God. This is horrible. I think I do it as a man.*

— Okay. You want to get to know someone and to have sex with him. How are you going to do that?

— *I will not tell him, "Let's go…" I have to see some kind of a signal in his eyes. I have to experience a very strong desire.*

— You are experiencing a very strong desire. What happens next?

— *I will probably have some crazy thoughts.*

— What kind of thoughts?

— *If this is to happen in a restaurant, I may get up and do something.*

— Will you break a wine glass, take your skirt off, or order a steak?

— *I will ask him to come home with me. I will ask for a kiss.*

— This is a masculine type of behavior. When you invite someone to perform a certain activity, you behave from a man's role. The most primitive masculine approach is to come to a woman and say, "I like you. Would you like to have sex with me?" A man suggests actions: let's go to the movies, let's go to a restaurant, etc. In the end, he takes a woman to bed. What does a woman do?

— A woman does it differently. She does something that makes a man take her to bed.

— She stimulates him. How does she do that?

— I don't know. I might do something that would manifest my desire.

— What kind of a desire? You are sitting there looking at each other. You start to feel that you like him. You keep looking at him. That's it. It's his turn to act. If, in response to your stare, he starts to do something, you respond to it.

— What if he doesn't do anything?

— That means you are not his woman.

— Can one activate this desire inside?

— What about an old friendship? I have an old high school friend. When we see each other, he always spills something on his pants. I don't do anything when it happens. I don't know how to explain it.

— It's a perfect time to ask him to take his pants off.

— He is just not himself. When we get together, he spills his food on a table. He breaks wine glasses. He turns chairs over.

— But you don't stimulate him to do that, of course.

— You should manifest your man. When he spills something, he offers you to be a man.

— I don't get it.

— If you don't manifest feminine qualities, he starts to manifest them.

My work is to activate dualities, so you can start seeing them inside yourself

— We are discussing the duality "man—woman", but almost no one can discern them from each other. If you cannot discern them, you don't know this duality. If you don't know the duality, you cannot see it. What does it mean to be whole? To be whole is to connect yourself. You have been divided into many dual parts. How can you connect something with something if you don't see it? My work is to activate dualities so you can start seeing them inside yourself. Presently, you are neither fish nor meat. What can you connect? What kind of a man can you

161

connect to what kind of a woman? You don't know your man, and you don't know your woman. Therefore, you cannot see them.

— *We know them, but we don't see them.*

— What does it mean, "We know them, but we do not see them"? When you see something, you can describe it. If you don't see it, you cannot describe it. You are in a fantasy world: "Perhaps I am aware, but I cannot say anything." This is fantasy.

— *I am not aware.*

— There is consciousness, sub-consciousness, and awareness. You can be conscious of something that happens to be in your consciousness. Let's look at the computer, for example. You turn it on, and a certain image pops up on the desktop. There are many other programs that operate inside the computer, but they are not brought up to the desktop. This is an analogy of consciousness and sub-consciousness. Presently, you don't even see what you have on your conscious level. Awareness offers the opportunity to bring consciousness and sub-consciousness to the desktop simultaneously and to see them together. You can look simultaneously at two files on your desktop. Awareness is simultaneously seeing two parts of duality. These two parts of duality are created in such a way that while negating each other, they complement each other. It is not easy to see the wholeness of the opposite sides of duality. For example, while in a woman's body, you start to see how you manifest a man and then how you manifest a woman. You start to discern these things in your own structure. You start to understand when and who you manifest.

— *I just saw that my woman is very insecure, while my man is very self-assured and haughty.*

— That's a good start.

— *Can a woman be self-assured? Isn't that a characteristic of masculine behavior? Is self-assuredness connected to oppression?*

— Natasha clearly demonstrates masculine behavior at all times. This is neither good nor bad. I do not condemn her behavior. As I have said already, each human being contains a man and a woman.

— *I find it to be more comfortable at the present time to behave as a man.*

— This is a model of behavior that was fixed in your consciousness.

— *I was thinking about what to wear this morning. I figured if I wear a skirt, I will have to put on pantyhose and heels. I put on what I felt comfortable in.*

— Your man made a decision. You should start seeing your woman.

— *This is so complicated. I will have to wear a purse. I will have to apply lipstick... I will have to watch how I walk.*

— Yes, but for one reason or another, you have chosen to come to this reality in the body of a woman.

— *I know. I know. I remember that I am a woman, but it is much more comfortable to be a man.*

— If you know everything already, I can leave.

— *I know my woman. She is charming and beautiful, but she is in my way right now. I was in a woman's mode yesterday, and I was unable to say a word.*

— *So, your woman is charming and unsure of herself?*

— *Yes, she is.*

— *You love her for her charms.*

— *I love her the way she is.*

— What is a charming woman? Is it a woman who gets enchanted or a woman who enchants other people?

— *My man likes her.*

— He likes her because she is enchanted by him.

— *Perhaps you are right. She feels good when she is with him.*

— A man feels good with a woman when a woman is enchanted by him.

— So, what can we do about these men and women inside us?

— I don't know. We are investigating.

— I was always torn between the desire to be a stay-at-home mom and having a career. As soon as I start to climb up a career ladder, I get pregnant and have to deliver a child.

Every conflict can be seen as a parental conflict

— A woman has many roles: a wife, a mother, a sister, a daughter, and a lover. You have mentioned childbirth. That's the role of a mother.

— The role of a mother is expressed very strongly in my case. I think it is my maternal qualities that attracted my husband. He frequently behaves like a little boy. He insists that I treat him like a child.

— You will not be able to understand why certain things happen to you unless you understand the role you are in. Every family conflict is a conflict of roles. We are dealing with four discrete conflicts here: the conflict between a mother and a child, the conflict between a husband and a wife, the conflict between two lovers, and the conflict between a father and a mother.

— I can see that, but when I tell him that he behaves like a child, he...

— Here you go again. You don't understand that **you are this child**. You don't understand that **you are also his mother**. Until you see a duality, you will not be able to transform it. The conflict will continue. This is life in a state of sleep.

— I don't get it. Am I this child?

— **If you are a mother, a child should be somewhere nearby**. You cannot be a mother if you don't have children. Otherwise, you are not a mother.

— I have three kids as it is. Why should I make a fourth child out of my husband?

— You have learned to play the maternal role well. That's why you attract men who exhibit the behavior of helpless children. You may have many men, but they will all be boys.

Your model of behavior is mother—child. You need to dig deep into it. Do you really want to do this hard work, or do you just want to talk about it?

— *I want to sort it out.*

— I don't see your desire to sort it out. You are not spinning the conflict which, like a rope, tightens around your neck. If you don't feel it like a tight rope, you will not have enough interest to solve it.

— *What does it mean to spin a conflict?*

— Why did you come here? Did you come here to get new information? If you came here to get new information, we are having a great dialogue. You receive new information, who knows about what, but you are interested. Does anyone have something important to say, something that greatly nauseates him?

— *Quite a lot was said yesterday, and by evening time, I was able to sort out my puzzle. I thought I was full. I rejected emptiness, but without emptiness there is no fullness. My body reacted to this information with constipation. I started to observe that I was getting bloated. I realized I need to pass it along to my friends. I asked myself, "What did I see in Pint?" I was looking straight at you, but I didn't see anything. I didn't see you in a single masculine role. I didn't see a man in you. I didn't see a brother or a father. I didn't see a lover. You were empty. I started to cry. I cried for four hours. What was that?*

— Then, who am I?

— *I don't know. I did not see father in you. I felt like an orphan. I really felt it. I cried through the whole night. I cried for every orphan on Earth. When the sun came up, I decided I had to do something about it.*

Why am I so afraid to accept you as a father? In my world, father is someone who offers retribution. He can make me upset. He can reprimand me harshly. Then I started to think. What kind of a father am I looking for? I had to look in the opposite direction too. I came up with the opposite image, with the image of the father who is always loving and who will never

165

reject me. He will accept me in any state. To a certain degree, I think I sorted out some of these father—daughter roles. I feel better now.

— What exactly did you sort out?

— *I can see father in myself and in you.*

— **I want you to pay attention to the fact that while investigating what is in you, you will project what you have in you onto someone else. Quite frequently, you will project onto me.** We should sort out what we have. Unless you figure out why you have specifically chosen this human being to play the role of your father in your life show, you will not be able to understand your personality.

— *Yes. You don't pay any atention to me. You don't react to me at all.*

— Great. I will invite you to package your dissatisfaction with me into certain roles. For example, "I see father in you, and as a daughter, I don't like the paternal quality you manifest."

— *I am not happy that you deprive me of your attention, care, protection, physical contact, and caresses.*

— Who is talking right now?

— *A young daughter is talking now. She wants to be held. She wants candy.*

— Okay.

— *I project a paternal role onto you too. My father has always been oppressed by my mom. My husband behaves like a child, too.*

— What irritates you? What hurts you? What do you hate?

— *I will act as a contrarian. I don't see you as father. I like the fact that you are wise. You can understand everything. You can be powerful, helpful, and empathetic. You listened to me very patiently yesterday.*

— *I see a brutal man in you for whom nothing is sacred. You frivolously talk about such delicate matters as sex. I see a man who can easily pick up a woman just to have sex with her.*

— *I do see father in you, a detached, impartial father who doesn't manifest his feelings. Your other side is helpless and needy.*

166

— I project the role of a husband onto you. This is a very strong energy. It's a husband I can follow and trust. I can see myself being a woman next to you.

— In the role of a mother, I am proud of you, son.

— I project a role of a friend onto you. I like your softness. That's precisely what I want to see in a friend.

— I have projected father onto you, a father who is not soft and who cannot express his feelings well.

— I see you as a strong, wise father. You have not received this knowledge from a book. This is your life experience. As your son, I know more about technology, and I can help you navigate through new inventions. As a father, you never solve my problems, but you can always point me in the right direction.

— I see a loving father in you. I can also see a son in you who is a bit insecure.

— I see the opposite side of my husband in you. I am always constricted inside. I am always expecting to be ridiculed. I am afraid of you being rude with me. On the other hand, I want to trust you. There is something in you that attracts me, but I am also afraid of rejection.

We always see our own parts in another human being

— Each one of you carries different and frequently opposite notions. You don't speak about me; you speak about yourself. We can only see ourselves in another human being. Each one of you has spoken about himself. I invite you to return what you have just said about me to yourself.

— I also saw that as a father you don't see a woman in me. You are only concerned with my career performance.

— I will ask you to return this statement to yourself and to become aware of the fact that it is you who don't see a woman in yourself.

Which qualities irritate you in other people? I will ask you to pair up and to discuss these qualities. Until you see and accept the qualities that irritate you in other human beings as your own qualities, you will continue to project these qualities onto them. You say, "Natasha is cheap. I don't like that." You condemn her for being cheap. But you have the same quality in you—you are cheap. Until you accept the qualities you don't like in other people as yours, you will continue to condemn them for these qualities. You should start to see these qualities in yourself. You should accept them as yours. You should see that the qualities you don't like in your partner are in you.

— *I don't get it.*

— You can only see in other people what is in you. You cannot see in other people what you don't have in you. You see a certain quality in your friend. You don't like this quality. However, you don't see this quality in yourself. I offer you something for which the School of Holistic Psychology was built. I invite you to see yourself holistically.

You have discussed qualities that you don't accept in your partner's personality. Now, I will ask you to manifest these qualities.

— *I see how I choose people based on my needs. I see how I use them. If I don't like something, I leave a man and find another one. I dumped my first husband. I am about to dump my second husband. I used to justify this behavior by saying that I am not beautiful, and I always chose men who were uglier than me. I had a crippled boy in my class. Everyone was laughing at him. I wrote a letter to him in which I told him that I loved him. Then I met my first husband, and I dumped the cripple. He was close to suicide. Then I found another guy. He was very ugly. I looked good next to him. I decided to marry him on our first date, and I married him. A couple of years later, I met another man. He was tall and handsome. I divorced my first husband, and I married this dude in five days. I have divorced him too.*

— That's exactly what you hate in other people.

— *I am very sarcastic and spiteful inside. I would never say it out loud, but I hate women who are prettier than me.*

168

— We have two opposite sides in us. You have to see both of them. Otherwise, you will always project some of your qualities onto other people and condemn them for manifesting these qualities, simultaneously experiencing the feeling of guilt for your condemnation. This is what I call "sleep". Did your attitude toward me change?

— *Perhaps it has changed slightly.*

— I want you to pay close attention here. You think your attitude toward me changed, and it may seem to you that you see everything. No. **The only criteria which will confirm that you see yourself clearly will be a change in your attitude toward other people and your full acceptance of them. If your relationships doesn't change, then you don't see yourself holistically.** Does anyone else want to share what he or she saw?

— *I said to my partner that he has a very sharp mind but no feelings. After I said that, I returned it to myself and I saw that the way I communicate with my husband is purely mental. On one hand, I want to communicate with him, but on the other hand, my feelings are totally blocked. I am afraid to feel. This is fear of attachment, fear of love, and fear of betrayal. Thus, I close up and communicate on the mind level. I appraise a human being based on what he does and how he does it. I do not get to the level of feelings.*

— Now you can see why you cannot perceive what I discuss.

— *For me, to see what I have said is to accept that I am a bitch. That's what I said to my last husband when I threw him out of the house. So, it is me who changes one family after another.*

— Yes. It is you, and until you see and accept this, you will direct all your energy toward preventing yourself from seeing it. This is you. You are the one who is doing this. But you say, "No. This is not me." That's the way our egos work.

— *I see what a I bitch I am now. This is horrible.*

— Do you think you are the only one? We are all the same.

— *I pretend to be nice and decent. I stage such a show.*

169

The end of pride is the begining of transformation

— This is what your ego says: "I am decent. I have never betrayed anyone. It's the people around me who betray, not me." That's what our pride is based upon. If you see and accept yourself fully, your pride will disappear. When pride dies, transformation begins. So, it is either pride or transformation. Presently, you manifest pride that is connected to the negative notions that you do not want to see and acknowledge in yourself. You carry positive notions about yourself, and as a result, you feel proud of yourself. You condemn others for the qualities that you consider and call negative.

— *I feel shame now. We come here, and you tell us something. It appears that we understand, but it is a pretense.*

— It appears to you, not to me. I see that you are not moving anywhere. Now you can also see that you are not moving and why you are not moving.

— *So, the only thing I can do when something irritates me is to take hold of it, to be happy about it, and to continue to do it.*

— This is hysterics.

— *What should I do?*

— You have to do something and that is what I offer you, but you need to understand exactly what you are doing and why. You manifest great level of activity. You pick up a slogan, and you run into action. But this is not so simple. Every one of you wants to receive a direct recommendation from me, but I don't provide direct recommendations; I push you toward self-understanding. Your desire doesn't get realized, and you feel irritation. I am not here to fulfil your dual desires. I don't give you what you want. I give you what you need—wholeness. Your desire is active again: "Tell me what to do and I will do it. End of story." I feel what you need, and I tell you what it is, but you don't hear me. I can say this about everyone here. Your desire begs, "Give me affirmation. Tell me what to do. Should I do it before dinner or after supper?" This is not so simple. What do you feel right now?

— *I clearly see that I didn't hear you before. I was awaiting something I expected without even understanding that I was expecting it.*

— You were waiting to receive something you want, but I didn't give it to you. I gave you what you really need.

— *I was waiting for it since day one. I was not getting it, and I was getting angry with you. I projected my anger onto you.*

— You need to sort out your projections. What do you project onto me? Until you see what you want, you will be angry, and you will continue to project your anger onto me. In that case, you will continue to be angry with me throughout the seminar because I will not give you what you want.

— *I was angry with you for getting under a table during our last seminar. I didn't see it before. What kind of a man hides under a table? I did not understand that.*

— Here you go. This is your angry side that is full of revenge talking. I do not condemn it. Awareness does not condemn anything; it simply sees things the way things are. **We didn't come here to be good. We came here to acquire a certain experience.** The way a human being is brought up in this dual reality is as though he came here to be good and only good. Thus, we have this so-called life here—life in a state of sleep. It's impossible for you to be good and only good. Thus, you condemn other people and yourself for not being good.

— *I am experiencing a conflict in my relationship with you going to Latvia. One side of me wants to go there, another side does not want to go there. The part that does not want to go pretends it doesn't care, but I feel anger, jealousy, and a grudge. Actually, it cares and it cares deeply. I feel this war that occurs inside me.*

— Why do you need to go there? What's your pride in?

— *I am a very important person. How come I don't go? What are you going to do there without me?*

— How can anything happen without you? Nothing should happen in your absence.

— *This is what the all-knowing and all-understanding part of me is saying. One part suppresses the other. It is saying it doesn't care whether I go or not. But for the other part, it is very important to be there.*

— What exactly is bothering you? What's behind your pride? Which specific duality has been activated?

— *It's about the money: "I have the money—I don't have the money."*

— How many more times do I need to repeat myself for you to understand something?!

— *There is a part of me that would not allow me to be quiet any longer. I see a harsh father in you who screams and condemns me: "You are a piece of shit. You don't understand anything. You should understand everything by now, and you should be ahead of everyone. How can you be so stupid?" I could not express this condemnation to you because you are the leader here. You know everything. I am nobody. You are the authority here. I cannot say anything to you.*

— You are number one here. That's why I yell at you.

— *When you yell and condemn me, I feel stupid. I get confused, and I cannot figure out what you want from me. I should keep my silence. Then I would not be exposed to such a harsh condemnation. This is way too painful.*

— You get stupid when I yell, and you get stupid when I don't yell.

— *I condemn Olga when I see my stupid child in her, a child who cannot make any money; she just sits there crying.*

— What does money have to do with this?! I am asking about the reasons for your unhappiness. What causes you to experience this unhappiness? Why are you so worried about your inability to go to Latvia? What is the reason? It turns out that this is about "Nothing should happen without me. I need to control everything and everyone." That's your pride. Am I correct?

— *You are probably right, but I am also interested in seeing a new country.*

172

Personage's deadend

— I am trying to introduce a new language here where we will be able to reach some kind of understanding, but you don't accept it. Each one of you sings in his own birdy tongue and holds on to it. Each one of you is unique. You are so exclusive, you have excluded yourself from everything else. What are we going to do now?

— *I don't think our group is one unified organism. Everyone's ego, i.e. pride, expresses its distrust. We are not fully open with each other. Each one considers himself tough but condemns others for being tough. Every one of us thinks his ego is tougher. I see no team work here. We bring the competition we experience in the outside world to the group. Instead of working with our higher "I", our conditioned minds compete with it. I saw my own condemnation and my own weakness today. My mind betrayed me today. It could not prove how tough it was to others. It is afraid to appear weak.*

— *The mind is afraid to admit its weakness in front of everyone. That's why we are not sincere with each other.*

— *It is afraid to admit its own weakness to itself.*

— *Naturally. When you say something that comes from the core of your being, you experience fear. Was I too sincere? The mind feels weak. It sees sincerity as a betrayal. It turns out that I have this horrible quality in me. The mind tries to block me from seeing it.*

— This is not only betrayal of the mind. One part of me won over the other. We are talking duality here. Exactly who and what did your mind betray? You have manifested weakness. Your strong side got activated and became indignant toward the opposite, weak side. Those are the weak and the strong sides of one duality.

— *Why do you reject what I say?*

— *I don't reject anything. I just want to bring some clarity into our discussion.*

— *You have to have clarity in everything.*

— *Why are we circling in the dark?*

173

— There is clarity, and there is no clarity.

— I don't understand what you are talking about. How could the mind betray you? Who did your mind betray? Did it betray your soul?

— I saw how horrible I am. I feel horrified. My mind horrifies me. I am ashamed. I have always agreed with it. I had no idea what I did. I have never grown out of this six-year-old girl.

— You are not open and sincere with yourself. Therefore, you condemn us for our openness. You condemn yourself for your openness.

— Can't you see what is happening here? We are talking, but nobody is listening to us. People have spread around the room, and nobody is listening to our conversation.

— Is it important for you that they listen to us?

— Yes, this is very important. We are one group, and we have gathered here for a reason, but everyone is on his own.

— One hears who one wants to hear.

— I cannot hear anyone because I am stuck in my own shit.

— I think each one of us has to hear another human being.

— Who said that? It's your program talking. What if someone is not listening to me? Should I condemn him for that? But who is it that doesn't listen to me? It's my other side. According to your notion, if someone is talking, everyone should listen to him, and whoever doesn't listen should be condemned and be forced to listen. However, the other side of you doesn't want to listen. It doesn't need it. Everyone here is submerged in his own stuff. Whoever wants to hear will hear.

— What are we talking about now?

— We are talking about nothing …

— We have discussed Olga's situation. Looking from the side, we can say that every seminar reinforces her pride: "Look at me. I come to every seminar!" I feel she is saying, "What kind of a seminar can they have without me?"

— Let's not deny it; each one of us is full of a similar pride.

— I don't deny this. I am just verbalizing my thoughts.

— Why don't we let Olga say what's on her mind?

— I don't understand anything. I am trying to observe myself.

174

— *I like your energy. It is very strong. You just don't know where to direct it.*

— *If you could only use this energy for peace. You are definitely not sending it in the right direction.*

— *I agree.*

— *Olga, you will definitely succeed. I am sure of that.*

— In what will she succeed?

— She will succeed in getting what she wants to get. She is running in circles. We are trying to sort out what she wants.

— You have said she is going to succeed in something. In what is she going to succeed?

— *Okay. Unless we succeed, we will run in circles until the day we die.*

— *You want us to start to desire things. Why should we do that if nobody can achieve anything here?*

— *We should believe we are going to achieve something.*

— *Isn't it better for us to believe that we are not going to succeed and to relax?*

— We are facing a crisis.

— *My personage is tremendously proud for his attempts to do something using other people. Consciously, when I am asked to do something, I do that. I get upset when people don't do what I ask them to do, claiming to be busy. For some reason, the mechanism of using other people to do things I need to do gets turned on in me. This mechanism is very well known to me. Consciously, I do not allow myself to do anything for another human being when I am busy.*

— Okay. We are watching a show now. What kind of a show is it?

— *Every actor is being shown the specific "not understanding" he is in and his inability to see the level of his not understanding. Every actor is given an opportunity to resolve this not understanding.*

— This is a personage's dead end. **Self-investigation consists of our living through something and then becoming aware of what we just lived through.** We have just

175

played something out. I will ask all of you to become aware of what just happened here.

Can our group become aware of what is happening in it?

— It is impossible to move on while being in the personage. I am trying to do something while I am in the personage. I have been shown that I will not be able to do anything unless I start to see my personage as a personage.

— Exactly. Our group is a self-investigating organism. Can the group become aware of what is happening in it? If it is not capable of becoming aware of what's going on in it, it is not a self-aware group. We have all gathered here under the slogan of self-awareness. If what's happening in the group is not enough for us to become aware, then we need to intensify something somewhere. We cannot get out of the dead-end until we become aware of what's going on. All of us are in the same boat.

— Yes. I see a clear separation here. I have always seen myself and other personages as separate from each other. We are observing the group and group processes now. This is something else.

— This is the most important thing. The ego always focuses on itself. We have just observed that every one of you is focused on himself and on himself alone. You are not capable of seeing the group process as a whole. Presently, our group is just a collection of separated and dissatisfied egos. If you cannot become aware of yourself in the mirrors of the group, you cannot participate in the self-investigation process. You have mirrors around you. What do you see in them? Can you become aware of what is happening to you when you see your reflections in so many mirrors? What kind of a mirror is in front of you, and what do you see in it?

— I see confusion, condemnation, and fear.

— I have only one word: "No Awareness". I am talking about myself.

— You are talking about every one of us.

— I am afraid to open up. I am not sure I can trust you. We are separated. Each one of us tries to stand out. I saw that Olga cannot accept her pride. It is very difficult to open up.

— Is it difficult for you to open up to yourself?

— Yes. I saw myself condemning you for the weakness you have manifested. I suddenly saw that weakness and power were two sides of one coin. I felt gratitude. I was afraid you would dig deep and find something I would be ashamed of, something I didn't want to see.

— Do you find it difficult to open up in front of other people who are sitting here, who you see for the first time and perhaps will never see again, or do you find it difficult to open up to yourself?

— I am afraid to open up to myself.

— What kind of life are you living if you cannot even open up to yourself?

— I am experiencing a strong inner conflict. I intuitively feel that there is trust here, but my mind doesn't trust anyone. My ego doesn't trust anyone. The conflict is in the duality "trust—distrust".

— Who exactly don't you trust?

— The conflict is inside me. I want to ask these two parts to cooperate.

— Look around. Everyone here is you. So, who is it that you don't trust?

— I don't trust myself.

— Then continue to remain asleep.

— Presently, I just see that there is trust and distrust. Both states coexist in me. I need to change it.

— Who don't you trust here and why?

— I trust everyone, and five minutes later, I find myself distrusting everyone. I condemn myself for this distrust.

— I want you to specify who you don't trust here and why.

— I don't trust Eugene. He is completely closed up.

— Who do you see in Eugene when you speak of him being closed up?

— I see myself. I see myself in him.

177

— And we call this craziness life. Do you want to continue this madness? Do you see this madness now, or do we have to intensify it further?

— *Who are you saying this to?*

— I speak to all of us. We are in the same boat.

— *I just saw that you don't accept us.*

— We don't accept each other, but at the same time—we are one.

— *The personage will never accept anyone else.*

— We don't consist of the personage alone. Therefore, we can become aware of what is happening to our own personages. I invite you to do that. We can only become aware of ourselves together. I, as a personage, am irritated by other personages because they don't understand anything and don't want to understand anything.

— *Yes. This condemnation is a rule of the game. Without us being so unaware, we would not have you so aware. This is the proud side of the ego. Let's not forget about your pride.*

— Yes. My personage is proud of his awareness in comparison with your unawareness.

— *Yes, my personage is happy that others don't understand anything.*

— My pride is happy that others don't understand anything. With you so dumb on the background, I am quite aware.

— *You are sitting so high, we cannot even see you.*

— I am great, but you don't even see it. I am sharing the pride of Pint's ego with you.

— *On the other hand, this pride is a defense. We should not reject it either.*

— Awareness does not reject anything. Awareness discerns and see the opposite sides of duality. It accepts both sides as equal. It cannot happen any other way in this dual reality. My personage would not be able to write all these books it has written, to continue working with the groups, and to create a school if this duality was not strongly activated in it. The wide spread of this duality led to the appearance of pride in my personage. But the personage would not be able to accomplish what it has accomplished without the appearance of pride. This is paradoxical. Pint's personage just shared its basic duality with you, but Pint is not only the personage.

— *My personage is the same. My personage also carries duality awareness—unawareness, understanding—not understanding. My personage gets very excited and happy when it encounters personages that don't understand anything. I condemn the group: "Where are we going? Why don't you understand anything?" But at the same time, I feel happy. "Great. Marina is so stupid she doesn't understand anything, while this dude is just sitting here with his mouth open." One part of me thinks, "Where am I?" The second part thinks, "God forbid someone outshines me and manifests himself as being more aware than me. I will not be able to bear that."*

I am also proud of being useful. I have organized this seminar, and I am very proud of that. The second part pops up occasionally and condemns my organizer part for being so full of pride.

I condemn myself when I don't understand something, and I condemn myself when I understand things.

— Okay. Next.

— *I have also condemned you for saying that I am me and you are you. You have divided us, but I understand now that only by dividing us you can connect us later. I thought to myself, "What's going on? Why do I feel such severe condemnation and hate?" I understand now. It is only through hate that you can unite and connect.*

— You need to activate the opposite side of a duality. Only by doing that you can see both of its sides and have the opportunity to come to a partnership.

— *I feel guilty for being stupid and for slowing the group down. I wanted to run away when you screamed at me. My opposite side, on the other hand, considers itself very important. It cannot bear it when I am not important. It has been squeezed now; it does not understand anything, it cannot become aware of anything, and it slows things down.*

179

— You slow the whole group down. The ego can take pride in this too. All by yourself, you are slowing down the entire group.

Can we feel the state "We are one"?

— We are talking about us. There are many of us, but We are one. I will ask every one of you to speak up.

— I spoke to Larissa during lunchtime, and she expressed her fear of getting close to people in the group.

— Where is "We"? Not "i", but "We"?

— It is impossible to move forward without this understanding.

— You can memorize the phrase "There are many of us, but We are one", and you can keep repeating it, without experiencing the state of unity. Can you feel that We are one?

— My personage is afraid to even think of such an experience. My personage will always insist on its own truth.

— My personage constantly keeps this internal dialogue going, discussing what it should say and how it should say it but never says anything.

— It looks like neither one of us understands or experiences our oneness.

— The first step is seeing that I don't understand that. If I think I understand, I don't need to do anything to understand because I already understand everything. To *see* that I don't feel it is a very important step. This is the first step. Everything starts there. The Process occurs as it occurs; it has nothing to do with my personage. We just happened to come to this point. The fact that we come to this point means that we are ready to enter something new.

— Why don't you change your own personage? Don't give us what we need. Allow us to express what we want to express, even if it is something very insignificant.

— Okay. Why don't you start?

— I can clearly see how divided we are. Every one of us is spinning on his own. On my way here, I observed people who were riding the bus with me.

We are so divided. Every one of us lacks attention. Everyone needs a kind word.

— Earlier today, I tried to imagine that We are one, but I was unable to feel it. This is a dead-end. I sat there, thinking. I saw some analogies. I heard a voice and a melody. The personage always wants to play his own tune. Melody is a process. Olga was talking a few minutes ago. Perhaps she doesn't understand everything, but this process is common for all of us. I must say something now. Someone will speak after me, and Olga had to say what she had to say. I say what I say now based on certain associations with music. I decided to figure out how I can accept that We are one, or that everything is me. I looked at Olga. Okay, she is my part, and I know her in myself. That was easy to do. But for some reason, I have a different attitude toward Eugene and Natali. I feel something, but I cannot define which part of me each one of them manifests. I never felt this way. This is a duality "me—another human being".

— It seems to me that every one of us is tired of sticks and is ready for candy.

— I don't know why you say we have come to a dead-end. I don't understand what that means. I came to understand that I can condemn any human being who is present here, in which case, we cannot be one.

— I, on the other hand, cannot condemn anyone.

— When music started to play, I decided to imagine how "We" can become one. What is my understanding of what "We" means? I see people who are happy. They are united by something that is common to all of them. Then, a thought popped in: "This happiness cannot continue for long." I felt a strong desire to manifest my not-manifested side. For some reason, my mind could not connect it with "We". When one is in the personage, one cannot feel "We". Every personage clearly senses himself as being separate from other people. The state of sensing another human being as me is not connected to the personage.

— I heard the word "We" for the first time when we started to explore the analogy of a theater: we are actors, and we play together. We play certain roles for each other. We help each other to see what it means to be separated.

181

We are so talented in this, that we really represent "We". Perhaps if we are given another script, we can play something else.

— I will use another analogy to explain what I see as "We": Alexander Alexandrovich is a canvas on which we represent different colors. We embroider this canvas as best as we can. Sometimes, we miss a stitch or two, or take a wrong turn, but each one of us paints his own color.

— I feel we are parts of one big automobile. Each part is separate by itself, but if we were to bring them together, lubricate, and assemble them, we will make one working mechanism.

— Those are all theoretical analogies. There is no real experience behind them.

— How can we acquire a real experience?

— I don't know. I don't like the fact that every analogy you guys bring up has never been experienced. You only talk about your weird notions.

— And what about you? How do you experience all of this?

— Don't you experience the state of "oneness" now? You have been living on your own for a while. It is only here, in the group, that you appear to be alive. How do you feel when you are alone? You told me yesterday that you feel very depressed when you are home alone. When all of us are here, we are something.

— What are we?

— We are something.

— When we are together, we can do something for us.

— Can you be a bit more specific. I have heard this word "we" many times, but I still don't understand what it means.

— We need to have a common aim. It would activate something in us. It would be good if this aim was connected to survival.

— Well, that's what we do all the time—we survive.

— We would get some kind of a result. We would scream at each other and push each other. We would live.

— Survival is a strong stimulus.

— When people started to talk about "we", I felt better. Something changed.

— *I am shaking. I want to cry. Something in me is asking to come out, but I cannot say anything. It is a dead-end.*

— *Where there is a dead-end, there should also be an exit.*

— *I also feel that everyone here can give me something, and my personage may not necessarily like this something. I can also give something to all of you. To do that, we need to understand what our interaction is based on.*

— *When we look at unity and separation as two dual sides, as a movement and resistance to a movement, we understand that one cannot exist without the other. In that case, we don't have to get rid of separation. We understand that.*

— *Then, we will face a need to feel the second side—Unity.*

— *I have a feeling that we don't notice it. Unity is always present here, paired with separation.*

— *We always act out of separation.*

— *The state of unity is perceived as a feeling that comes out of the heart. It appears spontaneously. Then, it quietly disappears. You can feel it constantly if you are not stuck in the personage. In that case, you don't care where you are and what is happening to you. You don't want to say or do anything, and it doesn't matter to you who says what. You experience kaif* just from seeing other people. Somehow, this is connected to you seeing yourself as a personage.*

— *I have a feeling that we talk about unity and separation as if it was a subject, not a state. The state of separation comes out of the state of unity.*

— *We can take a look at what characterizes the state of separation, investigate it, and learn it thoroughly. That's what we do here. We investigate our thoughts, feelings, and manifestations that accompany our states. They are opposite to the state of unity.*

— *Being in a state of separation, I am always looking for a profit. Being within a part with which I am identified, my personage determines what I need.*

— When we speak about our experiencing the state of love, there are no thoughts there. As soon as the mind starts to talk, we leave the state of unity.

183

— Every word we say separates us.

— As soon as we start to think, we enter separation.

— Is it even possible to think or to act when we are in a state of unity?

— When you think and act out of the dual mind, you cannot experience yourself holistically. You can only experience separation.

— But we cannot live without the mind.

— In that case, we cannot feel Unity. Everything we say will sow a seed of separation. As soon as a word is spoken, it separates. Every thought that comes into our head separates. There is no Unity in the mind. There is no Unity in the word. By definition, every word here is a lie, i.e. half-truth.

— It looks like separation can help us. We think while we are in separation, and we explain things using words of separation. If that is the case, then doing something in separation can bring us to the state of Unity. Separation is a working zone which prepares us for transferring to the state of Unity where we can feel love.

The state of unity cannot be expressed in words

— Love is present everywhere all the time. Without it there would be nothing here. We don't feel it because we think and talk using the dual language. No conversation here can lead to the state of Unity. Any conversation, including our conversations here, can lead to a more detailed discernment, but not to the state of Unity. The state of Unity is the state, and it is not expressed in words. Words can only express something that is separated.

— Our last seminar exacerbated something very strongly. That allowed us to manifest something new. Yes, it was the separation that we experienced at the time that allowed us to manifest something new.

— Until you see Unity, you act out of your personage, hoping that there is some kind of truth here. It looks like we need our personage just to see

what we are in, to see the entire separation. We need to see that there is no satisfaction here and can never be.

— But at the same time, it is precisely here that satisfaction is present.

— *For the personage?*

— I have told you before that no one will be able to tell you the Truth. It can only be felt. What I say is not the Truth. My words are only the pointers that can direct you toward it.

— *It looks like to experience wholeness, we must maximize separation first.*

— *How far can we go? Isn't it enough for you?*

— I show you the mechanisms of the functioning of the ego. I have offered you a special terminology that will help you solve this puzzle, but this terminology becomes an obstacle when we try to feel the state outside the duality. This is a paradox because the state of "we" is an experience that is outside the dual notions, while the picture of the mechanisms of the dual mind is a mental construct. Irrespective of how clear and precise this picture is, it will never replace the experience. No one here will ever be able to compile a mental picture that would lead him to feel Unity. Unity is an emotional state. Connection with a Soul occurs through the heart. The heart does not talk in dual words.

CHAPTER 4
EXCLUSIVE MEANS EXCLUDED

•◆•◆• •◆•◆• •◆•◆• •◆•◆• •◆•◆• •◆•◆• •◆•◆• •◆•◆• •◆•◆• •◆•◆• •◆•◆•

If you consider yourself to be exclusive, you will not be able to feel God inside

— I want to start by verbalizing my intention to see things the way they are irrespective of how they are. I intend to see illusion as an illusion. I intend to see duality and to connect my mind with my heart.

— I would like to discuss the Process we are in. I have thought about the question you asked during the last seminar, "Can one see reality without investigating duality?" and the opposite question, "Can one clearly see how this dual reality is made and at the same time not be aware of the reality?" The way I understand the Process is that you come to be aware of who you really are. You begin to experience it. You are in it. You start to be present in "this world". To do that, you have to find a special interest for your personage. You, Alexander Alexandrovich, have found this interest in the process of self-investigation, and that is what you do. At first, you were not able to see things clearly. I read the books that you wrote twenty years ago. That's why I say that. You had a vague notion of duality then, but you didn't see it clearly. At the same time, even though your ability to see things clearly was not yet fully developed, you were in touch with this reality. The ability to see things clearly is limitless. You will see things better and better. I used to think that if I were to start to see things clearly, I could end this process and enter the real world. I know better now. I understand that to be aware is to see dualities clearly. Unfortunately, the state of awareness cannot be described in words.

— Okay. Who is Pint? Pint is a personage. As I have told you already, we are in the same boat, in one reality, in one jail. As a personage, I was born in this jail, and I am a product of this jail. I am a product of separation.

However, my other aspect is in the "Other World". I had a conversation with this other aspect of me during which the following was said: "If you consider yourself to be exclusive, you exclude yourself." That's why you experience the state of separation or suffering. You can consider yourself exclusive, but in that case, you will experience suffering and the state of separation. You will not be able to understand what "WE" means." I am talking now from the point of view of the voice that is not of "this world", the voice with which I happen to be in constant contact now.

This voice says, "If you consider yourself to be unique, you cannot feel the state of Unity. Unity is a state. When you stop to consider yourself as unique, you will see Me in Everything. I am present everywhere. I am in every human being. I am in everything that exists. I AM. It's precisely the exclusivity that prevents people from seeing the presence of 'WE' or God in everything." As a personage, I asked, "Why do I do what I do?" I received the following answer: "Presently, the mission of your personage is to bring people to understand duality." The paradox of your mission is that you must express nondual vision through a dual language. A word can express only one side of duality. Whatever you say and whatever language you use is only half the truth. This is the paradox. The Truth cannot be expressed in words. It can only be experienced by heart.

As human beings, we are both the macrocosm and the microcosm. As the microcosm, we are just a part of the Universe. We are a macrocosm for the organs of our body. Our body is a very complex mechanism. What do the organs of our body experience? What do our kidneys, liver, and gallbladder experience? Every cell and every organ receive a certain experience. We only pay attention to them when they call our attention to themselves in the form of pain or disease. The state

187

that our cells and organs experience is a state of "WE". Looking at ourselves from the point of view of the macrocosm, we can start to understand what Earth with its organic life, people, and other forms of life experiences. What does it experience? Earth is also an organism which, as a human being, consists of many systems, organs, elements, and in particular "WE" — Humanity. The Earth is "WE", our organism is also "WE", but it is a different "WE". For the Earth, everything that is in it and on it is "WE". For us, our organism is also "WE". At the same time, psychologically we are in a state of separation because of the divided perception we use. The conditioned mind works on the principle of separation; it uses and supports the system of separated perception. As personages, we cannot understand what is "WE" because our personages see everything through a very narrow window of dual perception.

— *I have thought about the state of "WE" for a long time. My mind has explored multiple options. I suddenly realized that something was wrong. You asked me, "How do you see me?" I answered that I see you the way I always did, but the question of how do we connect to "WE" would not let me rest: "What kind of a connection am I looking for using my dual mind if I am not even grateful for what's going on? My gratitude is mental and very formal: "Thank you for helping me to see this and that."*

— This is not a state of gratitude. This is a mental notion expressed in words.

— *Yes. My heart is closed. How can I even connect to "WE"?*

— What kind of a mission does Pint's personage perform? Pint's mission is to bring clarity into the twilight of consciousness submerged into the lower vibrations of separated perception. When you talk to a human being, you see what happens in his consciousness. He hallucinates. What does my personage do? My personage says, "Consider the essence of the question. Every hallucination is connected to a certain law of functioning of duality." I introduce clarity into everything by seeing myself as a dual personality. Since I was a child, I was amazed when I saw

188

how clearly light and shadow get separated in the forest on a bright, sunny day. Shadow is clearly demarcated from the light. I show very clear separation between plus and minus in every dual personality, and in the process, I improve the quality and clarity of your vision. But even the clearest vision of separation will not allow you to feel the Unity or the state of "WE". The state of "WE" deals with feelings. This reality is perceived by the dual mind, but people don't see clearly how the dual mind works. In investigating the mechanisms of the work of the dual mind, I bring in understanding of how this dual reality functions. This understanding comes as we become aware of the mechanisms of the work of the conditioned mind. But to become aware of these mechanisms is to see the intellectual component of a human being. We also have an emotional component. One can intellectually describe the state of "WE", but to understand what it is, one has to experience it. **The state of "WE" can only be experienced.** You must conduct the work of separation by seeing and becoming aware of yourself to understand what I discuss now. The heart or the sphere of feelings is under the control of the dual mind; it is presently within the constraint of fear. We need to figure out how it works. If one of you suddenly feels the state of "WE" or Unconditional Love, know that this state will pass quickly, and you will submerge into separation again. We happen to occupy one jail that I call dual reality, and we need to understand the way it is made. I will repeat that the intellectual investigation of this question will not lead you to experience the state of "WE". The mind investigates the mechanisms and the makeup of this dual reality intellectually. **The state of "WE", on the other hand, can only be experienced when you are out of your mind, out of your personage.** To experience it, you need to cease being exclusive. Every personality here is unique in something and fights to prove its exclusivity. Every personality strives to be exclusive and wants to attract the attention of other personages to its exclusiveness,

189

reinforcing its pride in that way. This is the basic trap of the reality of separation. The personage excludes itself from God and from "WE" and thus cannot recall this state. It is personal pride that prevents you from feeling the state of "WE". You can feel the state of "WE" only if you are not excluded from "WE". If you are not in exclusivity-exclusion, you see God in everything. God is everything!

Feel the pain of the people you condemn

— I cannot experience gratitude. Today my son confessed to me that it was my husband who killed our cat. I knew my husband was cruel, and I always condemned him for that. But today, as my son was describing what his father did, I felt my husband's pain. I cried. Recently, you talked about people with alcohol dependency, who drink because they are in severe pain. I experienced something similar today. I have felt his pain as my own pain, and then I experienced compassion.

— His pain is your pain.

— I didn't condemn him. I empathized with him: "How severe must his pain be to reach such degree of aggression?"

— Aggression is a cry for help. How bad should one feel to take somebody's life? **To approach compassion, we must start feeling the pain of those we condemn. We always condemn ourselves. We only condemn ourselves. When we start to feel and experience the pain of the people who surround us, we can come to compassion. Do not get closed. You must manifest your feelings. Many people restrain their condemnation for a long time. You must see and manifest your condemnation, understanding that you condemn yourself. Recall what we discuss the next time you condemn. This will prepare and open your heart.** It may seem to you that the work we do is mental. Many of you have complained that our work is devoid of feelings. No. Feelings such as condemnation, guilt, and fear are always present here. Express your condemnation in such a way that you feel it as

190

condemnation. It seems to you that you don't condemn and do not feel guilty. This is an illusion. You are not in touch with your feelings. You cannot open your heart to Unconditional Love right away. You can move in that direction by becoming aware of the feelings of condemnation, pity, and guilt that you experience toward yourself. Don't be afraid to express your feelings. Otherwise, you are not going to become aware of them. Do it, but be aware of what you are doing and understand why you are doing it. A mechanically functioning human being does it without awareness. That gives birth to a vicious circle. The experience continues to recur. A man can understand what I say on the level of the mind, but if he prohibits himself from expressing aggression, guilt, and pity, he suppresses his emotional center. He doesn't manifest something that is present in his personality, and he doesn't see it.

— *What about "don't do to others what you don't want to be done to you"?*

— You are trying to run away from manifesting negative emotions, but you have to manifest them in full awareness of what you are doing, knowing why you are doing what you do. Our Process will help you to open your heart. It will teach you how to connect the mind and the heart. The mind provides you with vision. The heart offers you feelings. The mind is awareness. The heart is Unconditional Love. Awareness and Unconditional Love always go hand in hand. When we walk, we alternate our legs: left leg goes first, right one follows. You cannot step into Awareness with your right leg and become aware of everything immediately. Use both of your legs to enter Unconditional Love. Each one of you is presently at the level of hallucination and misunderstanding that he currently needs. This is not bad. This is the way it is. We will climb out of sleep step by step. Every step of Awareness is followed by a step of feelings. You cannot understand and become aware of something if you do not experience it. You are trying to understand something by using

191

your intellectual center. Do that. That's necessary, but that is not enough. To understand something in our Process, you must experience it. Our movement occurs step by step. Do not try to jump three steps at a time. You will be returned to step one. In the process of making these steps, your personage changes. Over the last twenty years, my personage changed significantly due to the steps I took toward Awareness and Unconditional Love. The life of a personage replicates the same thing over and over again. Let's become aware of this "thing". This step by step movement is spiral and ascending. We experience something, and then we return and experience the same thing again. But when we return to it, we see more than we saw before. In this way, we ascend to a higher level of the spiral of Life. In a few months or a few years, we are going to face this situation again. If we have experienced it, we will recognize and pass through it to another level of understanding. Our understanding is relative and not final. Every one of us has his own rhythm, and everyone's step is of a different length. I do not offer you the Truth. I provide you with pointers. As you catch them, you see the direction in which to take your next step. Then, you will get another pointer. How many pointers will you need? No one can tell you that. We are moving nonstop. The conditioned mind wants to be given the aim and recommendations on how to reach it faster. This is not what happens in our Process. You must experience one step. Then, we are going to discuss the next step. You take a step, and then you take another step.

— *I have started to openly manifest my condemnation lately, and I saw that guilt and condemnation are the same thing. I used to think that to experience the feeling of guilt was good but to condemn was bad. I used to block condemnation and experience guilt. I thought I was doing the right thing, but lately, when I express condemnation, I see that condemnation and guilt are the same thing. Guilt is another form of condemnation. The only difference between them is that guilt is directed inside. Instead of condemning someone, I condemn myself.*

— In the illusion of separation in which we happen to live, the feeling of guilt is the consequence of self-condemnation. When we condemn others, we direct condemnation outside of ourselves, but it returns to us in the form of guilt.

— *It's always the same, always the same...*

— No, it's not always the same. You must make a discernment here. It's different, but the mechanism of it is the same. The more you condemn someone without understanding that you condemn yourself, the more guilt you experience. One state gives birth to the other. Some people get inculcated with the notion that they need to experience the feeling of guilt while others get inculcated with the notion that they must condemn others.

— *A thought just came to my mind that I must allow myself to feel condemnation and guilt and to start to express them brutally. I always behave meekly when people are hard on me, especially when they yell at me.*

— Yes. That's exactly what you need to do now. You have the notion that you have to experience the state of guilt that is habitual for you. This part of your personality creates certain situations. It attracts other people and projects its own harsh part onto them, receiving aggressive condemnation in return. You do not see yourself in people who aggressively condemn you. You scream at yourself. You are not familiar with your own aggressive side. You must start to manifest it. Currently, you condemn yourself through other people. Do it, and you will start to swing your emotional center. Thoroughly feel both sides of the duality. Feel what the man who condemns you feels and what the one who experiences the feeling of guilt feels. This pain and suffering will show you what you do to yourself. You will experience empathy only once you experience heavy suffering. To do that, you need to know why you are doing it and what you want to achieve. Many people suffer while in this dual reality. They don't understand the reasons behind their suffering. They look for ways to lessen their suffering. They are not trying to find a way to

193

see why and how their suffering appears. Many people close themselves off from suffering; they stop manifesting themselves emotionally. The pain that was fixed in them and that they remember appeared in them while they suffered. This pain lowers emotional manifestation and sensitivity in general. These people close the diapason of their heart sensitivity, i.e. they close their emotional center. They become insensitive. They have several explanations as to why this is happening. Many of them claim to be nice. They say they never harm other people. They just don't feel how bad things are, or they feel it in a very narrow diapason. Such people cannot reach empathy without going through intentional, aware suffering. Suffering is downloaded into the structure of every personality from its inception. It is fixed in it by its painful experience. You must get in touch with this experience and activate it. You will have to do this by activating the sides of the dualities that you consider to be bad, sides that you were not in habit of manifesting. If you are used to people condemning you, you must start to condemn people. You must do it with full awareness and an understanding of why you are doing it.

How can I condemn someone and be aware of it?

— *How can I condemn someone and be aware of it?*

— Find someone here and condemn him or her.

— *Let me condemn Larisa.*

— Start to express your condemnation and intensify it. You can scream at her. Show us the diapason of feelings you have.

— *Larisa. You are a cold, insensitive log. When we spoke about my problem, you were very cold and …*

— Don't try to explain anything, just condemn her. By trying to explain to her why you are condemning her, you are softening your condemnation. Condemn her. Use profanities. Profane words carry strong energy. This energy scares many people. They

194

are just words. Why do they shock people? They shock people because they are usually connected to some negative, painful memory. Insert your emotional state in your condemnation. These words will help you to do that.

— *Why can't you do anything? You cannot even condemn. Do it! Do it! Damn you, just do it!*

— *Are you crazy? Stop it, you idiot!*

— *You are an idiot yourself!*

— *Calm down.*

— *I will kill you! Do what you have been told! Hit her!*

— *This is horrible.*

— She has just demonstrated what's going on inside you. This emotional storm is inside you. You have it contained now. You contain your inner aggression the same way you have just contained her aggressive words and behavior toward you. What do you feel now?

— *I am scared.*

— *Don't try to calm yourself down. This is not the end.*

— Who is it that feels scared? One of your own parts believes that you are calm. Your second part is going crazy inside you.

— *If you try to resist me, I will beat the shit out of you.*

— Speak up! Verbalize every sensation you just experienced.

— *I am scared. I am shocked. I feel nauseated.*

— What caused you to experience this unpleasant sensation of nausea? Who is she? Who is it that just attacked you?

— *I thought about the physical body. I thought about blood and bruises. It wasn't pleasant.*

— The unpleasant feeling is connected with the threat to the body. The aggressive display of emotions is connected to the potential bodily harm perceived by your structure. Can something happen to your body?

— *Yes, I am afraid for my body. I am not afraid of anything else.*

195

— Then, you are afraid to manifest these emotions because of the fear of receiving something similar in return, such as your body will be in danger. What can happen to your body? What can she do to your body?

— *She can break my arm or my nose. She can ruin my appearance.*

To be beautiful or to feel?

— You will not be beautiful anymore. You will be ugly.

— *Yes. That's what I am afraid of.*

— You have the notion that if you were to express your feelings through physical aggression, you may suffer disfigurement of the physical body and lose your beauty.

— *Yes.*

— You have a dilemma: to be beautiful or to feel. "If I start to feel, I may become ugly. If I continue to be beautiful, I will not feel." That was inculcated into your personality.

— *So, how can I connect these two ... ?*

— This dilemma creates fear. One part of your personality, the beautiful part, is afraid of the other part, the feeling part. These parts fight each other constantly. Can you accept the notion that you are ugly?

— *But this is my exclusivity ...*

— This is precisely what excludes you. Remember the script with the guy you attracted and who you did not know what to do with afterwards. You had a fear that he could cause strong emotions in you, and that could have lead to you losing your attractive physical appearance. If you are afraid of being physically abused, he will physically abuse you. He will beat you up. You have an inclination toward cruelty. You will search for a tough, cruel guy not because you want to be beaten up consciously, but because of the way this mechanism works. He will physically abuse you, and you will not be so attractive anymore. By feeling that, you prohibit yourself from being further acquainted with any man you like. You don't let him get close to you because he can give you a black eye.

— *That's true. I attract men, but I don't know what to do with them afterwards.*

— No one will hit you without a reason, but we cannot exclude you being treated harshly if you get in a relationship. You allow yourself to attract a man's attention, and in that way, you reinforce your pride of being physically attractive. The fear of ruining your physical appearance prevents you from having a close relationship with a man because it can lead to physical abuse. Most likely some man you will find will abuse you because you are afraid, i.e. you desire to lose your attractive physical appearance. Are you ready to feel it?

Shock therapy that opens the emotional center

A very effective method to loosen up the emotional center is for two human beings to hit each other on the face with love while feeling what their partners feel. This is not a fight. A human being beating another human being while standing in front of him feels what his partner feels. Pick someone who will do that for you.

— *Anna.*

— Okay. Are you ready?

— *I don't know. I will try.*

— Are you willing to do it?

— *I am willing, but I am afraid.*

— Do you understand what your fear is connected to? I have just described the dualities your fear is connected to, but you must see them yourself. This is an abscess you must open. I am offering a procedure that will help you to quickly open these dualities. You will start to express the states of condemnation and guilt significantly better than you do now.

— *Okay. What do I need to do?*

— Are you ready for it?

— *I don't know. I have never done it.*

— Are you ready to do it now?

— *I am ready to do what needs to be done.*

— Stand in front of each other and look each other in the eye. Feel each other as you would feel yourself. Act out of the state you have. Do not restrain yourself.

....

— Okay. What do you want to say? Describe your state.

— *When I landed my first blow, I experienced excitement and fear. Then fear left, and I felt pity for her. I wanted to hug her.*

— Pay attention here. When you hit, you condemn. When you hug, you pity. This feeling of pity is generated by the feeling of guilt. The diapason of emotional expression can vary from wide to narrow. The diapason of your emotional expression is very narrow. You manifest these types of emotions in a very constricted form. Do you feel that the diapason of your manifestation of these emotions widened?

— *Perhaps just a little bit.*

— You have made a step forward. It was a small step, but it was a step forward. What were you afraid of in the beginning of this procedure?

— *I was afraid of pain.*

— Okay. And what happened?

— *As I was hitting Anna, I thought she would experience pain.*

— At one point, you got out of the fear of pain. You started to fear that Anna would experience pain.

— *Yes. We were asked to slap each other only on the face. If it was not for this condition, I could have manifested a wider range of emotions.*

— Do you want to hit some other part of her body? Where precisely do you want to hit her? Why don't you mark the spot on her body where you want to hit her?

— *I don't know. I am very afraid of being hit on the face. I am also afraid to lose my attractive appearance. The reason behind these fears is the same.*

— If Anna agrees, you must manifest yourself freely. Hit her anywhere you want, but remember—you are hitting yourself. Both of you should manifest what comes from the inside.

— *I want to grab her, flip her over, and bang her against the floor. I want her to stay there. I have also observed a desire to let her get the upper hand. I want her to force me down.*

— Do it! Do what you want to do!

— Enough! Enough already! You wanted to experience this roughness, and you did. What do you feel now?

— *I am afraid of her ruining my face. I am afraid of bruises and disfigurement.*

— What will happen if you were to be disfigured?

— *I don't know. It seems to me I would not exist anymore.*

— Why do you think so? Will you lose something very important?

— *Yes. I will lose my attractive appearance.*

— What does appearance give you? You will still be able to eat, drink, and work.

— *I will not be able to work where I want to work.*

— Where do you want to work?

— *Appearance plays a significant role in my line of work.*

— What kind of work do you do?

— *I am an assistant to a CEO of a big corporation.*

— Are you working there, or are you an escort?

— *I am working there.*

— Are you looked upon as an escort?

— *Yes, I think my appearance helps.*

— What are escorts used for? They accompany businessmen to business meetings. Their physical appearance and sexuality are very important.

— *This is not the only important attribute of my work.*

199

— Nevertheless, this is a very important element of your work.

— *You are right.*

— That's precisely what you are afraid to lose. You are using your physical appearance to make money.

— *There is another element here. The people who hired me expect their employee to have an attractive appearance.*

— Exactly. This is one of the motives behind business people hiring attractive women.

— *If my physical appearance is damaged, I will not find a job.*

— So, you are selling your appearance?

— *Yes.*

— And if you were to lose your attractive appearance, you would have problems finding a job. You are afraid to lose your beautiful physical appearance because you are identified with it. That's where your fear is coming from.

— *I had moments throughtout my life when I wanted to have a regular appearance. I thought it would be easier to live with a plain face. Everything would have been simpler. For some reason, everything that happens to me is connected to my appearance.*

— During the first day of the seminar, I asked you to describe how you manifest your physical, mental, and emotional spheres. You are primarily active in your physical manifestation. The main center that is active in your life is your physical center. If it was your mental center, you would hold on to the mental concepts. But, in your case, it has to do with your appearance.

— *Yes.*

— *What if I were to tell you that your appearance is not so great? It's mediocre. What would be your reaction?*

— *I think I would need to see it myself.*

— Beauty depends on the point of view. There are no objective criteria to appraise attractiveness. One man considers a woman to be unbelievably beautiful and loses his head over her, another doesn't even look in her direction.

— *She has her own opinion, and what you have said is not important for her.*

— What I have said has not even touched you. You have a clear, solid, and unchangeble understanding of the subject.

— *Her understanding is supported by men. If what you have said was said by a man, she would have reacted differently, but she behaves in such a way that no man would say it to her.*

— *Yes, men only say good things to me, and this is very important for me.*

— Yes, that's exactly what the story with your guy shows. You say it's important for you that he reacts. You need reciprocity. You are afraid to approach him because he can say "no" to you.

— *I think he would only say that because he is afraid himself.*

— This is another level of defense. You are projecting your notion onto him. He can say that you are not his type. He may like voluptuous blonds.

— *Yes, perhaps he doesn't like me anymore. At one point, he did. He used to say that he liked me. He used to say, "Look in the mirror. Can a man trust someone like you?"*

— Why "look in the mirror"?

— *It reflects my physical appearance.*

— So, a man cannot trust someone who has such an appearance?

— *I don't know.*

The problematic beauty

— The problem you experience in your relationship with this man is related to your appearance. On one hand, you are sure that you look good, but on the other hand, you are equally unsure of that. On the conscious level, you think that you are attractive, but on the subconscious level, you carry the opposite notion. Fear, that comes from the subconscious side, gets projected onto this man and other people.

201

— Does it come from the subconscious side?

— It comes from the part that considers you to be unattractive. As we have discussed already, the conditioned mind is dual, i.e. in every situation it gives birth to two opposite notions. One notion manifests itself on the conscious level, another on the subconscious level. The subconscious notion reminds about itself by spilling into consciousness. The subconscious part doesn't stop its work, and it will lead you to meet a guy who will not like your appearance. You will be connected by the attraction of opposites, even though consciously he will do everything that you do not like. In not understanding your inner duality, you will not be able to understand why this is happening. The subconscious part of your personality—the unattractive part—also works. By reinforcing the attractive part of your personality, you simultaneously reinforce the opposite part—unattractive. Thus, you will appear attractive to men to whom you will not be attracted, but those who you find attractive will not find you attractive. That's the law of the dual reality we have entered. The life of a personality is to experience the script inculcated into it. Since the most important things in your life are your physical body, its appearance, fear of losing attractiveness or damaging your body, and fear of cruelty, you will be haunted by these fears throughout your life.

You cannot change your personality to another one, but you can transform it.

— Why? The personages changes ...

— What people believe to be a change here is just a change from one polar side to the other. What you use to have on your subconsciousness ascends to consciousness, and what you had on the conscious level moves to the subconscious level. These changes are always one-sided. They do not offer a full vision of your inner duality. Something will happen, and you will suddenly consider yourself unattractive. The side that considers itself unattractive will manifest itself consciously, while the side that considers itself attractive will move to subconscious. In the process, in considering yourself unattractive, you will suddenly meet a man who will love you dearly. You will be surprised: "How can this be possible? I am so ugly. Why does he love me?" Those are the paradoxes of this reality. Remember when I asked you, "Why did you come to the seminar?", you told us about your relationship with this guy.

— *That story woke me up. I started to ask questions and search for the answers.*

— Every personality contains basic dualities, which will be activated irrespective of whether or not you understand them.

I do spiritual surgery. I open "inflamed" dualities.

— *I want to say something about the fight that just occurred here.*

— This was not a fight. We have opened a duality.

— *When these girls were fighting, I saw me fighting my twin. We used to fight until blood would come out. If I were to choose someone to fight here, I would pick Olga. Why? I suddenly saw myself wanting to hit her fat butt. But then, I realized that it was my mom who I wanted to hit.*

— *I was shocked when three big guys pinned this young girl down to the floor. The scene of my rape flashed in front of my eyes. I am looking back now, and I feel pleasure. I fought him all night, but I felt pleasure. I think if I were in her shoes now, on the floor, I would have found it pleasant. I thought I became cold because of that incident. I used to condemn my mother for screaming at me. The image of the man who raped me haunted me for years. I don't look at that situation as horrible anymore. I have a feeling all of this was thought up and exaggerated. In recalling and reexperiencing that episode again and again, I had the opportunity to stay in a victim role. I experienced a certain kaif there. Now, I have a feeling that pain doesn't exist on its own; it's just a notion. I used to feel constant pain. I realize that this*

203

was just an illusion. As I sort it out more and more, I feel lighter and lighter.

— Exactly. You are breaking through. The most difficult part is to start to look your fears in the eye. You were encapsulated by fear, and you needed a shock to open you up, like an abscess that needs to be lanced. I do spiritual surgery. I open dualities of the mental and emotional spheres. I am not sure you are ready to be opened yet. I would say you are at the stage of diagnosis. For a duality to open, we must spread its opposite sides wide. Until this is done, the painful experience continues to be encapsulated; it encapsulates itself further and further by using multiple psychological defenses.

— *I experienced a strange reaction during the fight. When these women started to slap each other, I felt nauseous. I've seen many fights in my life, but I have never been nauseated by them before. When three men pinned this little girl to the floor, I projected myself onto her, and I felt that she didn't resist them. I felt as a wild cat. They would have seen my teeth and nails.*

— *I felt proud for them. They were able to overcome something.*

— What state are you in right now? Do you want to do that now?

— *Do what?*

— Do you want to do what they did?

— *I don't know. When two of them were slapping each other … that was a joke… I could have taken both of them with my right hand …*

— Wait a minute. We are not fighters here. Look at her. We've got ourselves a heavy weight fighter here. What you saw a minute ago was not about the fight.

— *She is so ugly, she has nothing to lose.*

— *I thought, "Why did I jump at her the way I did?" It turns out, I was as callous as she was. I thought I was very sensitive, but I didn't feel anything.*

— *What about your appearance? Can you say something about it? You jumped at her with such anger. You probably felt a certain impulse to do that.*

— I spoke to Larisa, and she has nothing to do with this. I just wanted to help.

— Tatiana was talking to Larisa. You went for Tatiana. What irritates you in her?

— I wanted to help her. I wanted her to divert her condemnation and aggression toward me.

— What irritates you about her? What irritates you about her personality? You wanted to kill her. There is something in her personality that is opposite to what you have in your personality. That's what irritates you. Look at her. Start to condemn her.

— You think you are pretty. You are ugly. You think you are smart. You are stupid. You think you are free. You are not. You think people will carry you in their arms. They will kick your butt. You think you can hold your ground. You cannot. You are a floor mop.

Being afraid to manifest your feelings

— What do you feel now?

— I feel that what I say is unnatural.

— You expressed what you felt. You said it, but you did not thoroughly feel what you said. Now, tell her what you want to tell her, but feel every word you say. Experience every word you say. It's one thing to say something, and it is a totally different thing to feel what you are saying.

— For some reason, I cannot do that.

— You can say words very well. Why can't you feel them?

— I don't know. I cannot express my feelings.

— You do not allow yourself to feel something about yourself. Your feelings are blocked. Okay. Start talking about yourself. You need to open your personality to us.

— I thought I was capable of doing everything, but I cannot even slap a human being on the face. I am equally incapable of pitying or hugging someone.

— You don't allow yourself to see your desires. Pick out one of the students here. Tell him what you want from him and

205

immediately say something opposite. You must see both sides. Speak not in terms of qualities but in terms of your desire to do it. Feelings come from the sphere of feelings. They are also opposite and dual. Say what you want to do and express your desires through actions.

— *I don't understand anything right now.*

— You are afraid to manifest your feelings. You express certain things in words, but you don't feel anything.

— *Why do you say that? She had so much aggression in her when she jumped me. She is not afraid to manifest her feelings.*

— She can manifest her feelings, but she does not allow herself to manifest them now. You are afraid of manifesting "I want" because next to "I want" stands "I don't want", which condemns you for wanting something or brings up frightening arguments that prohibit you from wanting it. Tell us about your desires.

The paradoxes of desires

— *I want to hug everyone.*

— Then you will suffocate them to death. Right? This is a duality. When we started to talk about desires of the personality, everyone woke up. I invite you to manifest your desires. Where is your personality? What does it want? You will see that every desire is dual.

Think of someone and tell us what you want to do to him or her.

— *I have a girlfriend and I want to help her, but on the other hand, I don't want to do that.*

— *As the level of my condemnation heightened, I started to feel guilty. I don't understand why.*

— *I want to dance, and I want to sit still.*

— *I want to be at the seminar, but at the same time, I want to be home.*

— *I want to hug Tatiana, and I want to kick Inna hard.*

— I want to see my friends, but at the same time, I don't want to see them.

— It's not "don't want to" but opposite to "want to".

— I want to be by myself.

— This "want" is opposite to the first "want".

— What about "want" and "afraid"?

— "Afraid" comes from the first "want". One part wants something but is afraid of its opposite side, i.e. the opposite "want". For example, you are consciously in the part which wants to be decent, and you are afraid of the desires of your indecent part.

— I want to be caressed, but at the same time, I am afraid of being caressed.

— Find the opposite side. **Always look for the opposite side.** "I want to be caressed, and I want to be beaten up." You must sort it out. Feel it. I ask you to get to the feeling level. Stop masturbating mentally about feelings. We are investigating the sphere of feelings in duality. I want this and I also want what is opposite to this. Pay attention to the fact that your mind immediately appraises what you can say and what you cannot say.

— I want to be with a handsome man, and at the same time, I want to be with an ugly midget.

— Here you go. Now you are talking. Next.

— I want to torture my mother. I want her to suffer. On the other hand, I want to love her. I want to hug her and cook for her.

— I want her to live in poverty, and I want to give her all my money.

— Sometimes, I am very passionate about doing my work, and sometimes I just want to find a quiet place and take a nap.

— One part of me wants to work hard, long hours without being paid for it. Another part of me wants to stay in bed and to be paid for it.

— I always start with fighting for something, and I always wind up dropping it.

— I want to go to work, and I want to stay home. I want to be with one man, and I want to be with many men.

— I am afraid to discuss what I want. I want to see my children grow up, but I am afraid to say that I want to kill them. I cannot feel it. I am afraid to feel it.

— Correct. This is the interrelationship of our opposite parts. They are afraid of each other. If you were to consciously harbor a desire to destroy your children, you would be afraid of the part that wants to nurture and love them. **Fear is a consequence of the war that occurs between our polar, opposite sides.**

Let's talk about sex

— Let's talk about sex now.

— *I love sex, but it is icky and dirty.*

— "Come to me"—"get lost".

— *I want to have sex every night, and I want to be alone every night.*

— To have sex is as pleasurable as not to have sex.

— *I want to have sex, but I don't want to get undressed.*

— I want to have sex with a black guy, and I want to have sex with a white guy.

— *I want to have sex with a man and a woman.*

— *I want to be an oppressor, and I want to be a victim.*

— *I want to have sex with a blond and then with a brunette.*

— I want to have sex with a fat woman, and I want to have sex with a skinny one. Then, I want to have sex with a girl who is fully dressed up followed by sex with a naked girl. I want to have sex being on top, and I want to have sex while being on the bottom.

— *I want to have sex with everybody. What sex are you talking about? I don't even want to talk about sex.*

— *I want to have a very feminine partner with elements of homosexuality in him. I also want to have a brutal stud as a partner. I will have to obey him.*

— *I want to be with a voluptuous, sensual woman. I also want to have sex with a log.*

— *I want to be with a pauper in a palace, and I want to have a prince in a dirty restroom.*

— *I want to have sex in a stadium with thousands of people watching, and I want to have sex in a dark room where I cannot even see my partner.*

— *I want to have a slow, romantic sex. I also want to have sex without debt—let's just finish this dirty business.*

— Great. I think we have had enough for today.

Chapter 5

Your Parents Are the Main Conditions of Your Assignment

•❖•❖•❖•❖•❖•❖•❖•❖•❖•❖•❖•❖•

Presently, you are just a set of someone's expectations

— Who is going to start today?

— *I used dirty language today. I observed myself mentally use profanities three times.*

— There are different levels of creation. You can do something in your mind, i.e. you can think of something, and you can also realize something in the physical world. You can think about something, but not do it physically. You can think about something, talk about it, and then do it. That's how every act of creation gets completed. So, at whom did you swear?

— *Today is Sunday. Yet someone called me from work and told me that I had to come to work. I spent two hours arguing with the administration.*

— Okay. Swear at your boss now. Do it here. You are speaking in a very soft voice now. That points to the fact that you don't fully manifest your feelings. Talk loudly and express your feelings. Express your state!

— *I don't know what to do.*

— You don't want to manifest your state. You feel irritated. You are full of anger and hate.

— *I am indifferent.*

— **Indifference is a form of defense that protects you from seeing your difficult state. When you are indifferent, you don't differentiate—everything is the same to you.**

Everything is equally grey. I invite you to discern now. You can do that by manifesting one side of your duality. You are presently in a state of indifference. We have started to activate your duality so you can manifest yourself somehow.

— *I am irritated.*

— Manifest your irritation.

— *How can I manifest it?*

— How does your mind work? It asserts a fact now: "I am irritated." To manifest irritation is to scream, yell, break things around you. You are just sitting here quietly yawning, saying, "I am irritated." Do you see the difference?

— *One doesn't talk about it. One just does it.*

— Manifest your irritation. Scream at your boss for asking you to work on Sunday.

— *Idiots! I am tired! What do you want from me?!*

— You want to be nice to everyone. You don't exist now. You just correspond to someone's expectations and notions of who you should be. Express how you feel about working on Sunday. Should we slap you again? You are telling me you are not going to argue because it is meaningless. I ask you to manifest your state, i.e. what's in you. Your aim now is to manifest your emotional state. What is your state now?

— *Irritation.*

— Express it! Express it to me! I got you, didn't I?!

— *Perhaps, I will do it later. I cannot express all of this now.*

— You can do it! You need to express your state! People don't express their states nowadays. They intellectualize, and so they are never in the present moment. The present moment is a present emotional state, but you don't even feel it. When you finally start to feel it, you cannot express it.

— *But you did not do anything wrong to me.*

— Okay. What can I do that will scare you the most?

— *I am not afraid of anything.*

— Nothing at all?

211

— If you were to kick me, that would be scary.

— I will kick you! I will kick you hard!

— I will not defend myself.

— Why not? Are you afraid, or do you want to be kicked?

— Looks like I want to be kicked.

Whatever we are afraid of is what we want

— I want everyone to pay attention here. We are dealing with a paradox. **Whatever we are afraid of is what we want. We can put an equal sign between our fears and our desires. Fear appears because of the interaction that occurs between two sides of a duality. One side of a duality wants something, while the other side wants the opposite thing.** One side is consciously afraid and doesn't want to be slapped, but the second subconscious side wants to be slapped.

— What do we do with this?

— You need to feel this and to become aware of this. I am offering you an opportunity to feel it. I will slap you now.

— I will cry.

— You have to start to discern. Presently, you don't feel the difference between a caress and a slap. You cannot discern between them.

— Is it because I do not allow myself to feel the second side?

— You do not allow yourself to feel either one of these two sides. They are interconnected. If you allow yourself to feel one of them, the second side will open too.

— Can I manifest it at home or at work? I don't want to manifest it here.

— Everything happens here.

— If someone were to scream at me or to hit me, I would retaliate.

— Who wants to hit her?

— No! Don't do that! I am not interested anymore!

— Here you go! Manifest it! Speak up!

— Don't do that. Stop! You are going to tear my shirt! Get off me!

212

— *Here you go! Did you have enough? You want more?!*

— Say what you feel!

— *What can I say? I am going to cry again.*

— Cry! Cry and talk. Scream. Yell. You can say what you want here. You can open your feelings here. Otherwise, you will continue to live in this suppressed state. Recall how you have experienced similar, painful situations before.

— *I don't remember any of them.*

— They are analogous. Someone was hurting you and tearing clothes off you.

A man and a woman. Who will win?

— *My mom beat me one time for losing the key to our apartment. She bit me so hard, I peed my pants. She beat me very hard with a stick a few times. This was very painful. I experienced severe emotional pain when my parents were going through a divorce. No one physically hurt me then, but I was in so much pain, I wanted to jump off the roof.*

— Why was it so painful?

— *Mom left Dad for another man. I felt she dumped me.*

— You felt betrayed. Did you stay with your dad?

— *There were five people in our family: Mom, Dad, me, my brother, and my older sister. I look like my mom. We were inseparable since I was born. My older sister looks like my dad. We were split. My brother, who is actually my step brother, was born from a different husband. When Mom left dad, she left me with him. Dad was cold to me. I was left all alone. We don't communicate now.*

— How old were you when this happened?

— *I was eleven years old.*

— Who do you live with now?

— *I live with my mom now.*

— How do you feel about your dad?

— *He is a weak man.*

— What's his main weakness?

— He drinks. When Mom left, he didn't think it was serious. He still loves her, but he cannot bring her back. That's why I pity him.

— How do you feel about your step-dad?

— I don't like him.

— What don't you like about him?

— He is also weak. He cannot make a decision. Mom decides everything.

— How do you feel about your mom?

— She works long hours. She is suffering too, because she loves another man but has to live with this …

— Your mom manifests a man, i.e. her strong masculine side, and she meets men who manifest feminine qualities. They are weak. They drink, cry, and submit to her without protest. Which model of behavior did you take? You had to choose a model of behavior from either Mom or Dad. Their models of behavior are opposite, and their incongruences in you creates your inner problems that reflect themselves outside.

— I think I chose Mom's model of behavior.

— If that's the case, you are running away from your problems by going to work.

— Yes. Work has always been my main priority.

— An attitude toward men was formed in you. You think they are weak, and you feel nauseated when you have to deal with them. This attitude was inculcated in you by your mom. She is a woman based on her physical body, but she manifests a masculine model of behavior. Your father, on the other hand, while in the physical body of a man, manifests a feminine model of behavior. You are dealing with a mix up. That's why it is so difficult for you to discern what's going on. Your attitude toward your dad, who manifests the feminine model of behavior, is negative. You consider him to be a weak loser. Your mother manifests the masculine mode of behavior. She is strong but unhappy.

— I would not call dad a loser. He has everything he needs.

— He has everything in terms of material things, but he cannot have a relationship with a woman. He wants to be with your mother, but he cannot. They cannot be together because there is no partnership between their inner man and woman.

— *Lately, Mom started to talk about her desire to return to Dad.*

— You cannot imagine what that would lead to. If they start to live together again, they would not be happy.

— *I cannot even imagine them living together.*

— But all of this is in you. That's the script your personage has received. You need to become aware of this script. That's the only way to get out of it. This is not easy. Otherwise, you can expect to experience something very similar to what your mom experiences. Your relationships with men will be similar. Your man will be weak. He will manifest a feminine model of behavior. He will want to be with you, but you will not want to be with him. What do you feel now?

— *I want to get out of here.*

— Please, do so.

Strong mother—Weak father

— If you don't become aware of yourself, you are doomed to repeat the scenario inculcated into you by your parents. This scenario will be realized with a great precision. You can only exit this script by becoming fully aware of it. This requires you to understand and to see the working mechanisms of the whole matrix of dual perception. Every script inculcated into a human being born in this dual reality is a script of separation. Everyone's scenario is different, but in terms of the presence of conflict between the opposites in them, they are the same. The old matrix is the matrix of separated perception, ruled by the conflict of the opposites. We need to become aware of the mechanism of action of the old matrix. That's the only way to move from the conflict between the opposites inside us to their cooperation and partnership. The only way one can become aware of the mechanism of action of the old matrix is to investigate one's own personality. The subject of investigation is not someone else's personality but your own. By investigating your dual personality, you can see the entire old matrix of the conflict and fight between the opposites. That's what we do here.

— *I am in a similar situation. My mother manifests the masculine model of behavior. My dad is weak. He lacks will power. He manifests the feminine model of behavior. A few years ago, Mom told me that she loved only one man in her life. He dumped her. After that, she decided to marry someone who would love her. That's how she found Dad. Her life with him is calm and quiet. My personage repeats the same model of behavior. The man I like doesn't care for me. When I am with him, I am always afraid of being dumped. When I look at my mom's life, I am not interested in such a life. I cannot get out of this situation.*

— Your mother behaves as an oppressor, and your dad behaves as a victim. A victim and an oppressor are two sides of one coin. A victim oppresses an oppressor by using her own victimhood.

— *My dad accepts his role of a victim. My mother accepts her role of an oppressor. He is constantly waiting for her to give him directions, and he does everything she tells him to do. They are a good team. A few days ago, he told me that he would not know what to do without her.*

— This is a relationship of two prisoners chained together. That doesn't mean they are happy. This is the scenario that was inculcated in you.

— *My mom does not like to have sex with my dad. She likes to talk to him. She hugs and kisses him, but sex with him is torture for her. She has created a gynecological problem, and she is happy she doesn't have to have sex with him. When she spoke to me about their sex life, she cried. She doesn't know why, but she was always repulsed by him when it comes to sex.*

— Take a look at this script. Your scenario is the same. Perhaps it is not so active yet, but you still have some time ahead of you. The script that every personage receives here is transmitted to him by his parents. You absorb both sides of behavior: maternal and paternal; one side is chosen as conscious, the other as subconscious. We attract the corresponding actors and play out the same scenario our parents played out. We live with an illusion that we have a choice in this dual world. We fool ourselves into thinking we can do what we want and not do what we don't want. We think we are free to change something in our life. We think we understand who we are and what we want. This is an illusion. Unless you are aware of yourself, you will drag through life repeating your parents' scenario. The background could be a bit different, but it will be the same scenario.

— *My situation is the same. My dad is weak, but sometimes he blows up. He was terribly angry when I was a kid. My husband is also weak. He is not physically abusive, but he drinks.*

— Your dad's aggression was directed outside. Your husband's aggression is directed inside.

— *Yes, that's true. His aggression is directed inside.*

— Power and weakness are two sides of one coin. It's usually a man who is gifted with power here, but a weak woman will force a strong man to realize her desires.

Parental conflicts are transmitted to the child

— *I was very upset with my mother's betrayal.*

— What is betrayal?

— *I call it betrayal, but I can see now that she just made a choice. But I condemned her for making this choice.*

— A man who is asleep cannot choose. "My mom chose another man, and my dad, a poor victim, was left alone." You call that betrayal.

— *I can feel what this young girl felt back then.*

— This girl is a child who reflects a conflict that occurred between her parents. The same conflict is inculcated in her now. Is this a betrayal? And what is a betrayal?

— *I don't know. At that time, I felt that both were very close to me.*

217

— You are discussing the situation from the point of view of a child, but this is not how your parents see each other. We are dealing with an interesting situation: if you are a father, it is for life, and if you are a mother, it is also for life. No one can change that. But spousal relationships can be changed. As a husband or wife, you can divorce your partner and marry somebody else. A child perceives parents as something whole, but parents do not see themselves as such. They get together to continue their bloodline. Animals do that too.

— *That's what we call love. We camouflage these relationships with traditional courting, romantic fantasies, and other attributes introduced by the conditioned mind.*

— A social animal that we call a human being calls this love. An animal doesn't call it a name. A child is a product of the union of two opposite sexes. A child feels pain relating to the conflicts that arise between Mom and Dad. In the child's perception, parents are one whole.

— *Why do people marry? We live with the common notion that up to a certain age, a girl must remain a virgin. Then she should get married and give birth to children. In that case, she is considered to be a good citizen of society. If you are not married by a certain age, you are an old maid in whom no one is interested. Moreover, a harsh notion was hammered into our heads. We should be virgins when we get married. If you are not a virgin, your husband can kick you out. You should not have premarital sexual relationships. It is dirty and unacceptable. It can lead to disease. That's what was hammered in me by my parents since childhood. This was hammered into the consciousness of girls and boys.*

— What is love? A girl is coming of age. She is waiting for her man. She is dating. She dreams about someone she will love all her life. We call this process falling in love, but this is just the instinct of procreation of purely animal nature. This is the instinctual process that leads to the continuation of the species. This process is supported by social arrangements that are determined by the cultures in which people are brought up.

218

Every child experiences a paternal conflict.

— *Dad loved me when I was a little girl. He used to play with me every day. Someone told Mom that he was cheating on her, and they started to fight. As soon as he would come home, she would pick a fight with him. He changed. He became irritated. I would run to him expecting him to pick me up, but he wouldn't do that. His face got darker and darker every day. Finally, Mom kicked him out of the house because of her suspicions. My dad was German. He was younger than Mom. Mom is Russian. Two of her brothers were killed during WW2. My grandmother hated my dad for being German. She used to chastise mom for being married to a German. Grandma was the commander-in-chief in our household. Mom was afraid of her. I took after my grandma.*

— Yes, but your mom took her model of behavior too.

— *Mom kicked Dad out of the house when I was two years old. I got to know him when I was fifteen. I lived with him and his second wife when I was in High School. He is a nice fellow. I just realized now that his second wife also manifests a masculine mode of behavior. He listens to her and he is afraid of her. He calls her Mom-Alexis.*

I followed a leader, i.e. my grandmother. She was very powerful.

— We take the model of behavior of one of our parents, and based on this model, we judge the behavior of the other parent.

— *"Dad is bad. He is a dog. He betrayed us." That's what Mom used to say.*

— *I picked up the model of behavior of my dad. My mom died when I was six years old. I don't remember her at all.*

— Here is another scenario. Every scenario here is a dramatic scenario.

— *I just realized that my daughter manifests a the masculine model of behavior. My daughter-in-law also manifests the masculine model of behavior. My son and my son-in-law manifest feminine models of behavior. They are soft, timid, and sweet. What are we dealing with? My husband is also soft. He is tender, gentle, and sweet. I, on the other hand, am harsh, capricious, and power hungry.*

— We are getting in touch with our personal experience. Quite frequently, this experience is painful. We need to de-identify with the personality. The way to do it is to investigate it. If you are in the personality, all you do is cry. You cry, and you cry, and you cry. You can't understand why you have been dealt with in such a harsh way. De-identification will not occur at once. It will happen gradually. You will face many painful moments. When your past recollections surface, you will have to become aware of them. Otherwise, you will not be able to sort out the mechanisms of action of the old matrix.

— *I feel that my sexual and emotional energies are being blocked by all these situations. I am turning into a mind machine.*

We open capsules filled with painful experiences. That allows our hearts to open up.

— Yes. Every child acquires painful experiences as he witnesses parental conflict. No one can escape that. This experience is so painful that a child tries to encapsulate, hide, and forget it. When a child, experiencing severe suffering, encapsulates this painful experience, the diapason of vibrations of his emotional sphere narrows. In repeatedly reinforcing the capsule by lowering the diapason of the emotional sphere, our child starts to use the conditioned mind and abstract notions to escape emotional pain. Instead of naturally experiencing irritation, grudges, condemnation, and guilt, you start to participate in abstract conversations. This substitution of feelings by illations leads to depression.

Why does it happen? The pendulum of the emotional sphere must swing constantly from condemnation to guilt, and back again. Some people are chronically depressed; their pendulum of emotional manifestations got stuck in one position—everything is bad. These people constantly condemn other people or themselves. They have blocked their emotional center in one position. What are we doing here? We are opening capsules of the painful experiences we have accumulated, and we allow the feelings constricted there to come out. This happens according to your readiness to sustain this pain at any given moment. You will not enter a painful experience that you cannot withstand. You will have to return to your painful experience again and again. You will have to reexperience it again and again, removing defenses layer by layer. That's the way to restore your emotional sphere.

As we have discussed already, the exit out of a dual, separated perception occurs through the deepest levels of the heart. At the deepest level of the heart, the emotional center is connected to Unconditional Love. That's where we are going. As we start to understand and to become aware of how the mechanisms of the conditioned mind work, our defenses drop one by one. Without awareness, you will not be able to understand why you live the way you live. Self-investigation removes defenses that were introduced into your emotional sphere. You start to remove them, and you remove as much as you can according to the level of your awareness. Gradually, you increase the diapason of sensitivity of your emotional center. Awareness increases the frequency of vibration of every one of your centers. By removing your defenses, you increase the frequency of vibration of your emotional center. Eventually, we will witness a connection between awareness and Unconditional Love, i.e. between the Mind and the Heart. This path consists of multiple steps. That's the only way to Enlightenment. You can only do it yourself. But to do that, you need a group and a leader who knows how to do it. I will repeat. That's the only way to Enlightenment. I'll repeat, our basic work here is to get in touch with our painful experiences.

Can you tell us, Tatiana, why do you need to do what we do here? How do you understand what I said? You have asked me,

"Why do you need to beat me?" Would you still say that we just dug up and scattered your pain, or do you understand why we did it?

— *By reexperiencing this pain, I am freeing myself of it.*

— Yes. You will liberate yourself from it, but in order to do that, you will have to reexperience the painful moments of your past while being aware of why you are doing it. We cannot stop here. We are constantly moving. We need to remove our defenses of the emotional center. This is the most important thing we need to do now. Liberation of the emotional sphere is necessary to connect to "WE". Each one of us will have to do that. What do you feel now?

— *I want to be by myself in the woods, where I can scream, yell, and hit the trees. I want the entire Universe to hear me.*

— Okay. Can you express all of this here?

— *Do you want me to scream here?*

— Yes, talk it through, yell, cry … everyone here passes through pain and tears. If you need to cry, allow yourself to cry. Liberation occurs through tears. How did you experience yourself when they were beating you? Did you experience yourself as mother or father?

— I experienced *myself as father.*

We must feel and understand the pain of our parents

— Can you feel what your father felt? It is very important for us to understand the pain our parents experienced. Mom used to beat you, but in the process, she experienced equal pain. We need to connect with Mom and Dad. They have inculcated two halves of our script. These scripts are opposite to each other. They create the inner conflict within us. To understand this conflict, we need to feel what each one of our parents felt. Neither one of them is good or bad. Both are unhappy because they didn't understand what was going on. **Being in this dual reality, we**

222

choose the model of behavior of one parent, rejecting the model of behavior of the other parent and internally condemning him or her. That's how separation is transmitted in the family. How many of you consider one of your parents to be bad?

— *I consider both of them bad.*

— From the point of view of my dad, Mom is bad. From the point of view of my mom, Dad is bad.

— *I think my mother is bad.*

— You have accepted the model of behavior of your dad, and you condemn your mom.

— *I have a really difficult time condemning anyone, but sometimes this condemnation spills out in a very aggressive form.*

— You have to sort out your relationship with your parents. Which one of them do you condemn?

— *I have never seen my dad. I don't even know him. I was brought up by my stepdad, and I see him as a weak man. He is a drunkard. He is physically abusive to Mom. I tried to protect Mom. I used to fight him. I would go to school covered in bruises, pretending the cat scratched me. I don't want to see the other side. I am ashamed to have such a stepfather. I studied well, trying to protect myself from feeling shame about my grades. My stepdad is much younger than my mom. Dad lives in Latvia. Mom told me he drinks and recently got out of jail for stealing something. Do I condemn my dad? I don't know. I think there is condemnation there, but it hides very deep. I don't see it. I felt fear when Tatyana and Anna were fighting. I feel calm when I am behind the wheel, but when someone else is driving, I feel nervous. I am not afraid of death. I am afraid of being maimed. My body is all messed up. I have had so many surgeries, I have lost count.*

I was sitting here quietly all these days. My facial expression might have manifested contempt, but internally, I admired everyone. The part of duality that I will call admiration came out. I have also observed the duality "strong—weak". It follows, the strong one drinks ... My first husband was weak. He didn't drink. He loved me, but he left me for a beautiful woman. I consider myself to be a grey mouse. Lately, I have started to drink. I cannot

223

open to him. I cannot tell him I love him. I don't know what happened to me. I am raving now.

— That's good. Keep talking.

— *Strong—weak, drunk—sober. I condemn myself for drinking. I don't want to discuss this. I feel very strong resistance. When I am not in the mind, I feel euphoric.*

— You get into this state for a very short time. Then you slip back into your script. While in the script, you do not see the exit.

"I am afraid to plug into her craziness …"

— *I went to Latvia to see Reda last month. She was not herself. She was shaking. She was in a weird state. Something was off, but I decided not to plug into her craziness. I had a different aim. I wanted to see the old city. But the next morning, I realized that I was not accepting my own part. I asked her why she invited me. I saw my disrespectful attitude and my contempt of her.*

— I am not this way. It is she who is crazy, not me.

— *I finally saw that she was asking for help. I invited her to express the hatred and aggression that were boilng inside her, but she said she was afraid. I invited her to scream at me and kick me, but she refused. Later, I realized I was not ready to accept my crazy part yet.*

— For some reason, you were attracted to each other. You need someone crazy next to you to project your craziness onto. In that case, you have an illusion that you are not crazy.

— *I was able to tolerate three days of her company. I run away from myself. All my life, I condemned people for smoking weed. I considered it to be bad. Then I tried it, and I think am free of this condemnation now.*

— This is the illusion of liberation. Where does condemnation come from? We get the script of our life from our parents. If you accept Mom's script, you start to condemn people for the qualities for which she condemned Dad. If you accept Dad's script, you start to condemn people for the qualities he used to condemn in Mom. You need to see both of your parents inside yourself. You need to understand which side you took and

224

which side you condemn. You must experience the side you rejected. You need to experience and thoroughly feel everything your parents felt. You condemn your parents. You think you don't have what they had in them. But they are in you.

— *I believe I took Mom's model of behavior.*

— Okay. You took a maternal model of behavior. Did she condemn your dad?

— *Yes.*

— So, you condemn people for the same qualities that your mother condemned in your father. You must feel the state that your dad was in. You need to find your inner victim, i.e. your second side, and to come to understand what it feels like.

— *I just came to understand that I behaved the same way my mother did, because originally I was in dad's state. I clearly see and feel that now.*

— What exactly do you want to say?

— *Currently, my parents are not in conflict inside me.*

— If they are not in conflict, you are enlightened already.

— *My parents are not fighting, but I fight with my mom.*

— Here you go. This is your lunatic asylum. You are raving.

— *I don't even know my dad. I have never seen him. How can I condemn him?*

— Okay. What about your stepdad? Look at him.

— *He is weak, and he drinks.*

— Based on what you have told us, your dad is the same. You think he is a weak drunkard, and you hate him for this. That's what we can infer about your dad. I will ask you not to define your dad's behavior based on the duality "weak—strong". Your father is in you. You need to experience him. Then you will start to understand him. What you say about your father now tells us that you don't understand who he is and what he had experienced. He lived a long life, and he experienced a lot, but you only talk about his drinking and him being weak. Do you feel why he drinks? You need to feel it. Then you will be able to say something else about him.

225

— I just realized that I don't want to drink because I am afraid of getting drunk. I can relax and start to cry, pitying myself.

— Do you even understand what I am talking about? I keep telling you that you need to feel what your parents felt. You need to experience the emotional states that they have experienced. What can you say about your parents now?

— My mother experienced fear. She was afraid to manifest herself sexually. She spent her entire life with the notion that woman's duty is to be a good homemaker. She performed her duty well. Dad was looking for something else. She condemned him for having sexual relationships with other women and for his drinking. She could not accept it.

Why did your father drink?

— Why did your father drink?

— He drank because my mother was cold. He drank because she didn't play any other role but the role of a homemaker and a mother who gave birth to three children.

— What is a good mother?

— She lived with the notion that she gave him three children and fulfilled her duty.

— Did she give birth to these three children for him or for herself? Why did she think she gave these children to him? You have discussed how you would get onto your dad's lap but he would neither play with you nor pat you on the head. What prevented him from doing that?

— He would not do it because of Mom.

— Is this a criteria of a good mother? Is a mother who prohibits the dad from caressing his child a good mother? Or is she good because she gives birth to children—the more children she delivers, the better mother she is?

— She had the notion that she got married to give birth to children, take care of them and her husband, i.e. to cook, clean after them, and to keep her house in order.

226

— It follows that a good mother is the one who delivers a child every year. Does she understand how she creates the relationship between her husband and her children? When a child feels that in the presence of his mother, that his father should not pat him on the head, a child develops severe inner conflict. A child cannot understand why this is happening. It turns out, a good mother prohibits the dad from caressing his own child.

— *Well, she did not push him away from me. Perhaps she was sending some kind of message to him, or her behavior told him not to …*

— She did something that led to his inability to caress you. She hated him and she didn't want her child to manifest the emotions that she didn't manifest toward him herself.

— *Yes. That is it.*

— Every child takes paternal conflict hard. The war that occurs between parents occurs through their child. A child experiences this war to the fullest.

— *I consider myself to be an ideal wife and an ideal mother. It turns out that I condemned my husband from day one for watching TV. I could have sat the couch next to him and watched a movie with him, but I always kept busy. I would do the dishes, cook, and iron just to be an ideal wife. I just saw this side. I am constantly trying to prove that I am a good wife and a good mother.*

— What is a good mother? I'll break into your stories from time to time to bring clarity to our discussion.

— *I want to figure out who I condemn. During my childhood, I condemned Mom. Dad would frequently come home drunk, but I saw him as a nice, good man. Mom, on the other hand, was always angry. She frequently screamed at him and on a few occasions, she would not allow him in the appartment. Sometimes she was physically abusive to him, slapping him in the face. He was a soft, kind man. He could not defend himself. Now, I condemn dad for being so weak. I condemn him for drinking.*

— You condemn him for weakness.

227

— *I condemn myself for being cold, and I condemn myself for being weak.*

— You condemn yourself for weakness the moment you consider yourself to be strong. On the conscious level, you identify with a "strong" part. When you are weak, you condemn those who are strong.

— *When I am weak, I condemn those who hurt me. I condemn him for being an oppressor.*

— First, you condemn your mom from the point of view of your dad. Now, you condemn your dad from the point of view of your mom. Dad is a drunkard, and he is weak. Therefore, weak is kind. Pay attention here. Our scripts are different, and our notions of what is weak, nice, and kind are also different. The meaning that you insert into these words comes from your personal experience.

— *In my case, kind is weak.*

— *I think kind is tender and gentle.*

— *Kind is defenseless.*

— *Kind is mean.*

— Here you go. That's why the only way to bring clarity into your notions is to clearly see all these patterns.

— *Both of my parents are weak. They cannot fulfill their desires. They cannot get what they want. My father wants to be with my mom, but he cannot. Mom does something that she really doesn't want to do.*

— This is a conflict situation. You call them weak, and you think you are going to be strong. Your mind calls them weak but thinks you are going to be strong. I will repeat what I have said before. You, as a personage, incorporate both of your parents into your structure; you are going to play out their scripts.

— *My mom always dominated my father. She refused to have sex with him. I decided not to be like her. But I see now that I repeat every detail of her script.*

— Children say they will not behave the way their parents did, but they turn into carbon copy of their parents.

228

— I went through some rough times during my adolescence. There was this incident when my father thought that my boyfriend hit him. I experienced a colossal feeling of guilt. Dad never laid a finger on me, but after this incident, he beat the crap out of me. It was my mom who initiated this beating. He really gave it to me. He was wild. Afterwards, in all my relationships with men, I always provoked a fight and had myself beaten. Looks like I am reinforcing the model of behavior of my father.

Your father and mother are the origins of your personality

— The "father—mother" model of behavior represents the duality of your script. This is a set of dualities that make up the structure of your personality or your personal script. **Your father and mother stand at the origin of your personage.**

— There is a sexual underlining here too. Dad had decided that my boyfriend had beaten him up, and my parents developed the notion about me that I am a slut who sleeps with God knows who and whose father suffers because of it.

— That means that the same problem was present in your parents' relationship.

— Mom was afraid of men. She was always afraid of being raped. Dad just turned seventy, but women still like him. I consider him to be weak because of his womanizing behavior, but I don't condemn him for that. I don't even know what I am talking about.

— No one here knows what he is talking about. It's not easy to see this mess holistically. Start to discuss it. As you do that, you will start seeing your scripts. Our discussions will help you. It's important for you to discuss all these issues. It is important to start seeing the models of behavior of your parents and to start to experience both of them in full awareness. You have picked up one model of behavior, and you condemn yourself for the second model. Start to recall the scripts of life of your parents. Talk about their scripts.

229

— *I have a feeling that I took the model of behavior of my mom, but I don't think it suits me well.*

— This is how you see it, from the point of view of the model of behavior of your dad. Your conditioned mind cannot combine two opposites: "I took something, but it doesn't suit me. What else can I take? Where do I get a new model of consciousness?" **I keep returning you to your parents. You will not be able to run away from them. There is nowhere to run. Everything you have in your personage comes from your parents.**

— *My mother is a powerful, goal-oriented woman. She always knows what to do. She always acts ruthlessly. She never compromises. She knows what she needs and she knows how to get it.*

— Tell us about your father.

— *When I was young, my dad got stuck between two women. He didn't know which one to choose. My mother made a choice. She filed for divorce.*

— How does this conflict manifest itself in you?

— *I try not to get into a conflict.*

— It's impossible. You cannot avoid conflict here. You can pretend it doesn't exist, but conflict is the essence of this dual reality. I keep telling you, "Escalate the level of your conflicts to become aware of them." Every conflict of yours, irrespective of what it is, is the conflict between the opposite models of behavior of your parents. I will ask you to pair up and to discuss one specific conflict of your life as a manifestation of the contradictions that exist between your parents. You play it throughout your life. You don't see it as your parents' conflict. **Every conflict that your personality experiences is a conflict of your parents. The problems your parents have experienced are your problems.**

— *The first familial conflict occured when I was born. My mom was nineteen years old. Dad was adamantly against her giving birth. He thought she was not ready for it. Mom insisted on giving birth, and she prevailed.*

230

— Let's take a look at your conflict. You are dealing with the same conflict in your life.

— *I do feel that it is there, but I don't see it yet.*

— You have to investigate your own conflicts and search for similar parental conflicts.

— *When I was dating Eugene, I used to condemn him for being weak. I kept telling him he is not manly enough. This was my mother's attitude toward my father.*

There was also a conflict at work which made me leave. I just could not stay there. The chief CPA was a woman. She was very powerful. She constantly attacked me. She used to condemn me for everything. I retaliated. I could not take it. I attacked her back.

— Were you manifesting your dad's model of behavior?

— *No, that's not how Dad behaves. He tries to soften the situation. He does everything he is asked to do. I don't accept Dad's role. I tried to fight her and to show her how strong I was. That would make her even angrier. I wanted to get down on my knees and make up with her. I wanted to tell her I would do anything she wants. I manifested one side, but I was feeling the other side.*

— *I was married. I gave birth to a boy, and when he turned six, I fell in love with another man and decided to divorce my husband. I married this guy and gave birth to my second child. When my second kid was six years old, I faced the same situation again. I divorced and remarried again. The third child was born.*

What do I do now? This is the way my program works. I cut off my ex-husbands completely. I don't communicate with them. I throw them out of my life. I look at my dad's situation. He is living with his third wife. My mom and his second wife have died.

— You have said you just throw them out of your life.

— *I do not prevent my kids from seeing them. They see their fathers.*

— Okay. What's the common factor between your conflict and your parents' conflict?

— *I feel that one part, my dad's model whose script I have chosen, condemns and is afraid of emotionality; it pushes career and self-denial.*

231

There is a deeply ingrained notion there that I should not depend on anyone. There is constant dissatisfaction: you ought to do this, you ought to do that ... On the other hand, I produce high emotional waves. I can restrain myself for a long time, but this is followed by an emotional splash that I cannot contain.

— You are dealing with a conflict between logic and emotion. When you fall in love and experience a corresponding emotional state, logic steps in and says that you don't need it. Then you fall in love again and experience another emotional manifestation. Your emotions only get activated when you are falling in love. As soon as you get married, feelings are exchanged for logical appraisals and definitions.

— *How is it connected with my kids' ages?*

— You will have to sort that out yourself. This is what self-investigation is about. You will only grow as a self-investigator when you start to conduct your own self-investigation.

— *So, there is a program in me according to which I have to marry a man, give birth to his child, bring this child up to a certain age when I don't need this man's help anymore, and dump the man.*

— Search for the same pattern in your parents. To become whole or enlightened is to accept two halves of our personage— our father and our mother—inside ourselves, to connect the mind and the heart, i.e. our intellectual and emotional centers. The level of development of the emotional and intellectual centers of your parents are different. One of the parents predominantly manifests the emotional sphere, the other— intellectual. A woman, while in the physical body of a woman, can predominantly manifest her intellectual center. This is a masculine model of behavior. A man, in the physical body of a man, can predominantly manifest his emotional center. This is a feminine model of behavior. This is a common occurrence nowadays.

— *Can I take any given event of my life and see it in my parents?*

232

— Yes. Any event of your life reflects the relationship between your parents. To see it clearly, you must acquire the tools and habits of a qualified self-investigator. When you become one, you will see that the entire life of your personage represents a script downloaded by your parents.

— *My mother has the body of a woman, but inside her hides a very emotonal man.*

— Emotionality is a feminine manifestation.

— *At the same time, she behaves like a man.*

— You have been entangled quite severely.

— *I have experienced another man's pain, and my mind brought me to a dead-end. My mind thinks that everything that happens occurs through pain.*

— I want you to note that the model of behavior you manifest is the model of behavior of an intellectual man. The life of a human being is a tangled ball of yarn. I invite you to untangle it. You, on the other hand, tangle it more and more. You grab one end, and you pull on it. Then you grab the other end, and you pull on it.

— *Neither one of my parents manifests emotions.*

— There are no people here who don't manifest emotions at all. If a man doesn't scream at tops of his lungs, it doesn't mean he doesn't feel anything; his feelings are suppressed, and he manifests them weakly.

— *According to my notion, if a man and a woman scream at each other, they are emotional people. If they don't, they are intellectuals.*

— You use what you have based on your vision of the situation. When you use common, daily language, you manifest your own incomprehension.

— *My parent's marriage was arranged. Mom got married because she was getting old. Dad was ten years younger than her. I also got married late. I was afraid to become an old maid. I also needed a roof over my head. I was in love with another man. I knew what I was doing. My husband was older than me. My parents divorced when I was five years old. My mom was*

233

jealous of my dad because he was younger than her. She created a situation that forced him to drink. Then her girlfriend told her that she saw him with another woman. Mom kicked him out after that. My situation is analogous. I was cold to my husband, and he started to drink. I became suspicious of him having an affair. I found something in our bed one day that was not mine, and I kicked him out too. I pretended to be a saint, "I do everything for the family. I don't see other men. I am not like you." Being so saintly, I forced him to feel guilty.

The kaif of condemnation

— Kaif of the ego is in condemnation. You can condemn anything. You don't need a reason to condemn. It is not about a reason. It's about the state you experience at the moment of condemnation. **When you condemn someone or something, you dump the guilt you have accumulated onto them.** Certain condemnations are traditional here. For example, "You cheated on me!" The ego experiences kaif in a state of condemnation. You need to feel it. Feel that it is kaif for you to condemn.

— *I create these situations to experience this kaif. I create high adrenalin situations, in which I can feel righteous and self-important.*

— *Do we inherit the program of condemnation from our parents?*

— That's what I have been telling you all along. We get into the world of separation where we experience two basic emotional states: condemnation and guilt. We learn how and why we experience condemnation and guilt from the scripts of our parents. We condemn others for our own experience of feeling guilt. That constantly allows our ego to experience kaif.

— *I can see why I have entangled everything. I did it in order to not condemn. My kaif is not to condemn. I invent logical reasons not to condemn. I will do anything I can not to condemn.*

— You experience kaif of exclusivity. Everyone here is up to his ears in shit, but you are clean. You are different from everybody else. You are exclusive.

— *My mind constantly searches for an explanation that would allow it not to condemn other people. I will do anything not to experience condemnation. I will look at a situation from ten different points of view in order not to condemn any participant. I have the notion that it is bad to condemn.*

— You don't condemn other people. You condemn yourself. I will ask you to condemn yourself. You can use the people around you as screens.

— *You wanted to hit me yesterday. Condemn me. There is something in me that irritates you.*

— Condemn him. Do it.

— *I can take anything. I can withstand anything ...*

— *Why do you need to withstand it?*

— Here you go, "I can withstand anything." This is where your entanglement lies. That's what prevents you from seeing yourself holistically.

— *Anna resisted when I tried to unbutton her shirt, but she didn't resist when people were beating her. She got very nervous. She didn't want to be seen naked.*

— This is the way the conditioned mind works. It works in the regime "yes and no" like a pair of scissors. Your mind got stuck in one side. That's why you cannot think paradoxically. Allow yourself to be weak. You are weak in manifesting your feelings, but you are strong in manifesting callousness. You show everyone what happens to the mind when your emotional center is blocked. The mind comes up with nonsense. What do you feel now?

— *Everything I was so sure of prior to this moment turned out to be just another house of cards.*

— Yes. That's what happens inside the mind. Assuredness transfers to unassuredness. You will take yourself out of the dead-end of the illusions you are in only when you become aware of the feelings you harbor. What does she react to more than anything?

235

— I tried to unbutton her shirt and she started to fight me right away.

— Okay. Unbutton your shirt.

— I don't want to do that. I'd rather go.

— You can leave, but you will remain in your naughtiness. What's behind it?

I am an ugly freak

— I have mentioned already that I am an ugly freak. That's what my mother used to call me.

— Condemn your mother for this. She put a curse on you. Tell her what you think about this. You must remove this curse.

— I don't know what to say.

— You will remain a slave to the curse your mother put on you unless you rebel against it. You are on a very tight leash and unless you cut it, you will remain a slave for the rest of your life. Moreover, you will pass it to your kids. What do you want to say to your mother?

— Let me play your mother. "You are ugly. Your body is ugly."

— I know that.

— You are not a girl, and you are not a boy.

— I've heard that before.

— Why did you put this white dress on? Are you trying to hide your ugliness?

— Yes, I feel better wearing it.

— How can it make you feel better? Look in the mirror.

— I know I am ugly.

— Then why did you come here? How can you show your ugly face to people?

— I feel okay when I am dressed up.

— You think if you are dressed up, a man would give you a chance? Who needs an ugly duckling like you?

— Nobody needs me. I know that.

— The only idiot you ever found ran away with another woman.

— Yes Mom, you are right.

— *Of course, Mom is right. You don't stand a chance.*

— Observe how "the ugly" part of your ego stands up for its rights. "I am right saying that I am ugly." Irrespective of which part of the duality with which we are dealing, it will always insist on its truth. By insisting on its truth, it experiences kaif of exclusivity and self-importance. It's not even about you being pretty or ugly. Irrespective of how ugly a human being is, someone will always find him or her beautiful. One part of your ego is fighting for being on top. It took "ugliness" as an arguing point of being right. Look how strongly you insist on your ugliness. It's not about the ego's inability to part with something it uses as an arguing point, i.e. "ugliness". No, it's about the ego's inability to part with its own importance. How it explains its importance is another question.

— *I didn't think I was so tough.*

— "I am very unhappy, but I can withstand anything." Did you say that?

— *Yes. That was me.*

— I am here to show you that the real reason behind all your suffering is the pride of your divided ego. You can be told a thousand times that you are the prettiest girl in town, but your pride will not allow you to perceive it because that would make you lose your toughness. Your ego would lose its exclusivity. We are unable to feel the state of "WE" here because our individual exclusivity prevents us from entering this state. Until you acknowledge that you are not exclusive and stop excluding yourself, you will not be able to approach the state of "WE". You will continue to recreate your exclusivity. You will continue to be separated from other people. You only see one of your sides. You call it "ugly". You don't see your other side. You are afraid of it. If you start seeing it in yourself, your exclusivity, which is built on the illusory truth of one side, will disappear. Your main problem is that your ego does not want to part with its exclusivity. Identified with the ego, you are afraid to lose it.

237

— *I don't see the connection between the ego and my physical appearance.*

— Look how you revel in self-pity. Eternal self-pity is the profit of the ego. You are the ugliest human being on earth. If we were to bring a thousand ugly people here, you would still say that you are uglier than them, i.e. you are the toughest of them all. This is what the pride of your ego is based upon. That's how the ego stands up for its rights. That what happens with everyone here. Some of you are laughing now, but your situation is no different.

— *I laugh because I would gladly exschange my physical appearance for hers.*

— Here you go. We have a contender for your toughness. Looks like you are not the ugliest woman here, Natasha. Olga thinks she is uglier than you. She wants to exchange her physical appearance for yours. Don't fight her. Let her drown in self-pity. She doesn't want to part with it either.

— *Recently, I heard Anna say that she doesn't desire anything anymore. I thought to myself, "Ah, if I only had her problems! She doesn't even know what a real problem is. My problems are real problems."*

— One more ego takes pride in its problems. Your problems are the worst problems on the planet. You can build exclusivity and toughness on beauty, or you can build it on ugliness. Exclusivity can be created on either side of duality. Tatiana builds her exclusivity on the side that is opposite to yours. She builds it on beauty.

— *What would you feel, Natasha, if we were to say that your physical appearance and your body are average?*

CHAPTER 6
A NEW HUMAN BEING COMES TO THE SEMINAR

•◆•◆•◆•◆•◆•◆•◆•◆•◆•◆•◆•◆•◆•◆•◆•

Does anything bother you in your life?

— I see new people here. Let's start with them. What can you share with us?

— *Life is beautiful. I have read a few of your books, and I decided to come here.*

— What interests you exactly?

— *I want to know why we need to do certain things in public. Why can't we deal with our own hang-ups on our own?*

— Can you deal with them on your own?

— *Of course, I can. I don't think we need psychologists to treat depression or anxiety. A man can take himself out of these states on his own.*

— Yes, he can. He can also succumb to another bout of depression in a few days. So, your life is beautiful and everything is great with you.

— *No, not everything is great. A man who is happy all the time is an idiot.*

— Does anything in your life bother you?

— *No. When something bothers me, I take care of it on my own.*

— In that case, why are you here? People who gather here are weak, depressed, and hysterical. They have a difficult time navigating out of these states. Everything is great with you. Why were you interested in attending this seminar?

— *How about curiosity?*

— Are you curious to see how the depressed part of society lives?

— *Yes, I want to see how they live in a group.*

— We had a big fight yesterday.

— *Who won?*

— We fought all day long. One woman was bitten so hard, she didn't come today.

— *You should have finished her off.*

— It is easy to strike up a conversation with someone who has problems, and it is very difficult to start a conversation with someone who doesn't have problems.

— *That's because you don't need that. You are in the habit of talking to people who have problems. You don't know how to talk to people who don't have problems.*

— Will I have to deal with depressed, aggressive, and hysterical people all my life?

— *This is a choice. You have made your choice.*

— Then why did we meet?

— *Did we meet?*

— Yes, we did. Moreover, we are talking.

— *I am just siting here, observing. I am a polite woman who replies when she is spoken to.*

— I work with unhappy people. You, on the other hand, are happy.

— *I irritate you because I am not unhappy.*

— Perhaps we are all going to the place where you already are, to the state of total bliss and happiness.

— *Actually, I just drove my friend Maria here.*

— Hmmm, what are we going to do now? We will be ashamed to talk about how unhappy we are having in front of us a human being who is very happy. How about we have a group conversation with Oksana?

I will not discuss my life with you

— This is very interesting. Do you have any problems?

— *Unequivocally, I do. I am still alive.*

240

— What, exactly, is wrong in your life? What makes you unhappy?

— *I will not discuss what's wrong in my life with you.*

— With whom do you discuss these questions?

— *I have some special people who help me carry my shit away.*

— So there is some shit in your life.

— *Unequivocally. Don't you have shit in your life?*

— No, we don't have that. We have dualities.

— *If you don't carry shit, you swallow shit.*

— So, you have shit in your life, and you have people who carry this shit away for you. And overall, everything is great.

— *Unequivocally. Some people shit, and other people clean up after them.*

— Okay. Does anyone have another question for her?

— *No. Looks like she can take care of her shit on her own.*

— *I have one problem. I need to get a second degree, but I am lazy. Time passes by, and I understand that I don't move anywhere with this second degree. I cannot move up a career ladder, and I cannot work with people I want to work with.*

— You also cannot get a man you want to be with.

— *Yes, you can say that. I need a man. On the other hand, I don't need a man.*

— Does anyone want to ask her a question?

— *Earlier, you said that you don't need anybody's help. You are managing all right on your own. What about the people who carry your shit away?*

— *These people dump some of their shit on me too.*

— *But you said you can manage on your own.*

— *I said I can manage on my own when I was talking about depression.*

— It follows that depression and shit are two different things, yet at the same time, you have cleaners after whom you have to clean up.

— *Unequivocally. This is my moral responsibility, to clean after people.*

241

— So, after you have shit on someone, you get his shit in return.

— *Unequivocally.*

— Everything is unequivocal for her, while in our case, everything is dual.

— *Perhaps this word speaks of her wholeness.*

— *Unipolar world.*

— Can you entertain the thought that unequivocal can be equivocal?

— *Unequivocally. One can entertain any thought. What's important is how one uses it.*

— *Are you bothered by begars on the streets?*

— *They used to move me to tears a few years ago.*

— *What happened since then?*

— *I figured out the reasons why they are there.*

— *What is the reason, if you don't mind my asking?*

— *When I see old women begging on the street, I still pity them.*

— Why do you pity them? An old woman is working.

— *I pity her that her life turned out this way. She doesn't have anyone to support her.*

— Don't you work yourself? Don't you do what she does at work?

— *No. When people give me money, they are happy to do that. They thank me.*

— Everyone and always?

— *Yes, always. This is what my job is all about.*

— Is your job to take money from those who are happy to give it to you?

— *My job is to take money in such a way that people would be happy to give it to me.*

— Have anyone given you money from a different state?

— *This happens when our firm makes a mistake. That usually leads to a scandal. But when people give me their money, they are happy.*

— What do you experience in these situations?

242

— I don't feel anything.

Bad things don't bother me

— Your business is to take money from people who happily give it to you. Afterwards, you don't need those people. They are not your business anymore. You only accept good things. Bad things don't bother you.

— Theoretically, I know that bad things exist.

— Theoretically, you know that bad things exist, but they don't bother you.

— I don't allow myself to be bothered by those things. If I have to experience bad, negative things, I will experience them.

— Are you experiencing anything bad now? Is there something bad at work that bothers you?

— Of course. I deal with some bad things.

— Do you accept them?

— Yes.

— What do you accept?

— I accept the fact that my boss doesn't want to evolve. He has the opportunity and financial means, but he is stuck. I cannot move him.

— He doesn't want to evolve.

— He doesn't want to evolve.

— How are the two of you related?

— We have known each other for a long time.

— So, you think you just know him. He is he, and you are you, and there is nothing more there than two of you knowing each other. What if I were to tell you that he is you?

— Everything is possible.

— That's true, everything is possible, but this statement will not get us anywhere.

— Perhaps we don't need to go anywhere. Life will solve everything. We need to accept things the way they are. I have a choice …

— What kind of a choice do you have?

— I can leave this man. I have prepared everything already.

— You can leave him and find another man, but he will be exactly the same.

— *I have found a great firm. I could start working there tomorrow.*

— You know it's a great place. Why don't you leave now?

— *I don't want to lose everything I've done. This firm was created by the two of us. We started from the bottom. We invested ourselves in it. This firm is my child. I know I can move my partner in the right direction. I just need to work on him. We will evolve.*

— Okay, what about your personal life?

— *I have what I want. I have a well-trained man next to me. He buys what I need and takes me where I want to go: movies, theaters, restaurants. He knows what to do in bed.*

— Does he love you?

— *I have never asked him that question.*

— Do you talk about anything?

— *We discuss books, movies. We have common interests.*

— Do you talk in bed?

— *Not really. Why?*

— What do you do in bed?

— *We have sex in bed.*

— Does he say anything during or after?

— *Afterwards, he sometimes says something nice, some words of gratitude.*

— Looks like everything is great in your life: at home, at work, and in bed.

— *I do everything well.*

— Have you ever seen him unhappy or irritated?

— *If I were to see him in such a state, I would not see him again. Why should I torture myself? We should find pleasure here and now.*

— Our entire life should bring us pleasure, right? If something causes us to experience displeasure, we should throw it out. Right?

— *This is the common outlook.*

244

— I repeat what you have said. If your man doesn't bring you pleasure, you don't need him. Correct?

— *Yes.*

— Things that don't bring you pleasure should be removed from your life.

— *Yes. This is a no brainer.*

— The problem is displeasure, and to solve it one has to chase it out of one's life.

— *We create our own problems.*

— You hold the view that everything unpleasant should be removed from your life. That's why you don't have problems.

— *Do not generalize, please. I didn't say that.*

— You said that if a man was unhappy with you, you would not see him again.

— *Yes, I was talking about one specific case.*

— That's what we are trying to sort out here—one specific case.

— *But you generalize. You apply it to my entire life.*

— I have a tendency to generalize. I walk from small parts to the general picture. So, if your man were to express displeasure with you, you would remove him from your life.

— *Yes. I would part with him.*

— What do you need him for?

— *I need him for physical health. I like to be massaged some times.*

— So, you only need him for health. You want to die healthy.

— *Unequivocally. He protects me from a heart attack*

— Great. You probably had a man before him.

— *Yes, I did.*

— Was he removed because he said something unpleasant?

— *Yes. Why should I hear someone saying something bad about me when I have a mirror in my house? I can see everything on my own. Why should I hear it from a man?*

— You are not a member of the "happy thoughts" cult?

— If you want to be happy—be happy!

— We are seeing the physical realization of this formula. I am interested in how you achieve the state of this unlimited happiness. Are you reaching it by removing unhappy thoughts?

— In this particular case, yes. But it is difficult to throw some people away.

— How far do you go, removing those who you find disagreeable? If one of your men were to tell you that you were an idiot, would you consider that a good reason to kick him out of your life?

— It would depend on why he said it and on the context of the situation.

— What if he were to say it to insult you and to bring the level of your health down?

— If that was said in the heat of an argument, it would not bother me.

— What if he were to give you herpes?

— This is impossible.

— What do you mean?

— People invented condoms to prevent that.

— Okay. What if he were to wake you up in the middle of the night and insult you. How would you react? Would you kick him out?

— No, I would reply in a similar fashion.

— So, what does he need to do for you to kick him out?

— I was in a situation where I was threatened with a machine gun. It happened in Tadzhikistan. People used to carry guns at the time. My husband got drunk one day and threatened to kill me. I told him, "Stop!" He froze. I knocked him down and put my foot on his throat.

— And what did he do?

— He picked up his gun, and he left.

— Afterwards, you only dated well-trained boys. Am I right?

— Yes.

— Do these well-trained boys become hysterical sometimes?

— No. I never insult them. I am very gentle with their manhood.

— What happens when they lose their potency?

— *There is always a reason for that. It means a man is not ready.*

— What happens if he is not ready the next day?

— *It can continue for a while, but eventualy he will recover.*

— Will it end up with him disappearing from your life?

— *Yes, he will be removed from the playing field.*

— Do you train them to suit your needs?

— *No. They come prepared. Every human being can give something to another human being. If a man has something to give me, great. If not, we have nothing to discuss.*

— *My dad would suit you well.*

— *The spot is not for sale yet.*

— You demonstrate a great way out of duality. We search and sweat here, but it looks like Oksana has found it already.

— *Are you afraid of anything?*

— *Of course, I am.*

— *What are you afraid of?*

— *Every fear is connected to a stressful situation.*

— *What is a stressful situation for you? People try to scare you with a gun, but you are not afraid; you scare them.*

— *We have discussed my reaction to the situation, but I have not said a word about what I experienced at the time.*

— This was just a report.

— *Exactly. I was asked, and I answered you. One has only few seconds to make the right decision in a situation like this. One's own life and the lives of other people frequently depend on these seconds. We usually experience a whole range of emotions and feelings at the time, without which we would not be able to make correct decisions.*

What are you giving your life for?

— Do you have anything for which you would give your life?

— *No. I only have one life.*

— Nevertheless, you slowly give it away.

— *I live my life.*

— You give it away for something you do in this life. You waste it for small change. Imagine you have a thousand dollars. Every day you give one cent away. You are paying for something. Your life, the way you spend it, is a payment for something. Your life is a payment.

— *That's right. There is no other currency.*

— So, I am asking you, what are you giving your life for? You just said that you will not give your life for anything, but I am telling you that you are already giving it away. Do you understand what I am talking about?

— *I am giving it for something I have.*

— Let's say you have a thousand dollars. You can pay to go parasailing. You can buy a nice dress. You can buy food in the supermarket. What are you giving your life for?

— *I am giving my life for my firm to exist. I am paying with it for my parents to live comfortably. I am paying for fresh air outside my window.*

— So, you are paying for comfort.

— *Yes. I love comfort.*

— You are paying for comfort with your life. That's why you were shocked by my question about giving your life at once. If you were to give your life for someone or something, there would not be anyone here to receive comfort. Therefore, it is better to give your life away piece by piece. In that case, there would always be someone here to experience this comfort.

— *Obviously, I will not give up my life for being kicked, beaten up, not fed, etc. I doubt anyone would give up his life for that.*

— Okay. Since you somehow wound up here, I will make it interesting for you. I will invite people to manifest every negative emotion they feel toward you. You avoid negative states, but you may find them interesting. You build your life in such a way that nothing negative gets into it. Obviously, you are bored with your life.

— *She came here to have fun. She is here out of sheer boredom.*

248

— *She is a callous animal. She destroys men. She mirrors a very interesting part to me.*

— *Her behavior shocks men into doing what she wants. As soon as a strong man shows up in her life, she immediately breaks off the relationship.*

— *She is a vicious manipulator.*

— It's easy to manipulate people who are shocked.

— *I think she lives based on the principle, "I agree with whatever you do, as long as you don't interfere with my life."*

— *I don's cross your road, and don't you cross mine.*

— *If you don't satisfy me in some way, get lost.*

— *She displays a severe fear of low self-esteem. She has very high opinion of herself. She doesn't accept her shadow side at all. She simply rejects the fact that she is an old, childless loser.*

— *Who told you that a woman owes something to anybody? You think that by the time a woman reaches old age she should have kids. I don't have to agree with you. I have my own opinion, and I don't care for yours.*

— *That's exactly what I am talking about: "I have my own opinion, and I don't care for yours." You care for no one but yourself.*

— I would ask you to express your thoughts and feelings in respect to her way of life. The way people live their lives differs significantly. If someone insists she can live this way and live comfortably, about which I have my doubts, why not?

— *I see her as a cancer cell inside an organism. If the organism is well, it will destroy it. If it is not well, the cell will destroy the organism.*

— Exactly. You see a cancer cell that says, "I lived like this. I live like this, and I will continue to live like this."

— *A normal organism will destroy a cell like that.*

— That's true. I have doubts regarding Oksana's wellbeing.

— *She manages to escape life, and she calls this escapism life.*

— She cannot escape life. No one here can escape life. She has created a certain worldview, and she defends it.

— *I create my own worldview, but I don't insist on anyone following it. I live the way I want, and I am comfortable.*

— Exactly. You put forward a certain conceptual life position and you assert that this is how it is for you.

— *Yes, this is how it is for me.*

— I have my doubts about that. I have the right to have my own vision of the situation, right? My vision of your situation differs from yours. We have encountered a phenomenon that exists in every human being. We discussed this phenomena prior to you showing up here. We don't invite people here. They come on their own accord, and they illustrate the Process that occurs here. I will invite you to use this rare chance. You have asserted what every ego asserts. Your statesments characterize the philosophy of the ego very well.

— *She took the side that life should only offer good things, and she uses all her strength to fight the second side. Her emotional center is closed.*

Let's cut off half of our life and throw it away

— She thinks life should only offer pleasure; everything else should be removed. This worldview is quite popular in this reality.

— *Her defense system is very strong, way too strong for everything to be cool.*

— You are seeing your own ego now. That's the way our ego walks and talks.

— *This is a good illustration to the theme "to have" that we discussed. I want this, this, and that. I want to have everything.*

— The ego only speaks of what it wants.

— *The verb "to be" has not been mentioned once.*

— The ego, as an illusory structure, is constantly concerned with its survival. Survival can only occur through "to have." The more it has, the tougher it is. It tries to have what it considers to be good here, and only what it considers to be good here. I will receive as much pleasure as I can! That's what every ego builds its policies on. There is a very well-known principle called "a carrot and a stick". The ego chooses the ideal—carrot. It dreams that with time it will have more and more carrots, and these carrots will be sweeter and sweeter. This is the philosophy of the ego. The ego will never acknowledge something it doesn't like, something it considers to be bad.

You might see another type of ego. This ego will insist that everything it has is bad. This ego will be very unhappy, but it will carry its load of unhappiness with pride. This ego can withstand anything. Some egos place their bets on markets going up, and some place their bets on markets going down, but every ego feels the pride of its position. Right now, we have the opportunity to observe the ego that places its bets on the market going up. "I had it all good, and I will have it even better," — it insists, thinking that it has created itself and controls its own life. Imagine that a pop star comes to stage and starts to cry, "I can't sing today. I have troubles at home. I am depressed." How long would such a star maintain his popularity? To maintain the image of a popstar, one must play a role of happy, successful, gifted singer.

— *No one knows how this happens.*

— I am showing you how this happens to you. Your ego has created an illusion of a life where everything is swell, bright, and rosy.

— *Not so swell, actually.*

— Really? Don't cross out your beliefs now. I am playing along with your world view.

— *You have brought this example and you try to force it onto my world view. I don't like that. I am used to playing only one hand—my own.*

— Have you met people who have your world view?

— *Of course. I don't need to go far. Plenty of people next door share my world view.*

— Are there people like you who are famous?

— *I don't know. I am not acquainted with many famous people.*

— You can feel it.

— *I cannot feel the TV screen.*

251

— You are an exclusive woman. I have not met anyone with that philosophy yet.

— *I suppose there are people like me, but I don't know them.*

— Very tough defense. One cannot even get close.

— *You remind me of a character from a movie I watched a long time ago. The main character walks through life laughing at everything. It isn't until the end that she notices that her boss has been crying throughout the movie. I am looking at you, and I feel empathy. Perhaps this is pity. I think you are showing off.*

— *I really feel good now. I don't know what will happen tomorrow. I can't know that.*

— You don't remember what happened yesterday. You don't remember where you came from. Do you remember the woman you brought here?

— *If I forget her, she will remind me of herself.*

— Does she only turn to you with good things?

— *She turns to me with different things.*

— Why don't you remove her from your life if she brings something unpleasant to your table?

— *Like I said earlier, there are people to whom you give your energy. You don't throw them away that easily.*

— And they dump their shit on you.

— *Yes, that happens sometimes.*

— You have been saying that there is nothing unpleasant in your life, and you are never unhappy, but nevertheless, it looks like your ego experiences some negative states.

— *I have mentioned that before.*

— You have also said that you immediately remove people who bring these states into your life.

— *I have said that, but you missed the part where I mentioned that some people are allowed to do that.*

— Why are they allowed to do that when it is bad for your health?

— Because I have enough energy for that. I cannot be good for everyone. I cannot be bad for everyone either. There are people who I can listen to and help.

— Will you happily listen to every trouble they bring you?

— I will happily help them although I will not be happy listening to them.

— You will listen to them while not being happy. So, you do have unhappy moments in your life?

— Yes, I am not that different from other people.

— What do you mean? I thought you were exclusive. I thought you were different from everybody else.

— I never said that.

I listen, but I don't hear. I look, but I don't see.

— Okay. Who wants to ask another question?

— I hear her cry for help, but I also see her showing off.

— How can a person help someone who has such a strong defense system?

— Someone inside her is calling for help, but we can barely hear it.

— Yes. That's what is happening to each one of us. **Every manifestation of aggression is a cry for help.**

— Perhaps you should allow yourself to hear this inner scream of yours. Perhaps you can allow yourself to acknowledge it.

— I listen to it.

— She listens, but she doesn't agree.

— I may agree or disagree, but I will not bring it here. You are trying to make me angry. You want me to do it here, but I don't want to do it here. I will not do it here.

— "I control the situation. The fact that I have a crazy, screaming, bleeding lunatic asylum inside me is none of your business." Is that what you think?

— Yes. I will not open up in front of all of you.

— "I will listen to you, but don't you think you can stir something in me. I will not open myself to you."

— *Yes. I will not open up here.*

— "I came here to take a look at your show."

— *Perhaps we should not spend so much time with her.*

— *I didn't come here to make a fast conclusion. I came to spend time with you.*

— You came to take a look at us, but we are looking at you too.

— *You came to take a look at people who open up their feelings. People open their souls here, and you came to look at these people. You are curious.*

— Actually, we are seeing the ego of the personage named Oksana. It says one thing, but there is something totally different inside it. This is not about her coming here to look at us. She came her to figure out what it is that she doesn't allow herself to do. It's important for her to see how other people do that.

— *She needs to feel it.*

— To take a look at something and to experience something are two totally different things. A man can look at someone being stabbed to death. That's what it means to take a look. It doesn't mean he experiences what someone who is being stabbed experiences. If he starts to experience what the bleeding man feels, he would end the execution.

— *I agree.*

In defending yourself from an external attack, you don't see the attack that occurs inside you

— *As I was walking to the seminar this morning, I asked myself why I came here. My ego said, "Let's see what will happen. I am not going to reveal anything. I am okay. I don't have anything bad to show."*

— Roman socialites used to go to the Coliseum to watch gladiators kill each other. Today's high society women attend ultimate fighting and pay a lot of money to see men maim each other. They like these shows.

— When one's defense is very strong, one's body gets depleted of the energy necessary to put up a resistance. If you continue to walk this road, your immune system will give up. It doesn't matter how good of a defense you put up. This will happen inside. You will not be able to defend yourself from your inner self. Pills will not help.

— Exactly. You believe that you are defending yourself from something external. Your defense is based on the illusory notion of your separation from the world and your need to defend yourself from this world. In reality, you are this world. You recreate what you are afraid of inside yourself. No defense system will help you. **Moreover, this is not what *will* happen, this is already *happening*.** That's the only thing that can happen at such a high level of defense.

— I am in full control of the situation. There is plenty of information on the internet today. I know everything I need to know.

— You can defend yourself from the external manifestations, but this attack starts inside. No science can explain anything here. All the information you have accumulated is useless.

— Let me tell you that prior to me turning into what you see now, I was anemic. I was not born anemic. I developed anemia. First, a human being makes a choice, and then starts on his way, passing every step, trying to sort something out. It's useless to talk about my problems now.

— This is another misconception of the ego, which thinks it has a choice, or free will.

— I will not argue this point.

— You can argue this point, but the loss of such a perception is death for you, and you are afraid of it.

— You might be right.

— Observe the level of uncertainty of your ego. You have used the word "unequivocally" many times. At the same time, you are constantly using words that carry uncertainty, words such as "perhaps", "maybe", "I may agree or disagree", etc. If you were to stop using these words, a serious inner conflict would appear. I usually don't carry these conversations, but today I want to illustrate to all of you what our ego does. I will repeat. This is what every ego does, not only Oksana's, and you can clearly see it now. I will invite all of you to see it inside of yourselves.

— *I can see that I strive for total control. I want to protect myself from every possible threat. The only difference between me and her is that she can do it better.*

— *Why do you think she can do it better? It depends. In Oksana's case, we are dealing with the sphere of comfort. One man considers himself to be strong while another consider himself to be weak or unhappy; to each his own.*

— **Notice that the conversation about safety and security starts when you are afraid of something. Since our personality is dual, fear is a normal state for it. Fear is a state that appears in the process of the interaction of two opposite parts of our personality. Personality lives in fear; it doesn't feel anything else. All we do in this dual reality is materialize our fears. This is a brief description of our life. What types of fears we experience depends on the structure of our personality.**

— *On the conscious level, we experience condemnation and oppression, and on the subconscious level we feel guilty and experience victimhood.*

— I invite you to see this in your own personality. Oksana just showed us the mechanism of action of the opposite sides of the personality. That's how this mechanism works in relationship to something each one of us is afraid of. Each one of you is fixated only on one side and rejects the second side of your personality. At the same time, you try to maintain constant control of that sphere of you, where something that you are afraid of can happen.

"I am afraid to be old and penniless..."

— *My ego is afraid of me being seen as weak.*

256

— Power of the ego is an attribute of control. The weak ego is unable to control anything. This is a duality "power—weakness". It is similar to the dualities "good—bad" and "positive—negative." By themselves, they are not really dualities; they point to certain dualities. Okay. What is your power and what is your weakness?

— *My ego is afraid of being a victim.*

— You are using common phrases. You need to be more specific. For example, in Oksana's case, we are dealing with comfort.

— *My ego is afraid of poverty and aging.*

— So, "I am afraid of poverty and old age."

— *Yes, my ego is afraid of poverty and old age.*

— Your ego will control the situation in order to not be poor and old. Whether you control it or not, you are already old. What does your ego think about that?

— *It is very angry. It cannot believe it.*

— "What happened? We are old already! Where is our control? What's going on here?" **Control is an action that is directed toward preventing something you are afraid of.** What are you doing to avoid your fears? Oksana has described an intricate system of defenses. You have a specific fear, which is the result of the fact that your personality has two opposite sides. One side considers itself young, while another side considers itself old. The young side tries to control the situation and to prevent the old side from realizing itself. Oksana is a good example. The old side controls the situation and tries to prevent the young side from sticking its nose out. Olga is a good example of that too. Two opposite tendencies exist in one body, and each one of these tendencies act with equal strength. Control appears as a system of defense; one side defends itself against the actions of the opposite side. The ego cannot control its own duality. The sleeping man thinks he keeps everything under control. No. You will only be able to do that when you recall your Supreme "I".

— *On the conscious level, my "old" side is fighting my "young" side.*

— If the "old" side is fighting the "young" side of your personality, you want to be an old woman.

— *Looks like this is the case.*

— What is old age and what is young age is not clear. As soon as the word "aging" is heard, each one of us comes up with our own notions of age. This is not easy to understand. We need to understand what you mean by that. For one woman, two wrinkles on the forehead is old age. For another, old age is physical disability. For the third one, old age is dementia. Yet, for the fourth, it is wisdom. What is your notion of old age?

— *For me, old age is associated with helplessness, disease, the inability to take care of myself, being a burden to my relatives, loneliness, infirmness, senility, and poverty.*

— *Are you talking about sex too?*

— *Yes, I am talking about sex too.*

— Are you still dating that guy you told us about?

— *Yes.*

— Why do you insist that no one needs you? I assert that men who need you do exist, but you create an impression that no one needs you.

— *This is part of my personality that I am conscious of. It forces me to*

...

— Do you understand that this is not the case?

— *You picked up a good looking man two weeks ago at a grocery store.*

— She doesn't remeber that. She needs to experience the state of not being needed. There are plenty of men around her. A woman who wants to be with a man will find a man irrespective of her appearance or age.

— *So, this is what one part of my ego does in order to not show what it wants or doesn't want.*

— Your defense system doesn't allow anyone to get close to you in order to perpetuate the illusion you have created that no one needs you. Somebody else is afraid to have his illusion of

258

being needed destroyed. Every ego is exclusive in its own way. We are discussing the basic structure of every ego. Exclusivity appears based on dualities. For example, Natasha says, "I can withstand anything. You can beat me. You can rape me. I will withstand anything you do to me." That is what her exclusivity is based upon. You need to be beaten, and you will be proud that you can withstand this beating. You control the situation from the position, "I am strong." Every ego controls the situation from the point of view of the side with which it is consciously identified, trying to prevent the other side from manifesting itself.

To fall in love is to lose the illusion of control over a situation

— *Are you telling me I am not allowing myself to have a man?*

— Yes, you are not allowing yourself to have a man because to have a relationship with a man would mean you failed to control your exclusivity.

— *Where is this fear to manifest my good side coming from?*

— "Good" and "bad" are technical terms. What's good for one man is bad for another. You need to specify what is good for you and what is bad for you.

— *I am afraid to love someone, and I am afraid to be loved.*

— *I heard her say, "I refuse to feel love out of fear of losing control. As soon as I fall in love, I lose control."*

— In reality, the ego doesn't know love. It cannot know love. This is another misconception. Another illusion.

— *To love is to be open, to trust your partner, and to be able to experience some kind of feelings toward him. However, love leads to loss of control.*

— What do people call love here? When people talk of love, they talk of an emotional interaction. The emotional interaction we call love here contains two sides: positive and negative. He will pet you, but then he will hurt you. He will compliment you, but then he will scold you. It's not clear what the word "love" means. I will repeat, this so-called love is nothing but an emotional interaction of the opposite sides of duality. Whenever you enter an emotional interaction, you are subjected to the action of both sides of the dual, emotional sphere. When we discussed the way Oksana interacts with men, we discovered that, in her case, these interactions are not emotional. They represent pure animal instincts. When a man insults her, she throws him away. But duality is present even in animal relationships. A man is sexually excited today, but he is not sexually excited tomorrow. We are social animals, and whether you want it or not, you will have to talk to your partner about it. You will ask him to tell you what is happening to him. He may say that he doesn't find you attractive today, or he might even come up with a worse answer. That's when all hell is going to break loose. You will not be able to bypass your emotions completely. To be subjected to the emotional interaction is to shed light on the subject of one's own inner duality: positive and negative. You cannot avoid facing these two opposite sides in the emotional interaction. That's why these relationships are so complicated. We face the most difficult emotional relationships with people who are close to us: our friends and relatives.

— *Oksana mentioned the fact that she wants to make her parents comfortable. Are you suffering from the feeling of guilt in front of your parents? Is it another fear?*

— *No, I am doing it out of gratitude.*

— She only has gratitude. She is positive, and only positive. She doesn't live with them. She sees them from time to time.

— *I live with them. Moreover, I feel good living with them.*

— *It's exactly on this emotional duality that my question popped up. I could not understand why relationships change so fast: he loves me today, and he hates me tomorrow. Why can't one have only positive interactions? This question brought me to this school. I could not figure out what I was lacking. Why does it happen to us all the time?*

260

— You cannot escape duality if you are living in the dual reality.

— *I didn't know about the school when this question appeared in my head. That was before I came here, and it is thanks to this question that I am here.*

— Now you know about duality. I keep telling you that being in the dual reality and having a structure of personality equipped with the dual perception, you cannot avoid being influenced by the duality. Therefore, whenever you enter an emotional relationship, you will experience both states: positive and negative, plus and minus. The ego doesn't want to experience negative states, and it will defend only positive states. This will lead to the exacerbation of your suffering. You may start to search for an exit out of this suffering. You may start to use alcohol, drugs, sex, or any other method to lower your emotional tension. If you find that none of these methods works, you will start to ask questions that we can work with here.

Two types of water: dead water and alive water

— *I felt a strange sensation after the slapping exercise. I felt my body alive and full of warm energy, especially those parts of the body that were slapped.*

— The slapped parts of your body are coming to life.

— *A thought came to me that in order for feeling to manifest itself and something new to be born, something inside us should die.*

— Exactly. What you experienced yesterday was not just a simple process of giving you a beating. Your body was brought to life. Your body is dead. That's why you are afraid to show it. This has nothing to do with your physical attractiveness.

— *I feel like I don't even exist. Some thoughts run through my head, but I don't feel my body. I don't feel my weight. I don't feel how I walk.*

261

— All your energy is spent on mental hallucinations. Some people are very sensitive; they feel the slightest touch. Others perceive a strong blow as a light touch. We have different thresholds of sensitivity. In the pre-Soviet Russia, village men used to beat each other up during the holidays. Why did they do that? They did that to experience physical pleasure. By beating each other, they were caressing each other.

— *As a child, I used to hear from mom, "What are you crying about? Look in the mirror. Look how ugly you are." When I was smiling, she would say, "What's wrong with your face? If you don't know how to smile, don't smile." I developed a defense against this when I was four years old. I didn't cry when Mom slapped me. I never showed my pain. That was my way to show that I was different, to express my exclusivity as you say. I was trying to separate myself from other kids at that young age.*

— I can see a very painful experience behind your story.

— *My brother used to play a game with me. He would drop on the floor and pretend to be dead. I would pretend to believe him and try to revive him. He demonstrated death. I showed the opposite state. I showed that I was alive. He used to play another interesting game, "Stay there—come here." He would yell at me, "Stay there!" Five seconds later another command would come, "Come here!" That's what I project onto you. I don't understand when I need to stay and when I need to go. I don't understand when I need to experience something and when I need to observe it.*

— You have been inculcated with a very painful and complicated script. This script is the subject of your investigation.

— *As I was experiencing slaps on the face yesterday, I was thinking about how I should react. My main hang up here, in the group, is that I perceive everything that happens here as a learning process. I don't believe this is serious. That's why I didn't fight back. I thought all of this was being done for me to understand something. The only man I was angry with was you. I wanted to kick you hard and ask you whether you could hit me back. I immediately justified you by saying that you do it for our sake, so we can get out of our habitual states.*

262

— Everyone here tries to pull others into his game. Your personality can only interact with another personality through the script that was introduced into you. You intuitively chose a human being to fill a vacant role in your show. I was chosen to play the role of an oppressor in your show. That's what your script needs.

— *I was able to explain it to myself. I said that you didn't fully believe me. I knew I could handle it. I knew I could handle even more beating.*

— You are discussing your script now. You don't know yourself, and you don't believe yourself. You attract exactly what your show needs. My job is to kick you out of your script so that you can observe it from the other side. You cannot exit your script until you become totally aware of yourself. You exit your script step by step.

Dead defense

— Do you want to experience something, or do you want to continue to observe?

— *I will sort it out myself.*

— You don't allow yourself to feel.

— *Do I need to behave in any special way to do that?*

— I am just asking for your permission. If you want to continue to sit there, you can do that too.

— *Based on what I told you earlier, I would prefer to just sit here. I don't want to get involved in what you are doing.*

— Okay. What scares you the most about me? You could have agreed to feel something. What stands in your way?

— *I don't want to talk to you about that.*

— Is it communication with me that scares you the most?

— *I am not scared. I just don't want to talk to you. As I have already said, I live based on the principle "I want—I don't want".*

— This is not true. You are lying. You are afraid of something.

— *I am not afraid of anything.*

263

— *She is dead.*

— She pretends to be dead. When hunted, some animals pretend to be dead. Tell me what you are afraid of?

— *What for? To make people laugh? I don't want to do that.*

— *She is totally closed now. Her arms and legs are closed. Her body is in a prenatal position. What are you afraid of?*

— *I will not tell you. I don't want you to know what I am afraid of.*

— She is so afraid, she cannot think straight.

— *You are right, I can't think straight.*

— Why is she so afraid of me, Marina?

— *Are you afraid of him?*

— *Should I be?*

— *I am the only one who is afraid of you, Alexander Alexandrovich.*

— *Are you afraid of yourself too?*

— *No, I can always come to an agreement with myself.*

— Who is going to agree with whom?

— *My mind will agree with my soul.*

— Your soul is not of this world. How are you going to come to an agreement with it? No, one part of your brain will agree with the other part of your brain.

— *One way or another, they will come to an agreement.*

— *I am also afraid.*

— What are you afraid of?

— *You can pull something that I don't want to see, something I will be ashamed to see. I am also afraid of being beaten.*

— We are going to shoot a new TV series "Beaten Up 2". Who else is afraid?

— *I saw that I am afraid of men. I am afraid of being intimate with a man.*

— Is it a fear of close physiological relationships?

— *It is a fear of deep physiological relationships.*

— What is a deep physiological relationship?

— *I am talking about deep penetration.*

— Okay. You are afraid of deep penetration. Why are you afraid of a deep penetration?

— *I am afraid of unpleasant sensations.*

— *I, on the other hand, am afraid of my sensuality, or I might be afraid to lose my sensuality.*

— "I am afraid to lose, and I am afraid to acquire. I am afraid."

— *On the conscious level, I am not sensual. I am callous. I am comfortable being with men with whom I don't need to feel anything. I am afraid to manifest my sensuality. On the other hand, I constantly talk about and manifest myself sensually.*

— What is sex?

— *Sex is penetration.*

— What are we doing here?

— *We are having sex: mental and emotional.*

— Sex is an interaction between two sides of a duality. In this reality, people define sex primarily as physical interaction. In duality, one side cannot exist without the opposite side.

— *Then, if I display sensuality, my partner cannot be sensual.*

— What is sensual?

— *When I use the word sensual, I mean bright, positive feelings.*

— What kind of bright feelings? What does positive mean here?

— *Erotic tension. Orgasm. I am scared. I don't want to discuss it.*

— Then let's end this conversation.

— *My ego is afraid to lose control. It is afraid to have sex with you. My ego is afraid because it understands that it will not be able to control you.*

— Don't be scared. I don't want to have sex with you.

— *I am not afraid anymore. That's why I can say that. The way Oksana does it, using only her mind, will not fly. If it happens with the emotional center turned on, the ego will have to let go. The ego doesn't want to relinquish its control.*

— What have we come to?

— *This is the fear of losing oneself, the fear of losing one's ego.*

265

What you are afraid of is what you want

— I will invite you to substitute the word "fear" with the word "want". If you are afraid of something, say that you want it. I will ask you to speak up.

— *I want to be a thief. I want to be a whore. I want to betray my husband.*

— Great. I want you to feel how strongly you want that. Don't hide your talents.

— *I want to divorce my husband, stay in my own house, ask men to visit me when I want and kick them out when I want.*

— *I want to express my feelings to a man. I want to say that I love him. I also want to insult him.*

— *I want all my friends and relative to die.*

— *I want to be ugly, unattractive, and lonely.*

— *I want to turn into a sick, poor street bum.*

— *I want to be able to not lower my eyes when a man I am with undresses. I want to be able to openly express my feelings.*

— *I want to fuck women and to be paid for that.*

— *I want to lose all my money. I want my parents to pay for me. I want my sister to kick me out of the house.*

— *I want to be a man and to love a woman without feeling guilty.*

— *I am afraid of being left alone with children without my husband supporting me. I am afraid to be thrown out on the street and to become an alcoholic.*

— *I want to blow up the world. I want people to scream in pain.*

— *I want to have rough, animal sex with a stranger.*

What is of utmost importance for you now?

— I will ask you to pair up and to discuss what is most important for you now.

— *The image of an old, ugly woman comes to mind. I feel older than Tatiana now, even though she is older than me. I am tired of life.*

— You have mentioned before that people initially perceived you as a young girl and then they started to perceive you as a woman. You have never experienced a state of a young lady.

— People still call me a girl sometimes, but you are right, I have never felt like a young lady.

— That's exactly what you need to feel.

— There is something in me that sees all of this as a game. Here is a man. I slap him, but he smiles at me benevolently.

— I see myself as a child, too. I feel like I am playing a game under your supervision.

— It is very important for me to open my emotional center. As soon as some emotional situation occurs, my intellectual center starts to search for a duality. In a few minutes, I hear, "Great. I found the duality responsible for it." That prevents me from thoroughly feeling both sides.

— If you use this approach, you will not be able to feel anything at all. You can only open a duality by experiencing both sides of it. This is not a mental process. I constantly remind you that you need **to experience** both sides of your inner dualities. The conditioned mind tends to think in abstract terms. It can imagine anything, but there is nothing but illusions there. You will only be able to understand duality when you experience both sides of it. You cannot do it by using your mind alone. **Understanding is the result of new knowledge and you experiencing this knowledge.** If you know that something is dual, and this duality is present in you, experience it. However, few people are willing to do that. All of you can discuss this mentally, but that's not enough. You will only understand what compassion is once you fully experience something. Compassion is a feeling.

— It was very important for me to feel that every human being has attachments. I felt mine. I used to block them out.

— I started to understand something. I started to see my exclusivity. I have been building it up all my life. The idea of my individuality and self-

267

importance got to be so high that it turned into a very strong defense. I defend myself from everyone around me.

— "I fight for my exclusivity."

— *I constantly deal with my defense. I have to lower it.*

— *My husband is very patient. Yesterday, I looked at myself through his eyes. I got scared. How does he tolerate me? I would have kicked this bitch out a long time ago.*

— You have a fear of being left without financial means. This fear gives birth to the desire to kick a man out. You have said that you change men every six years.

— *I don't want to depend on a man.*

— *She mentioned that her mom died when she was six years old. She took her father's model of behavior. She kicks men out the same way her dad kicked her mom out. He kicked her out so hard, she died. Now, even though physically she is in a woman's body, her inner man kicks out a man who is embodied in the male body.*

— Exactly. As soon as you start to feel dependent on your husband, you want to become independent. Exchanging one man for another, you get into another dependency out of fear of being left without means of survival.

— *I find myself in heavy dependency now. I have never experienced anything like that before.*

— Every subsequent dependency will be stronger than the previous one.

— *The state of supressed guilt causes you to experience aggression toward your husband.*

— You have to become a self-investigator. To do that, you need to begin sorting out yourself. No one will provide you with knowledge about yourself. When you self-investigate, you receive priceless information about yourself. Your self-investigator gets stronger and stronger. Each one of you will have to complete his own path. No one will do it for you. I will tell you how to do this work. I will share my experience of self-investigation with you.

— It is important for me to experience what a woman who condemns everyone around her for her troubles experiences. On the other side, she makes everyone feel guilty in order to get what she wants. She looks like Oksana. She is money-oriented. She doesn't care about other people's feelings.

— I have to start to feel another human being. I look at the man next to me, and I don't feel him.

— It means you don't feel yourself. You cannot feel what another human being is feeling if you don't feel his sentiments yourself. When you look at another human being, you look at yourself. The other human being is you. When you start to feel yourself in different manifestations, you will be able to feel different people who have similar manifestations.

— Is that why we need to experience dualities?

— You need to experience everything that is in you. That's the only way out of partial, one-sided, separated perception. As a result, you will become aware of the wide diapason of dual feelings you harbor. You will start to understand what happens to people who are submerged in a one-sided perception. You will not be able to understand the pain of other people unless you allow yourself to experience their pain. You will not be able to feel their pain unless you start the self-investigation process. When you start on the road of self-investigation, your defense system will fire up. It will try to block the feelings that will emerge any way it can. Our work is to add to ourselves our own parts, the parts that have created this defense system to protect themselves. You can remove this defense system only when you recall that you are not "of this world." You will have to be "in this world, but not of this world." You cannot see this world from this world, since in that case, you would only see it dually. That will give birth to the familiar feelings of condemnation and guilt. You need to get to the state of Awareness. The road to Awareness lies through self-investigation.

— *I look back on my life, and I see how I destroyed everything around me. I see how I destroyed my family. I see how I destroyed my daughter's family. I see how I destroyed mechanical equipment at work. I see the financial troubles that we have in our group as my own doing too. I am carrying this destructive force in me. I see it in the outside world, but destruction occurs inside me too.*

— You have to start seeing it inside yourself. That's the only way for you to manage this force. As ego, you cannot control anything. How can you manage something you don't see? When you start to see your dual ego, you will be able to do something about it.

— *I am afraid of my own feelings. I am fighting myself, trying not to manifest them.*

— To be afraid of manifesting your feelings is to be afraid of self-investigation. Start to see how you create destruction.

— *This is exactly what I do.*

— So, describe how you do it.

— *On the conscious level, I am good, morally upright, and law abiding man. But I don't see how I manifest my sub-conscious side.*

— You have said it thousand times already. I am asking you to tell us how you do that.

We are running out of time now. I want to thank all of you for the work we have done at this stage of our self-investigation.

www.ingramcontent.com/pod-product-compliance
Lightning Source LLC
Chambersburg PA
CBHW072117270326
41931CB00010B/1584